CANIO'S
SECRET

**A Memoir of Ethnicity, Electricity, and
my Immigrant Grandfather's Wisdom**

GREG GRIECO

EDITED BY SIDONIE SMITH

Front cover:
Castle in Brindisi di Montagne, Italy, 1995
Back cover:
Greg Grieco, c. 1976. Photograph by Joan Albert. By permission of the estate of the artist.

Edited by Sidonie Smith

ISBN: 978-1-4834-8225-5 (sc)
ISBN: 978-1-4834-8224-8 (e)

Library of Congress Control Number: 2018902882

Lulu Publishing Services rev. date: 03/23/2018

To Sidonie, David, and Tony

Happiness is all that's required.
—Canio Grieco, Summer 1953

CONTENTS

LIST OF PHOTOGRAPHS

Front cover: Castle in Brindisi di Montagne (1995)

Back cover: Greg Grieco c. 1976. Photograph by Joan Albert. By permission of the estate of the artist.

Figure 01. Grandpa Canio, Grandma Marie, and Greg, c. 1956

Figure 02. Kathryn Heaney, early 1930s

Figure 03. Gerald Grieco, c. 1930

Figure 04. Uncle Jack, 1940

Figure 05: Greg and Gerald, 1944

Figure 06: The Griecos, c. 1950 (left to right back row: Gerald, Canio, Kathryn, Marie, Gussie, Enzo; in front Regina and Greg)

Figure 07: The Heaneys, fiftieth wedding anniversary, 1950 (from left around table: Greg, Topper, Regina, Uncle Tom, Thomas Sr., Eva Mae, Kathryn, Aunt Rae)

Figure 08: Greg, Regina, and Tommy, 1952

Figure 09: Sugarbush, the Farm, 1950

Figure 10: Linden Avenue, Oak Park, 1960

CHAPTER 1

CANIO, IN AND OUT OF TIME

As boys of eight often do, I imitated my father. He maintained a commercial art studio in our home, and so I set up an office of my own in my bedroom closet. I created projects, first making toy boats from crate scraps and then doing experiments with Christmas lights. In the spring of 1950, Johnny Mulkerin and I tried to string a telegraph from his house to mine. With most of his friends, Johnny used the phone or the echoing alley to call and get someone to play with. But he couldn't call me because our phone was for business and we weren't allowed to use it. Hanging on the phone kept it busy and might delay a client's call, although the clients mostly wrote or returned artwork by special delivery when it needed corrections. What's more, Dad's business was seasonal, taking perhaps three to four months at different points in the year. But the rule about not using the the phone remained in place year-round.

As a consequence, building a telegraph was a scalable idea for an eight-year-old, combining both secrecy and cunning, the sort of challenge young boys like. Of course, there were technical as well as ownership difficulties. For one thing, the neighbors might not be so happy about having wires strung across their yards, and then there were telegraph keys and sounders to build and codes to master. I'd begun to tinker with a telegraph set, trying different combinations of bells and springs from Heitbommer's hardware store, which was what I happened to be doing the day everything blew up.

I was sitting at the dining room table, keying in dots and dashes, which made to Dad's ear a clatter of incomprehensible noise. Suddenly, springing from his drawing board, he stepped into the dining room and reached into the wires and batteries of my telegraph set. Pieces of it sprang up and flew in all directions.

Sensibly, I ran and hid in my *office*, in the bedroom closet. It was a white enamel room, the only one in the house with smooth walls. All the others had swirled plaster. It was the only room where if you lost your balance or were pushed, brushing against the walls didn't tear your skin off. High up on a chain there was one light bulb with a pull string. I leapt for it. Sometimes the light burned out like a flashbulb. This time it came on. I closed the door secretly, not letting the latch click, and then froze into the silence.

This was one of my free days, a holy day or Columbus Day—I can't quite remember which—that I'd been looking forward to for weeks. It was a glorious, chilly yet sunny day, a perfect time for fooling around or lazy experiments. I'd thought perhaps Dad would lend me a hand because he'd once worked for Western Electric, where they made telephones and where they knew how to solve serious technical problems like the ones Johnny and I had. As it turned out, all that didn't matter.

I hid out silently, trembling for a long time before I noticed I was gasping for breath and screaming silently to myself. I stopped breathing to see if I was still screaming, and then I screamed without breathing some more. Even if I screamed without a voice, it was as if some echo could still be heard. I wanted to wrap myself in the hanging clothes and hide like a bug. I tried to, but I was afraid my snot would mess things up or if he came in the bedroom, I might not hear him. That would make him angrier still. After a while, I slipped out from the hanging clothes and flipped the hook on the door to my room, even though he could smash it open if he wanted to. And still screaming internally—at him, at me, at I couldn't have told you who—I listened down the hall.

It was exhausting to stay here, but I didn't know where to run. Crying wouldn't help. I would still be a fool. I had to stop crying. Standing as quietly as I could and slowing my own breath, I finally stopped moving. I waited inside my head.

I spent much of my childhood waiting for Dad's explosions, surviving by living inside my head. What happiness I glimpsed I associate with my grandfather Canio Grieco, whose movements through the neighborhood constituted the grounds of my tenuous sense of belonging.

———————

Growing up in Chicago in the 1940s and 50s, you lived in parishes, even if you weren't Catholic, because the dominant architecture in Austin, as in much of Chicago's West Side, was the parish church. Its towers were reference points before you remembered north and south, pointing the way home from hockey or caddying, and its bells broke time into thirds—morning, afternoon, and night. Except, of course, on Sunday. On Sunday, the bells counted out the masses you'd missed, even if mass was the furthest thing from your mind.

Civil rights and foreign affairs were foreign to us. For our parents those topics were easily overshadowed by a new Ford Fairlane or the Cubs winning three times in a week, never mind three in a row. In those years during the Cold War and before JFK was assassinated, Austin was our country, kept together by votes that went to Democratic mayors like Kelly, Kennelly, and Daley and by young men who fought race wars in Garfield Park. It was a place where you bet with a bookie on the corner, where a small-timer like *Uncle Joe* showed up dead one night on the steps of Resurrection Church, shot and left there not as a symbol, mind you, but just because that was where they happened to catch up with him. It was a place where you lived within walking distance of your bakery and grocery store. And it was a place where, in lieu of falling in with the mob, going to school, or joining the army, you could usually get ahead in a union if you kept your head down.

Keeping your head down, in fact, was the key to everything, for both children and adults. We lived surrounded by hundreds of voices whose authority affected us but whose purposes and outcomes were beyond our control. Parades and memorials prepared us for patriotism, banks lent us money, and the mob fed our vices. If you were unhappy with this, you married up and out or kept your business small and friendly, which meant, for the most part, quietly accepting the racial and cultural epithets of white Chicago.

What my sister, Regina, and I learned came mostly from our parents, from our grandparents who lived downstairs, from the aunts and uncles we were told to attend to, and from the nuns who taught us. Of all these people, the one from whom I learned most was my grandfather Canio Grieco, and it was his life and character that opened windows on my world and formed a lens that focuses my attention to this day.

────────── ● ──────────

As Canio's grandchildren, Regina and I learned our first lessons and indeed lived out our early memories bouncing on his knees. We listened as he began stories of his childhood, set in a place that seemed no more than a postcard.

He had been born in a mountain village in Basilicata, in the impoverished south of Italy. And though Pythagoras had formulated his theorem just down the road and the birthplace of Horace was twenty miles away, Canio came from other stock, serfs who had been forced to migrate from Albania by a Norman queen late in the twelfth century. To the Lucani, the local people who were distant descendants of Pythagoras and Horace, these Albanian serfs were Greeks, and so they were called Grieco.

Near Canio's childhood home in the hilltop village of Brindisi di Montagna, you can still see the Norman castle from which the Griecos, pronounced *Grecco* or *Gree-ecco*, were pressed into servitude and also the hillside to the east, which is all that remains after a devastating earthquake that came in the middle of the night, burying many of the Greek-Lucani families that lived there eight hundred years ago. Grandpa Canio—tender, sometimes explosive, almost always hoping for a laugh—had been born of an earthquake.

As best I remember, here is the first story Canio told us. I was five or so.

"I was a little boy when we came here. We didn't have birthdays or cakes or parties or anything like that. That was later, much later. In America." This made Regina sad, and she snuggled up to Grandpa.

"One day we came out from our little town in a wooden cart with a donkey, bouncing up and down, all the way to the bottom of the hill. I didn't want to go, but my father said we had to go. To America. I wanted to stay with my mother and eat the pears and figs and all the fruit I loved.

"The figs were so good I used to eat them right off the trees. I would creep out of the house when everyone was asleep. We used to take a little nap in the afternoon, called a *siesta*, but I would creep out into the orchard when I knew the figs were ripe because I wanted to have some. One time I climbed up and got some in my lap and kept eating them and eating them until I got so sick I couldn't eat anymore. I was so sick I moaned and cried, holding my stomach and rolling around on the ground." At this point he would pinch and squeeze our tummies if he could. But we soon knew this story, and though we were on his lap, we learned to squirm out of the way. "Then my mother came running out and carried me into the house."

Regina and I thought it comical that though Canio was Italian, he'd gotten sick on figs. (*Comical* was a word our mom taught us so that we'd know what we were talking about.) As far as figs went, we had no idea what ripe figs were. We'd seen only dried figs, and we couldn't stand them. They were too sweet. They made your teeth stick together, even more than peanut butter did. Regina and I figured that since fruit was constantly being pushed on us by adults, Canio's getting sick was a good excuse for not eating fruit. Pretty soon, though, I had to go it alone because Regina gave in and decided she liked fruit after all. I didn't, swore I wouldn't, not never.

Canio would lift us off his knees so he could go over to the desk covered with bottles of colored ink, pens, airbrushes, and Ross board for his drawings. Further back on the glass top were his subjects—shoes, some still wrapped in green and tan tissue paper, others propped up on boxes so that the light would make them glisten. Young as we were, we knew we were never to touch anything there. Canio opened a drawer, the one where he kept the Chuckles, the jellied candy squares of different colors and flavors he would bring us from Featherstone's. He reached under bundles of string and tape for a postcard.

"Here. Right here. You see this place?" He ran the edge of his thumb along the bottom of the photo on the front of the card beneath the ruins of a castle. "Just here. This is where we lived."

"On the way over on the boat, I stood way in the back by the rail, with the water splashing everywhere and the little fishees jumping in and out of the ocean. 'Goodbye, little fishees,' I cried. 'I'll never see you again. Arrivederci, little fishees. Arrivederci, bye, bye.'"

It was through stories like these that we came to know our grandfather. And although we played "giddyap, horsey-horsey" on his knee many times before then ... and after, it was at age five that he became clear to me.

In retrospect, I now see how Canio cast himself theatrically—as the little boy crying to the fishees at the stern of the *Alesia*, which no doubt reflects how he felt, and his childlike persona as he imagined it to have been at the time. In fact, he was thirteen when he made the crossing, not a young child. He was mythologizing the childhood sense of loss and displacement he had experienced, protected now only by eliding memory and his eager grandchildren, much the same age as his remembered but really misremembered persona.

———— •• ————

In the 1940s, the Griecos were particularly proud people, proud of what Canio had accomplished. His was a common story. He had come from the old country and had become a successful businessman, so just to talk about that transition was somehow patriotic. That story, often told, reminded us of how we came to be Americans. But more than that, Canio was an artist, had a special talent, in a time when almost no one knew an artist. And as the family lore stressed, he had been successful, not in Europe, "where everybody was an *artiste* ... and broke," but in America, where being an artist implied something between Raphael and Michaelangelo and where he was a monetary success as well. Like most family stories, these proud acclamations were wisely reserved for the children of the household, who absorbed them with wide eyes and enchanted ears, in resolute belief.

So this figure in a business suit with a navy blue beret and poppet of Venetian red had a special significance to us and to the community around him that in varying degrees understood who he was. As a consequence, when events of cultural and artistic significance occurred, they always had a special meaning and interpretation in our household, and we were expected to be informed about them, repeating them as dogma, even if we disagreed. There was, in fact, plenty of wavering from the party line.

In 1950, when the towering sanctuary of St. Thomas Aquinas church came to be repainted, we were reminded that Canio's grandfather had been a skilled artisan who had painted church sanctuaries in Italy. What's more, Canio, who was an avowed anticleric and never went to church, took it upon himself to inspect the work. He looked critically at the figures and perspectives, at the meaning and glory of it, and when he returned, he reminded us that the Sistine Chapel had nearly crippled Michelangelo, "painting up there on his back," and probably did no good for the gold leaf-layers and the other fellows on those scaffolds either.

Always gregarious, Canio took pains to "make the acquaintance"—a phrase used by his wife Mary (whom her grandchildren always called Grandma Marie)—of a few of the artisans, and after several, secular trips to church, he admitted that "these fellows seem to be pretty well paid and know what they are doing." But in his view, the real point of the whole exercise was to remind us of Michelangelo, another Italian sacrificed to the self-agrandizement of the papacy. Naturally, the parish clergy, not to mention most of the wives in the neighborhood, would have none of this, and Canio was shuffled out of the way by the bustle of Catholic women, who had religious opinions of their own and no time for sacrilege, no matter how high the art.

Far up in the sanctuary, behind the altar, and not far from the image of the glorious and risen Christ was St. Paul, whose face had taken on the likeness of the bulbous-faced Monsignor Long, the pastor of St. Thomas when the restoration was commissioned. "It's the custom to make one of the apostles look like the pastor," Grandma told us, one eye on Canio. She was aware of the potentially bad effect the example of his anticlericalism might have on her grandchildren, although she herself was not entirely convinced of Monsignor Long's newfound, earthly glory. For that matter, she had never thought of St. Paul as an Irishman or in gold leaf, though in that the monsignor was much improved.

"Well, perhaps being priests," she said, "with all that wine," her voice trailing off as though her mouth had preceded her thoughts. Conscious of Grandpa's sullen, stalking reticence, expecting he would pounce on Monsignor Long, the church, or St. Paul at any moment, she remained on the defensive. Canio simply looked at her, at us, and chuckled. "You know what I think," he seemed to say. No need to argue. Or perhaps considering the healthful benefits of a glass of wine now and then, he was in a mood to be forgiving. Whatever his view, we were too young to ask.

"He's a little higher up there than he should be … for a priest," Marie conceded, half enjoying Canio now and a bit relieved to have the floor to herself. "Ah, but then for a *monsignor!*" She rolled her eyes from heaven to earth and back to heaven again. Suppressing a smirk of her own, she slapped a towel across her arm and retreated to the kitchen.

Enough said.

The dreaded moment of agnosticism had come and gone, and Marie, who prayed novenas every Friday for her husband's return to the fold, had scandalized us more than his Nietzsche or Spinoza ever could, more even than his complaints about the priests, whom we thought were entertaining. We especially liked them when they came during spelling class or when they told stories that made Sister Mary Catherine or Sister Immaculata giggle. The fact is that Canio's agnosticism was a tough sell and no great threat to the hearts and minds of Catholic school children. But Grandma Marie and her doubts about a tipsy monsignor—those things we remembered.

Because of Canio, civic art attracted our attention as well. When Pablo Picasso visited Chicago it was a public event, one which even Mayor Richard Daley, heretofore unknown to the art world, applauded. But in our house, where the only Modernists worthy of discussion were figurative artists like Auguste Rodin, Frederic Remington, and James

Milton Sessions, Picasso was universally scorned. Leaning over the drawing boards, you could hear the sarcasm in Canio's voice as he and the other artists spoke of Picasso and the mayor of Chicago. "Picasso! What's so big about him? The guy can't even draw!" They had only seen his later work, never his precise, exquisite, youthful drawings.

In this way, cultural events became issues of pride, taste, and patriotism for us and for our Italian relatives. For me, this pride was like a fusillade fired down the hallway of our long railroad apartment. Through the fusillade, a kind of reignment descended, perhaps no more than confetti but a reignment nonetheless, to be carried on in the family name. I was five or six and the oldest. I understood my responsibilities.

From the age of five, I learned that the time I lived in was Canio's, and I basked in the halo he cast over us. An artist in a world of practicalities, he lived out his values in the entangled relationships of an often hostile community, and he left in his wake threads of discovery for his grandchildren.

I spent decades fleeing the violence of my father, the oppressive scrutiny of the neighborhood in Austin, and the crushing self-loathing so internalized in my 1950s Catholicism. I have now spent a decade of return, bringing Canio back to me. Thinking back, I remember him most clearly and unmistakably as he was when I was about fourteen. He seemed to be at the peak of his life then, though in fact he would be dying of cancer in just a few years. Stepping away from his desk and the shoes he was drawing, he would walk down to the corner where Featherstone's Drug Store stood, dressed in his brown suit, as though dressed for business, with a navy blue overcoat and a French beret, a coat and hat that announced his character to the neighborhood. His beret was navy blue as well with a tiny, irridescent poppet at the center, a poppet of perfect Venetian red. He would buy the afternoon papers and perhaps a Garcia Delicias, a Cuban cigar, for later that evening. And he would tip the paperboy, not merely out of generosity but because he knew what it was to make a living, having once made a living that way himself. But now he was an artist, the only one anyone had ever seen in Austin, as much at home here as any artist in Montmartre, and a fixture of enterprise and character in the neighborhood.

I can see and feel and hear the tilt of his beret, the sensation of his embrace, the sounds of his baseball devotee's attention, and in my own writing, imagine him in the words he gave me. I have put him in motion in Austin. Inhabiting a place between agnosticism and anticlericalism, sensuality and reason, art and technology, Canio came to be reflected in an almost exclusively Roman Catholic mirror so that for a long time the full dimensions of his character remained difficult for me to see. I have conjured him through all the maps of Austin—geographical, economic, emotional, familial, intellectual—and followed him through that neighborhood where clothing, languages, verbal styles, styles of hat and of the heart became subject to scrutiny in the eye, the ear, and the flesh.

Consequently, this memoir arises *in illo tempore*, in that time in which Canio walked the earth. Without that time, I have no shape. With it, I'm willing to take all reasonable responsibility. This is probably exemplified nowhere more clearly than in the search for and ultimate acceptance of my father, even *in extremis.*

Immersion back into the time of my grandfather and the responsbility for crafting stories of Canio and of Austin have been an antidote, and in the end a stay to sluggish depression. In the midst of notes upon notes of ideas for my portrait of Canio, I find two poems about depression and self-image.

Kindly

As if on cue,
depression
the demon in the drawer
of Czesław Miłosz has arrived.
Arrived?

How nice to see you!
I greet the daguerreotype at the door.
Now there is no one
but me and the silver psychopath
in the house

to kill.

Kindly Two

That is not enough, he replies
Rebuffing my bromides
my greeting, my poetic delights.

I am swept aside by his melodramatic
Renaissance. He darkens the room to a whisper.
Less than a whisper, to a whisker
writing on an invisible plate, or is it
the thrush of a dead hair
run along skin?

Along mine.
Along his.

These charades …
I am disgusted with myself.
I am disgusted with my sentences. Indescribably
indigested I am.
In another room the wolf-child
plays at being.
I play at …

At what?
Suppose a world.
What is this I see when I close my eyes?

The fundamental human drama is self-knowing. Without it, happiness can only be shallow, transient, beyond ephemeral, more transient than the ephemeral. It makes no difference what powers we exercise, what tempests we control, what sophistication we command. The mystery of self is made to gnaw at you, at me, at us all as we await discovery.

Emanuel Levinas speaks of the discovery of the cryptic, by which I understand him to mean the infinite in every human face. Why is it that we find it so difficult to embrace that recognition of the infinite in every human face as a necessary path to our own self-understanding? In most instances it is too big, too immense, too uncontainable to comprehend, too difficult, too foolish to talk about, and too impractical and unmarketable to make us a living. Yet the discovery of the other in ourselves remains a transforming idea in many cultural traditions.

My grandfather was a familiar, approachable figure. He and Grandma Marie lived downstairs from us for ten years, providing the context of my childhood and youth until I was sixteen. Virtually everyone who had an impact on my formative years, except for one or two girlfriends, was known to Canio and was subject to his consideration, reflection, purview, and review. Canio was and is the lens through which virtually everything in my life came to be reflected, and so he has become the lens of my narrative. This pressure of personality, judgment, and desire structures the quality of my remembering and my storytelling.

Coming from somewhere inside my bedroom closet, inside my head, as I await the next eruption of my father, of the demon in the drawer, this memoir has been my effort to conjure a world, the world of Canio, my own world with and without Canio, the lost world of 1950s Austin, and some worldly and usable vision of happiness.

CHAPTER 2

ITALY IN AMERICA

Gerardo Grieco, Canio's father, brought his family to the New World only to find one very like the old one. As Mikhail Gorbachev famously observed, "Under communism man oppresses man, and under capitalism, it's just the opposite." For Gerardo, that observation ran to his life as a laborer and to his new home. In Brindisi, man oppresses man, but in Chicago, it was just the opposite. In Italy, he and his children left behind one form of political despotism for one equally familiar. But the pay was good in America, and the work was steady. A strong back would make a man a living. Long sacrifice would buy a small six-flat building, now remodeled and still owned by my brother Tom.

Canio's parents had made a modest living in Brindisi di Montagna, the mountaintop village east of Potenza in Basilicata in Southern Italy. They brought what they could with them to America. His grandfather, himself an artist, was a professional of sorts, who apparently lived off paintings commissioned by small churches in Southern Italy. But it must have been a nomadic life, in a time of cart-and-donkey transportation. In any case, there wasn't much left of it for his young son when Canio the Elder died sometime in the 1850s.

As a young man, Gerardo bought some land or perhaps inherited it, a distinction that he purposely addressed on his marriage certificate. Though neither he nor Carolina (pronounced Car-oo-LEEN-ah) could sign their names, he made certain that their marriage certificate said, "Gerardo Grieco, landowner," thus casting his identity out of the peasant and tradesman classes of the village and among the mostly absentee property owners, the minor royalty and otherwise politically connected people who often lived as far away as the Court of Naples and who in the summer paraded themselves before the village during the evening ritual of la passeggiata.

Whether they paraded or not or whether the crops were bountiful or impoverished, the nobility nevertheless exacted rents from the peasantry. Gerardo had a hectare of orchard as his claim to nobility, which he combined with significant personal traits, prescience, and determination. He was twenty-five when he married, and before his second child was born, he was on a ship bound for America.

Out of all this, there is only one story that has survived about Gerardo. It's as though, once settled in Chicago, not a word, a picture, or any other artifact of him survived. As it happened, a certain kind of nobility did survive him, however, but in Brindisi di Montagna, where he is still remembered.

According to a story in the village, there was nothing at all for their widowed mother in those days, except the same backbreaking labor that women still do in rural Basilicata.

Occasionally, between prayers for her husband's rapid release from purgatory and the thin soups that were all she had for her children, she would send one of her sons around the corner to an old widow, one more alone and poorer than she was, with a bowl of soup.

One night, according to the story, her husband appeared to her in a dream.

"Today you did me a great favor," he said.

"What?" she asked, hoping her fervent prayers had finally been answered and he'd at last entered heaven.

"Today you fed my son."

Annantonia was confused.

"Today, when Gerardo took the soup to the old widow, he ate it on the way."

When she awoke, Annantonia remembered the dream and rushed to find the boy. Grabbing him, she shook him by the shoulders. "What did you do with the soup! The bowl I gave you for the old widow?"

Resisting, then sobbing, her son finally admitted he'd eaten it on the way. Suddenly realizing what her dream had meant, Annantonia stopped, her hands slipping from his trembling shoulders. From that day forward, she fed her children first and worried no more about her husband getting into heaven.

Antonio Sarli, the guide who showed my wife, Sidonie, and me around Brindisi di Montagna in 1995 during my first trip to Canio's home, told me this story of purgatory and soup when he realized that Canio's last home in the village was in the house beneath that of his aunt Graetzina. For three generations it has persisted in the village, embodying at once the peasant balance between heaven and earth, the realization of happiness that Canio required of life, and the implicit anticlericalism that excessive devotion sometimes produces. In some ways, this story and its transformation still persisted in my grandfather.

Though he never told the story of the old widow, his favorite joke, the one he endlessly repeated to his grandchildren, began this way:

"I cannot eat the soup!" exclaimed a diner.

The waiter rushed to get the maître d'. "'What's the matter?' he asked.

"I cannot eat the soup!" the man shouted.

The maître d' called for the cook. The cook called the chef. The chef got the manager. The manager called the owner, and still, the man wasn't satisfied. Now the entire staff was scurrying about, arguing one with another. Out of the corner, the dishwasher, a small boy barely able to speak English, appeared. He tugged at the chef's apron.

"What's a madda?" Canio would say, imitating the dishwasher in a slangy dialect he himself never used.

"He cannot eat the soup!" the chef said.

"I know. Here," said the boy, and then he handed the chef a spoon. The chef stared at it for a moment and then handed it to the manager, who handed it to the owner, who handed it to the maître d', who handed it to the man, who to everyone's amazement, ate the soup, his spoon moving assiduously up and down until the very last drop.

———•●——

By all accounts, Gerardo was a classic immigrant success. After several years in Chicago, this immigrant who appeared here as just another broken-toothed, railroad laborer sent for Canio. Contrary to the story that Canio told us about the little fishees, he wasn't five or six when he left Brindisi di Montagna, but ten years old. And he traveled on the *Alesia* not with his father but with his uncle, Lorenzo DeStefano, and his older sister, Annantonia. A few years later, Gerardo sent for his wife, Carolina (née De Stefano), along with Canio's sister, Celestina (whom we all called Gussie). Gussie, though very young, remembered her arrival in Chicago.

"We were walking with all our things. Everything we had, all the way from Union Station to Grand Avenue (about a mile) when my mother saw him coming toward us.

"'Run and kiss him,' she told me. 'It's your father.'

"I was a little girl. What was I? Five or so? I wasn't going to run and kiss that strange man."

The year was 1898. From that point forward, Brindisi along with all of Italy became a land of myth and dreams for the Griecos.

———•●——

A short time later, Gerardo bought the six-flat building, which we called 13-48, on the near West Side of Chicago. As they had in Brindisi di Montagna, Gerardo's family occupied a precinct sprung from a church called Santa Maria Addolorata. At that time the parish extended west along Grand Avenue all the way to Western, and it was the leading edge of the second Italian diaspora in Chicago. In those years, it was said that "you could hear nothing but Italian from one end of Grand Avenue to the other." From the third floor there, you can still see the monumental buildings of the era, the Palmolive Building casting its beacon around

16

Chicago's Loop, Insul's Throne, the home of Kemper Insurance and Chicago's Lyric Opera, and the Morrison Hotel, all of them skyscrapers, transcendent emblems of America. His purpose settled, Gerardo died here, once again situated in view of nobility.

The Grand-Noble neighborhood had begun with Italians crowded into the immigrant ghettos on Taylor Street, back of the Chicago stockyards, but it had its true roots in the corruption of both the church and the state that kept Italy divided well into the twentieth century. And it was this fact that formed the central political premise of the Italian families we knew. Like most Italian immigrants of that period, every promise and threat the future held was framed in those terms.

From the nineteenth century well into the 1960s, long after Gerardo died, Italian immigrant families still came to 13-48. Those families had heard of Gerardo and Carolina's Chicago house in the old country, and when they arrived here, they thrived on the low rents, the familiar dialect, the wine-making cellar, and the smell of Italian cooking. But it's important to recognize that this welcome environment was secured by Carolina's refusal to speak English (though she understood what she chose) and her decision to accept only Italian tenants. The tradition was sustained after her death by her accomplished daughter, Gussie, who inherited the six-flat and who for fifty years continued to take in Italian immigrant families.

In a few years, these tenants often grew prosperous and migrated west to the outer ends of Grand Avenue, leaving behind photographs of their children with Aunt Gussie, who, having no children of her own, had taught them how to sing, how to play the piano, or simply how to get on in English in a place that was still strange to them. Over the years the Griecos lost track of these families. For decades, I thought I would never encounter them, though I heard stories of them, but then I rediscovered some of them in the stories their relatives told me during my visits to Brindisi di Montagna in the 1990s.

After Gussie died in 1971, another generation of Griecos would take up residence at 13-48. Along with my son David and his mother, Anna, I moved back to the old neighborhood in the late 1960s. But by then, we were culturally and politically far removed from Italy. We were the only

Italians at 13-48 who didn't speak the language. That's a marker of sorts, a familiar one to Italians, many of whom so longed to forget their past pain and deprivation as they struggled to meld into this country that they suppressed even their language and did so with a vengeance.

There's a kind of curse in this. The language Italy might have contributed to America, so perfectly whole and sonorous, has been replaced by one that is unusually mean, guttural and common, and has been carried forth by many nationalities as an argot of contempt, almost synonymous with criminality. I sometimes think there is no other liturgy of gesture and expression associated with immigrants from Europe that has so cursed its progenitors and so maligned its place of origin. And this is all the more ironic since Italian is the seed from which some of the most beautiful music in the Occident was born. In part, this is the result of historical divisions between peoples in Italy, and the exploitation of the power to unite, which contempt of *the other* readily generates. So even now when we despise the Mafia, we fail to realize how we encourage the unity and allegiance of its members. And conversely, when we speak its argot, Italians unconsciously take on its moral mantle. Perhaps the only solution is self-effacing humor, a mantle of irony. Grandma Marie almost had it right—neither despise nor assent to this view of us. "Stay away." "Leave it alone, or stay on the right side." "Make a joke of them."

So even in those hippie days when I returned to 13-48, I was still El Greco to some—who often relied on other names, not my last because, like the mafiosos it brought to mind, Grieco was a word either unspoken or difficult to pronounce.

———————◆●◆———————

Grandma Marie's father, Joe Navigato, had begun life in America as a rag picker and junk collector, fresh from Naples, Italy, and barely able to speak English. But in a few years, he could speak English, and his daily walks through Chicago's alleys had made him familiar with its real estate. He soon became a realtor. Then in the late teens and early 20s, founding a private bank became a natural addition to his booming real estate business. Joe had twelve children, the oldest of whom was Marie.

Of course, banks weren't insured then. There was no Federal Deposit Insurance Corporation, and there wouldn't be for a long while to come until the massive and widespread financial collapse of the Great Depression. Joe Navigato held on. This was his baby. In 1933, when the inevitable run on the bank came, he paid out what cash he had and closed his doors for good.

"And he went back to junk dealing," Marie said, still bristling at the ignominy of it. "What could he do? And even though he didn't have to, he paid back every dime of deposits he'd taken in." She paused a moment, and then both wistful and longing for a lost fortune, she added soberly, "He died a poor man."

From Grandma Marie, I learned that "the mob," as we called it, was never to be spoken of; that I needn't accept knowledge of or responsibility for its despicable acts, no matter how justified or glorified in film. Nor need I accept any oppression whatsoever, real or presumed, from its existence.

Indeed, her father, Joe Navigato, was the model for her. Her father had succeeded, had failed, and repaid every depositor in his bank personally for its losses. He held himself and his family to a standard, higher even than America's banking law required. In his name as well as in the name of the Griecos, we were Americans—more than Americans—since Joe had given more than even America required. Why, with that heritage, should we have anything to do with a mafioso identity? Marie's insistence on our independence from *central casting* has also given me a special kind of liberty.

CHAPTER 3

CANIO IN CHICAGO

In 1896, Canio arrived in Chicago as an illiterate thirteen-year-old. With that transit, what remained of his grandfather who had painted churches in Italy or of the castle was swept with the fishies into the American maelstrom. Perhaps those times could be recovered, but none of us returned to Brindisi di Montagna until a hundred years later. Sooner or later though, the question had to be asked. What happened to Italy?

Whatever the postcard he kept of the castle represented, it and the operas on bakelite disks, spinning at 78 rpm, were among the few remnants of Italy that remained to him. Even his accent was so meticulously excoriated that it would hardly appear, not even as he and his brother-in-law, Enzo Stasio, argued.

Slowly, they would swing from English to Italian and back again, moving more and more into Italian as they fought and fought again the Risorgimento, from Garibaldi to Verdi, from Verdi to Puccini, from the Popes to the Bourbons, and back to Garibaldi again. This generation had come as youngsters to America, full of hope in the New World, only to have their better angels vanquished, their rising voices quashed in what seemed to them a kind of industrial madness. Enzo himself went nearly mad, and then in a moment of lucidity, he took passage from the family coffers and returned to Italy. Canio's son Gerald, seemingly abandoning the old country, was more interested in chemistry than great artistic themes, and I, his grandson, made motor bikes and wind surfers, endlessly hacksawing in the basement. If Marie, Canio, Gussie, and Enzo had a dream of themselves and of Italy, it was probably better realized in Gerardo's generation. Though he labored all his life with a pick and shovel, Gerardo managed to return to Brindisi di Montagna often, to send his daughter to opera school and Canio to art school, and finally to inject this family, wholly Italian, into America.

———◆————

The streets of Chicago in the late 1890s were filled with every kind of hustler—organ grinders and monkeys doing trapeze tricks, newsboys on stilts, card sharks, diamond merchants, craps players, and fruit hawkers, and sidewalk artists. In the 1890s, newspapers had a massive and enthusiastic following. At the time, they were the only mass media. But for many Americans, they were a strangely silent media, wholly inaccessible to thousands of illiterate immigrants, except as the big stories were succinctly summarized by a chorus of urchins. Paper boys with spectacular theatricality brought life to the often massive headlines of the day. Newsboys climbed lampposts, hung their wares on fish poles, sang, danced, and did handstands and whatever else they could to sell the lead story or any story at all just so long as it attracted attention.

By his midteens, Canio, now comfortable speaking English, had developed a prized skill. He could draw. Quickly. With massive, colored chalks, he stroked Chicago's sidewalks into action paintings, panels of color and concrete depicting everything from corn huskers in Iowa to Teddy Roosevelt and the Rough Riders storming San Juan Hill. The work required speed, an operatic style, and a grandiose aesthetic. Bright colors, broad strokes, fast-moving lines, and a willingness to draw while the crowd gathered were all essentials. And it took more than a flare for performance. After all, you had to jump up and sell a paper every now and then … and then draw some more and make change. People applauded the outcome of the headlines he animated as though a moving picture unfolded before them. In appreciation, they threw money on the pavement for this patriotic immigrant boy.

In a short while not only was he only selling newspapers, but his pastels became events in themselves. The more political and propagandistic they were, the more attention they gathered in downtown Chicago amid cheers for Teddy Roosevelt and the Rough Riders and "Remember the Maine!" Canio's street art made money, drawing crowds that cheered half for Canio, half for the events he depicted, half again for the players in his tableaux. It was heady stuff for an immigrant boy learning the meaning of new words now flying at him in English.

Performance art didn't exist yet, but much like that evanescent form that would rivet audiences half a century later, his work could be suddenly washed away by a rain shower or smeared into a confused blur by a gust of abrasive papers blown along State Street into the Windy City. There was still something of that performance left in him forty years later as he strolled down Lavergne Avenue in his navy blue beret.

His youthful talent soon brought serious employment. He became an illustrator for catalogs and newspapers, working for several of Chicago's advertising houses, and a few years later he established his own firm, the Grieco Commercial Art Company. His craft in those days was honed on sensitivity to minute detail, a sensitivity that was closer to Vermeer, though unfortunately without that subtlety of purpose. True to his urchin roots, however, and perhaps to deeper instincts, Canio retained a belief in the simple pen stroke, the single, unbroken line that from its verdant beginning to dusty end was nothing but expressive action. One wonders what his grandfather's saints and martyrs must have looked like.

As it turned out, drawings and bold brush strokes were easily transferred to engravings and rapidly reproduced, so in Canio's youth newspapers were full of drawings too. Everything from shoes to soap and horseshoes to iceboxes was illustrated in pen and ink. It wasn't long before Canio found himself in the advertising agencies and large catalog houses sprung up to serve the even larger mail order firms, Mandel Brothers, Sears Roebuck, and Montgomery Ward, burgeoning enterprises in the emerging rail center of the nation. In less than a decade, Canio's newly founded studio was successful enough to support a dozen or so artists drawing illustrations for his accounts. By the time Canio married Marie Navigato, he was an American success story. Meanwhile, his sister Gussie was preparing for a career at the Lyric Opera, and the image, the hope, of Griecos as artists transposed from Italy to America in a mere generation was emerging.

———•———

In the 1930s, when their business was threatened, Marie became Canio's bookkeeper and business manager, bringing her father's financial skills to her husband's otherwise flamboyant, sometimes fanciful mission. While he spent his lunchtimes watching the vaudeville comedians and occasionally sketching the rest of the show, she collected the accounts. As her son Gerald would say, she "made sure the trains ran on time." But there were darker clouds upon them and closer than the horizon.

Canio's aesthetic in those years, though shaped by the commercial demands of Chicago's rapidly expanding advertising industry, was not limited to it. Although reasonably trained in the history of fine art and with what access the Chicago Art Institute could give him of painterly traditions, he sustained a lively if somewhat private artistic vision. He preferred Rodin, for example, to the excessive abstractions he saw in Picasso, preferred the action of color and line in Sessions's watercolors to the rhythm of form in the Modernists. In works such as *Nude Descending a Staircase*, he saw a plurality of forms lacking unity and precision, qualities he required of painting as it had been perfected by Da Vinci and the High Renaissance. In other realists, like Remington, he saw paintings and watercolors of great vitality, energy conveyed in the very brushstroke, and also relevance and accessibility through American subjects. These values, which may have arisen from his newsboy days, were rooted in a notion of popular art and in his own loyalty to the best Italian figurative traditions. To him good art was populist art that eschewed the extravagant and esoteric demands of high culture. Like many of his era, he found those who strove for those ideals somewhat suspect.

He read Ruskin and he studied Da Vinci. And as he read and looked critically at art through their discriminating eyes, he thought about what illustration should be. But when it came to drawing itself, he mostly marveled. I remember how he would stand immobile at times, his head back, examining the distortions and exaggerations light produced in some structure above him. Like his Renaissance predecessors, he marveled at the possibility of transposing open space on paper. High art in the twentieth century, the Modernists, and the Surrealists may have been swirling around him, but Canio could give a damn. The magic of space and action on paper was all to him.

I wish I could say that my most important memories of Canio's generation were the excerpts from Verdi's arias. But the artistry I remember most vividly was in the tall and mysterious closet kept by my grandfather. Even before I was told not to go in his room—Marie had long since moved across the hall to a bedroom with my father's sister, Aunt Rita—I had been told not to go in the closet because it contained "important business papers." From the hallway I could see a cream-colored room within the bedroom, hung all around with suits and overcoats that seemed to me a great place to disappear during hide-and-seek. But we were forbidden to go in Grandpa's closet (or until he was dying, even to cross the threshold into his bedroom). Later when I was not much older, he would retrieve a fedora and some drawings he meant to work on, and once in a while, he showed them to me. They were frequently of nude women, something which at the time didn't register with me at all. I wouldn't even have known they were nudes, except that Grandma came thundering down the hall, shouting at him to "put those things away" and asking what he was doing "talking of such things to little children!"

"Ah, g'wan!" Canio would mutter.

But she persisted, backing him and the armful of manila drawings into the closet from whence they'd come.

I hadn't any idea what the fuss was about. "Those nudes," after all, was Grandma's phrase. Canio, making summary excuses, buried his flagrant women in the lower drawers. There must have been several incidents like this because I eventually remember getting a glimpse of the long flats of vanilla newsprint, some like pages, joined in sections to make up his drawings, perhaps six feet in length. They were absolutely unrepresentative, depicting the barest hint of a figure lying prone on an equally invisible,

24

flat surface. To Grandpa, that single unbroken line, steadfast in purpose, varying only in width and intensity from head to toe, was an exquisite expression of the human form. For me, the form was almost indiscernible and certainly nothing more. It wasn't until twenty years later that I saw the work of a woman photographer from the Illinois Institute of Technology and recognized in her thinly exposed nude photographs the same essential shadows that Canio's drawings evinced.

In the last weeks of his life, when Marie won his soul to the Catholic church, the grand prize must have been those drawings because no one in the family ever saw them after he died. Whatever they were, they disappeared completely, and not even my father, who wasn't averse to the beauty of the human form, managed to recover them. In the end, what survived to tell us about this generation were a few notes, some discarded pen and ink illustrations of Canio's, and Enzo's love letters from Rome.

Amid these artifacts there are preserved stories. The story of Gerardo—or was it his brother?—that yet survives in Brindisi di Montagna and presumably resides there still along with the hat I wore there that refused to be caught as the wind whipped it from the castle keep, rolling down the ancestral hill where Canio's thumb once slid along a photograph, and where his beloved fig trees still grow.

CHAPTER 4

104 SOUTH MENARD STREET

When I was born, we lived in a house at 104 South Menard Street, on the western, upscale edge of Austin, next to enforceably Protestant Oak Park, and it was here that Regina and I formed our earliest memories. The fact that we began life during World War II and in the shadow of the Great Depression was almost unknown to us.

During the war we got US savings bonds for Christmas. We could only get so many car rides and so much meat because we might be out of ration tickets. We went to army parades, sang songs with the bands, and played with extra parts from Western Electric. Our dad worked there, a place that was important to the war effort, so he didn't have to go.

Meanwhile, our mother Kathryn's brother, my uncle Jack, was on his way to Europe and to a little place called Faverolles, France. All Regina and I knew was that he was in the army because he'd sent me his soldier's cap. I wore it now and then for pictures and other occasions. "Why doesn't he wear it himself?" I asked Mom. That was when she told me I had been named for him, and he'd wanted that. The past tense in which she spoke was lost on me. To me he was tall, rode horses, and was a hero to live up to. Even if his hat was kinda scratchy, I'd get used to it, and I'd grow up to be a tall hero who rode horses too.

Our heroes were flesh-and-blood people, aunts and uncles and people on the block. Across the street lived Dr. McGrath. He was the doctor for Grandpa Heaney's company, so that made him our doctor too. Whenever we had a cough, he came over with his black bag, his big eye peering through shiny glasses that sometimes had blue and gold rainbows when he peered down at us. We were his special charges because he'd *delivered* us both. Regina and I didn't know exactly what that meant, but we discussed it and decided he'd probably brought us across the street in a cardboard box or something, and left us in the hallway. Except it was cold out there. So why would he? But neither of us could remember that part.

Cardboard box or not, life was fragile in the 1940s. Its simple circumstances could turn a cold into a life-and-death matter. Although sulfa had just been invented, "the first miracle drug," you didn't want to rely on miracles. Grandma Heaney, our mother's mother, had lost two sisters as infants and lost more than enough loved ones of her own to break her heart after, so our mom was especially vigilant and protective. It seemed to me Kathryn watched us constantly. It must have made her feel particularly confident to have Dr. McGrath just a neighbor's short walk away. As it turned out, that wouldn't be enough.

I can still remember a time when no one else had names and the world was only as large as my toys and the rooms I played in. Not even the rooms had names yet back then, and I didn't have a sister. When Regina was born, I was a year and a half old. All I remember now about those early years was my dad and mom setting up lots of lights, taking picures of her and her pigtails before she could even sit up. I wanted to be in the pictures too, but they wouldn't let me.

For years my first memory of anything at all was of being knocked over by a dog, a rambunctious black German shepherd that jumped to lick my face in the snow in Columbus Park just down the street. I was terrified by the noise and the growling. I still get goose bumps from dogs and see this little kid in the snow with bloody teeth coming at him. As far as that goes, dogs seem to get goose bumps from me too, at least until we pet and make up in a proper display of interspecies symbiosis. The first time I heard about necking and petting, I thought it had to do with goose bumps and dogs. I was pretty sure petting was something like that. No wonder I ended up in analysis! Not that I mistook my girlfriend for a dog or my wife for a hat. Nothing quite like that. But my head needed some body work just the same.

But there were other events before that, and only after it was pieced together twenty-five years later with the aid of a superb psychoanalyst was I able to break with that time. By then, Jack and Canio were long gone and thought blessed. I couldn't ask them what they believed and who they thought I should be.

The realizations of identity run deep as do the habits formed as a consequence. While sometimes productive, my habits of mind from those days were well hidden and difficult to reverse. I say all this "just so you know who's talking," as we used to say in Austin, and so you know who made the choices to remember and to forget.

After the dog, I remember, more or less in order, making a mess with spaghetti and blaming my sister for starting it, trying to escape from toilet training by running into the front room, playing in the sunlight and dust beams there, and trying not to think about the scary Indian in the corner, which in fact, was a bronze bust of Dante that my parents won as a door prize at a bridge party. All this was long before I knew one word of Italian or even knew of Italy. When I could finally stand to look at Dante, I noticed he had braids just like my sister. Dad was crazy about her, and as I soon concluded, had a lesser view of me.

Just before Christmas when I was three, I found an orange and black box of tacks on the dresser, but they were part of a secret I wasn't supposed to know. That night a white sheet sealed off the arched entrance into the living room, so I couldn't run out in the sunbeams anymore because I'd bother the Brownies. Brownies were little men with big ears. They were like green leprechauns but with brown suits and bronze buckles on their belts and sometimes on their shoes too. They helped somebody called Santa make gifts. Brownies seemed friendlier and more my size than Santa, so I was curious about them, and I was really tempted to sneak under the big sheet. But after Christmas, they and the sheet disappeared, and I played with my cousin Topper's Lionel train for days, making it go faster and faster until it spun off the tracks. It smelled like sparks. I was always happy in ozone and sunlight. Now, I guess, sunlight alone will have to do.

That spring I chased Regina around in her diapers until she crawled under the table. When I tried to catch her, she crawled over a lamp cord and got away, but when I crawled over the cord, it messed me up. I tripped and broke the lamp. When Dad came home, I tried to blame it on her because I figured he'd be on my side. But it didn't work. It took twenty years before I came to realize the effect these patterns of blame and denial had as they were set in place those days—patterns, as most anyone could recognize, that diminished my view of women and my sense of personal responsibility.

In the backyard I once hit someone on the head with a hoe. And the house across the street burned to the ground. I don't know why, but I believed that couldn't happen to us because we had doctors that kept us from getting hurt. The lady who lived there went back inside the next day, even though it was still smoking. Mother took us over to see her. Her face was drawn and streaked with soot like one of Walker Evans's Appalachian women. Mom told her how sorry we were and asked if there was anything we could do to help. They talked and talked, but I just wanted to run away from that putrid smell.

That, the hoe, and Halloween were the first things I remember outside our house. Oh, and Gotskin's Shoe Store "because they had a box with a window in it to see your toes." It made your toes green right through your shoes, and it even made your bones green if you wiggled them.

———————•••———————

One winter our Plymouth broke, and my dad overhauled the engine with a guy he knew who was a mechanic. They did it in the garage. But when they finished, the engine kept knocking. Dad hoped it would break in, but after a week when it didn't, he said he was going to go to work and take it apart again. The whole car was cold and dripping with icicles that Saturday afternoon, so I was glad I didn't have to stand out in the garage and watch. Later on, he told us that when he dropped the pan, he found a bearing that was in backward. He put it in the right way, and the knock went away. I thought this was really, really smart, especially since he had figured it out even when the mechanic couldn't. So now I had to listen to him even more.

I remember from that time outings with the Heaneys, picnics with creamy potato salad, and watching baggy, shining elephants at Lincoln Park Zoo squirt water with their trunks at sunrise. Dad and his buddy Otto Schmidt came back from a long trip to Colorado and crept like Indians out of the woods to our picnic table. They'd saved a year's gas rations to go to Pike's Peak so they could take pictures. And they made it too, mostly by shutting off the engine and coasting downhill to save gas. I didn't like the Plymouth much because it had prickly, brush seats that stuck to you through your shorts.

My dad was often fun then. He wore a fedora and a leather bomber jacket and had an infectious smile, one of the warmest people ever saw or could imagine. What's more, his touch was like the hands of a doctor, light and ruminating, gentle as air from a spring window, like breath on the skin. Once he brought home brass couplings from Western Electric, rejects he'd picked out of the bins, toys for me to play with. I would endlessly put them together and then separate them. I came to love the glow and the tinkling sound of those couplings as they mingled in the day with his smile. They remain the first toys I remember, though photos tell of others as well.

When Dad came home we were often in bed. And he was gone in the morning. On weekends there were rows sometimes. Shoes and other stuff would fly out of the closet and slam, sort of kerplunk, and then jump around on the floor. You had to be careful you didn't get hit. But it was funny, except you couldn't laugh because you'd get in trouble and then someone would come after you too.

I'll show you, you bully, throwing your junk at me!

So even though I'd been wrong about chasing Regina and I liked the couplings, those days on Menard marked the dawning of a sense of estrangement from my father. Even so, for a long time the explosive shouting and the flying objects remained merely an anomaly to me as though they came out of another world, some locale of mind or other mysterious place where objects had a life of their own.

This strange explanation for the discontinuity between the father I loved and the person throwing the furniture turns out to have arisen from what I now believe to be my earliest memory, a terrifying dream of animals and monsters, orange and green visages stretching and bulging in grotesque directions. The animals and monsters turned into people's faces, swimming in and out of the dark. Horse faces acquired sweet red human mouths that were transformed into nothing but flairing nostrils. Orange devils shifted into snakes and then galloped toward me like antelopes and then turned into friends with horns or into gray dragons that morphed to human faces. I thought they all were howling at me. Why, I didn't know. Mother, sheepish and guilty, said she had dropped me on my head when I was little, not with malice aforethought but probably without much forethought at all. She sometimes asked if it had affected me, which was perplexing because it wasn't a day I remembered and thus not one to be compared to a time before.

Though this was a very early dream, it turned out to be a primitive explicator, providing, in retrospect, some bizarre kind of rationale for the otherwise inexplicable behavior of people I knew. If voices raged or shoes flew, if faces I knew turned to terror, it was perfectly sensible, no different than the orange, grotesque dreams I remembered. When I was two or three, dreams seemed to make sense of observation, and they gave rise to congruity and explanation.

And yet most of the time on Menard Avenue, we were surrounded by all that was Kathryn's. And in this way, before we were Griecos, we were Heaneys, or so it seemed. In fact, my mother resembled Katherine Hepburn, though that didn't mean much to us when we were learning to walk. She just looked like our mom. Her leg was warm when I wrapped my arms around it, and her cotton prints were a place where you could hide and snuggle. "Katherine Hepburn" was just something other people said.

In all those days on walks in Columbus Park or between the stores on Madison Street, Kathryn moved us along with proverbs. "April showers bring May flowers" was made to help us withstand rainy walks home. "March comes in like a lion and goes out like a lamb" was meant to predict the weather and also tell us about animals we'd only seen in pictures. "Take deep breaths to keep warm." "Warm hands with cold water." "Cool hot brows with cold wrists." Don't be a "pig in a manger." It was as though the whole world was a moral fable, fitted out with good habits, a landscape built on moral character.

How she had come to live in a garden apartment with a wringer washing machine by the back door and a screaming husband throwing stuff around inside was a mystery to me. And there are parts of this story she never fully revealed.

***

Uncle Jack didn't go ashore on D-day or for several days after. And as time would reveal, the reason he was in northern France was more out of duty than heroic conviction. In the 1930s, he had joined the Black Horse Troop, which was then a ceremonial part of the Illinois National Guard. For him, joining the troop was an opportunity to wear an impressive uniform, much as he had in high school at Campion, a Jesuit boarding school in Prairie-du-Chien, Wisconsin, and also a chance to ride unquestionably superb horses with his friends. After Pearl Harbor, the horses disappeared, and the troop was mechanized into the 106th Cavalry, US Army, and sent off to train in Louisiana. Whatever his commitment, Jack's words to my father before he left were clear. "Stay out of it if you can."

Uncle Jack never left Louisiana until the 106th shipped to Europe. His wedding day in Alexandria, Louisana, was the last Tom and Eva Mae Heaney saw of their six-foot-four son. By mid-August he was deep inside France. Paris would soon be liberated, and the future of the Allies seemed secure there while the war in the Pacific was taking a hopeful turn. C Troop always went back for its wounded if they could get to them. So late on the afternoon of August 17, Jack and either Ed Zawilla or George

Hawkins volunteered and took a jeep out to the fighting. In the troop's journal entries for that day, there is no mention of what exactly happened, but both men were killed by a Luftwaffe pilot. As a child, I imagined the plane coming over a hill in the sunset. I imagined it strafing them, hitting them in the back, lifting them off their feet the way waves make a surfer out of you just when you least expect. As a child, I often supposed that they were swept along just like that, horsemen tall and optimistic, as though, even in death, life remained a given.

My grandfather and grandmother seemed stoic. In fact, they were simply private, not approving of grief in public displays. All the Heaneys and their spouses were the same way. "What's done is done." What grief says to grieving, alone in the ending of the day, was all that was permitted. There, life could return to all its grotesque flesh if you cared to let it but not if it disturbed others. Only in privacy was life a given. For the rest, God only knows.

Beyond the songs and parades we knew as children, that was the real war, though it wouldn't become real to us for years to come. Not until we read about it in school and saw it in the movies. It wasn't until I was eleven (in 1953) that I had any serious awareness of the Holocaust. Even at that, World War II still wouldn't be real for another decade and a half, not until Vietnam. The whole subject, like the subject of race, had cast a shadow over us and our possibilities for the next forty years, but in our infancy it was remote, a plaything to us, and sometimes the subject of games. "Let's play war." Mostly, we played cowboys and Indians, a racial game.

Late in her life, Kathryn told me about Uncle Jack and Aunt Jean, stories delivered in fragments.

"They met before the war," she told me. "Jack worked for Steifel and Nicolaus, investment bankers, a post I think Doug Casey got for him. There was a bar on the North Side. Jack had friends he'd meet there, and that's where he met his wife, Jean. She didn't go out with him at first, but she asked around and found out he was all right, so then she agreed to see him. They were married in Alexandria, Louisiana. I think mother and dad went down there for the wedding. Anyway, Jack left for Alexandria in

November the year before D-day, but he didn't go to England until that spring."

I asked her if Jack had written to Jean when he was in England and after Normandy. "I remember we were all sitting around, Dad and me. Jean was there, and she had a letter he'd written. Poulos, I think that was her name. Later she married a man named Gee, and they moved to Salt Lake City, Utah, where they became very active in the Mormon church."

The last time I asked Kathryn to tell me about Jack—that was in 1994—Ezra Taft Benson, the Mormon prophet and president of the Mormon church, had just died. Mixed in the news that week along with the fiftieth anniversary commemorations of D-day (which the British still call Project Overlord) was speculation about who would succeed Benson. As Kathryn spoke of Jack and his widow, it felt to me as though England, the war, and even the Mormon sanctuary were being cut loose, separated from their roots, cast adrift like a gnarled trunk thrown up on the seashore. Cut from sand and sod, they seemed to thrash about and then float serenely out to sea. Perhaps they would never come ashore again.

The theologically unmitigated fact was that Uncle Jack and his scratchy hat were my first encounter with god—not the Christian one with a capital G but the real, unknowable one—and with Fate. How then to hang on to his hat and to his words?

The war itself eventually ended. Jean married Mr. Gee and went off to Mormon Utah. I missed her, whoever she was. I was named—my middle name, that is—for Uncle Jack after all, so I always thought I'd grow up to marry a woman like Aunt Jean, beautiful and accomplished, the way she looked in pictures.

In 1949, Jack's body finally came home from France in a long, ribbed copper cylinder, sealed like a sardine can around the edges. It was the first time I saw just how tall I might one day be. We all gathered for the reinterment, first at the funeral home and then at the Heaney plot in Mount Carmel Cemetery. It was pretty exciting for Regina and me. At the end, there was even a four-gun salute. I remember sitting on metal folding chairs in the funeral chapel. I was still a little boy, so I wasn't old enough to wear long pants like men did. I had to wear shorts. Like the casket, the chairs were cold.

It didn't matter where Uncle Jack was buried. For a long time to come, he would be with us all.

Bang the drum slowly, play the pipe lowly,
To dust be returning, from dust we begin.
Bang the drum slowly, I'll speak of things holy
Above and below me, world without end.

Until we moved to Canio's house and in some ways long after, Uncle Jack remained the focus of my identity. He was the first person I ever tried to be. Kathryn, virtually his sole interpreter at the time, said "he was a good listener, and you will probably be one, too." For some reason, not born out by his letters, she also said, "He wasn't really smart. He did okay in school, but nothing exceptional." I took these ideas to heart and tried to be a good listener too. Whether I was smart or not seemed to me an open question, but *good listening* I could do something about. Whenever I happened to think about Jack or when I played detective or hide-and-seek or when I had to figure a way around adults, I took advantage of being like him and listened. And I listened to avoid the terror I felt, usually when Dad was at home. Soon I learned to memorize every word, every momentary pause and intonation adults uttered. So from Kathryn's simple suggestion about Uncle Jack, I built my first identity, *reading the signs*.

Life at 104 Menard came to an end just after I reached the age of six. Leaving it behind, I leave you with pictures. Some you've seen, like the dog's red teeth. There was a Halloween once when candy corn spilled on the rainy sidewalk. You could still see it even in the dark, and it grew big like Dr. McGrath's eye grew behind his glasses. We'd never been to the movies, but we watched *Kukla, Fran & Ollie* on TV. And Ollie looked like the horse who came in my scary dreams, but not so bloody, while the goofy puppet dragon was black and white with a friendly voice instead. In the living room, there was the Dante Indian that had braids like my sister's and was really scary too, but in the sunlight the dust was fun because it spun in every tiny color. If the sun was gone, however, then there was no dust at all. And in the bedroom there was a tool chest my Uncle Tom had given me. So when I was too sick to get up, I got up anyway and cut wood to make ships. I didn't know what wood was, though I still have the plane that went with the wood, the plane that wouldn't fly. And behind all that was Uncle Tom, tall like Uncle Jack, like I would be one day.

Pictures.

Some with stories I've been telling and others seen "through a glass, darkly" (1 Corinthians 13:12 KJV).

THE WORLD OF THE HEANEYS

The Griecos called all their houses by the numbers, even though they were more like the flesh and blood we lived in, and they stayed flesh and blood for us long after we left them. When I was little, we lived at 1-0-4 South Menard. After that, we moved to 50-0-7, Grandma Marie's two-flat. And before 1-0-4 Menard, my dad grew up at 13-48 Ohio Street in Chicago's second oldest Italian neighborhood, where our great aunt Gussie still lived.

These homes smelled as wet and familiar to us as our dog, Scottie. They were as sure to us as cristales on Christmas and as aromatic and certain as the mild gurgle of water simmering under Grandma Marie's Italian sausage on a Wednesday afternoon. Like the homes of our childhood friends, these were places where the rug was worn so predictably at the doorways you could find your way in bare feet in the dark by the feel of it, and you could find your way as well by the smells that arose along the walls as you passed and disappeared as you crept by.

When we visited my German grandmother, Eva Mae, I wondered what was wrong with her kitchen because it felt more like just the number over the door without a smell of fruit or waffle syrup or for that matter, cooking of any kind.

Everyone's kitchen has smells, I thought. Grandma Marie's was like garlic and powdered sugar. Mulkerin's was like soap and potato soup. Donaldson's was … I dunno. Aunt Flo's was like pink powder and lilac perfume. To my nose, houses always had distinctive signatures. Well, maybe not Conboys'. I could never tell about that one. As we sat at the table in Eva Mae's kitchen one gray afternoon, I asked what Grandma Heaney did here.

"Cook, of course!" my mother answered. "What do you think?" The counters and cabinets were so clear of food and utensils that even if you took a deep breath, hoping to smell something, anything, all you got was the dry, brown prickling of Chicago soot. That didn't come from here, a place too clean by far. It must have seeped in from the outside. Burnt breadcrumbs in the distance—that's what Chicago smelled like in those days. Except when it rained. Only then you couldn't tell Chicago from any other rain-soaked place. In Eva Mae's kitchen, burnt breadcrumbs was all I could get.

This kitchen was the beginning of a sense of difference. Around the table the adults were talking about Grandpa Konning, Grandma Heaney's father, and his young wife, Anna Haase, and about railroads and engineers. I loved trains. I'd always wanted to be an engineer in a white-striped hat and wave at children ever since I'd seen the steam engines roar past on the high banks of the Great Northwestern line. In this kitchen, another world, a world wholly different from mine, odor-free and speeding like a zephr, was seeping into my head.

This was Jack's house, and since I was partially named for him, it required thorough investigation. I wanted to figure out everything I could about him. At first I thought it was just his name I got. But I remember looking around the oriental rug in the hallway, hot in the dust and glare, and the sunlight bouncing around the living room. How was I supposed to be like him? They would tell me, of course, because he was a hero in the war. But now he was dead. I had his khaki dress cap with the colored bars on it. I figured I'd probably grow up and be a hero too, rescuing people like he was trying to when he got killed picking up the wounded. I wondered if he had a panda bear to talk to like I did? The trouble was that when I thought about him, I thought it was a pretty bad idea getting killed.

Wandering around the rooms, I had no misgivings about the Heaneys. They were all tall and important-looking. Jack had been the tallest of all at six foot four. They had to make a special bed just for him. Grandpa Heaney was chief ranger of something called the Catholic Order of Foresters, a famous Indian chief, I figured. He had big jowls and white curling hair like flags whipping over his blue eyes, eyes just like mine. Uncle Tom was handsome and dashing in impeccable suits, with his long hands and cigarettes from a silver case, hands that moved like slow music around his words. He was the one who gave me the tool chest on my third or fourth birthday. It was a pine box filled with tools, one he'd made himself, which convinced me things could be made, even if it was a lot of trouble. It had saws, a drill, and a vice to fit on our playroom table. It might take a long time, but I'd figure out how.

They were all playing gin rummy in the dining room, and between hands, Aunt Rae was getting neat things to eat from the kitchen. Along with my uncle Tom came my cousin Tom, or Topper as he preferred to be known, who was five years older than me. He did scary things on Halloween like make bodies come out of coffins when kids came trick-or-treating. And he painted pictures of parks with dinosaurs hiding in the trees. He and Aunt Rae, who always said funny things, played guitars and sang songs together. Mostly cowboy songs like "Red River Valley."

Then come sit by my side if you love me,
Do not hasten to bid me adieu,
Just remember the Red River Valley
And the cowboy that's loved you so true.

They made me sad when they sang those old songs … and a little nervous because I worried they'd forget the words or hit wrong notes. They didn't, but listening to long songs made me nervous anyway.

This was the Heaneys' world, numeric, pristine, and pure like the definite whistles of my American Flyer train, two short blasts and a long one as it rolled by on schedule from semaphore to train station, through small towns and switch yards, around the track and back to me again. Without smells, this household always seemed on time, engineered, and official.

"My father had the gift of gab," Kathryn often said, occasionally adding, "and he was accustomed to using it."

Thomas Roland Heaney was the third son of Michael Heaney, and he brought forth his father's military posture, his piercing eyes, and determined countenance. He had grown up among the Irish, who were desperately poor in his youth, and just beginning to come into their own in 1900.

As a child of eight or nine, young Tom had passed out handbills after Sunday Mass with his father, who was attempting to found an Irish burial society at Holy Family Parish. It was commonplace for men, who in those years made perhaps eight or ten cents a day, to die penniless and leave their families without so much as the means to bury them. Begun first as a charity and then with considerable foresight reorganized as a fraternal insurance company, Michael Heaney's insurance society and its vision of generous fraternity would come to sustain Tom Heaney throughout his lifetime.

But early on, like so many other young Irish American men, Tom Heaney became a civil servant working for the post office. His brother Bill, also recognizing that path toward upward mobility, became a policeman.

At the end of the 1890s, Tom Heaney courted Eva Mae Konning. They met at one of the numerous athletic clubs that organized social life in the German community in Chicago. Well-financed, with substantial meeting halls, the clubs sponsored dinners, dances, and of course, athletic competitions. Eva Mae had gone to one of these dances with her friend Edna Mae Turner.

At 6:00 a.m. on the sixth day of the sixth month, in the year of our Lord 1900, Tom Heaney and Eva Mae Konning were married. For their honeymoon they took a carriage ride around Chicago. After Eva Mae and Tom left St. Charles Church that morning in 1900 and after they took their carriage ride, they moved in with Eva Mae's father, and they would live with him for the next twenty-five years.

It was Edna Mae who walked down the aisle as bridesmaid that day in 1900, and it was Edna Mae's death that would forever link Eva Mae and Tom to the deadly Iroquois Theater fire on December 30, 1903, the now legendary conflagration that claimed upward of 602 lives. Typical of the enormous uncertainty and tenuousness in which Eva Mae and Tom lived, Edna Mae's death must have had a profound impact on them and was surely part of what would eventually draw Tom into the fraternal insurance business to which his father had dedicated himself.

———◆———

In retrospect, Eva Mae Konning had married beneath her. Whether this was an act of defiance, a reflection of her long-standing independence, or the result of her keen and confident good judgment is not altogether clear. What is clear is that all her life, Eva Mae was intuitive, clearheaded, and purposeful by nature and grace. When she married Tom at age twenty-two, she had been the keeper of her own house since she was twelve. She was used to standing on her own. It's doubtful that her decision about Tom Heaney would have been compromised by social pressures. As for her father, he must have seen the qualities Eva Mae saw and approved not only of a son-in-law but of an additional boarder.

Grandpa Konning, head of the household, was an émigré from Germany, a practical man of no particular religion, and a self-made professional who had Americanized his name, legally changing it from Koenig to Konning. A man of slight build, he was taciturn, introspective, and frugal.

No one seemed to remember his past before he arrived in America, and most of what was said about him was in the distant past as well. He had started out as a switchman, but he became a fireman and then a locomotive engineer. Along the way he married a Catholic named Anna Haase, who gave birth to three daughters, two of whom, Emma and Florence, died in infancy. Nine years later Anna died of tuberculosis. In that year Eva Mae was twelve. Up until then, her father had been driving trains on long runs, often to the West Coast, and would be away for a week at a time. To care for his only daughter, who was now for all practical purposes an orphan, he arranged for Eva Mae to live with the Schultzes downstairs. In time he took over the Galena run for the Northwestern

Railroad so that he could be home with his daughter in the evening. Though he was successful and respected, life was fragile and tenuous in the deepest sense, filled with the presence of these dead.

Despite his agnoticism, Charles Konning saw to it that Eva Mae was raised Catholic, probably out of reverence for Anna. Though it was most likely not something Charles ever foresaw and hardly the intended outcome of that noble gesture, that decision would make marriage to Tom Heaney possible and thus make their daughter Kathryn's marriage to our father possible as well.

Eva Mae finished four years of Catholic high school and grew to be a robust woman with wide eyes and theatrical features. Tall for her times with beautiful carriage and posture, she seems even in photographs a bit larger than life. She had strawberry blonde hair that grew lighter, more effervescent, and more colorful as she aged. And she was remarkably, intelligently attentive, always reaping some personal insight from her gaze, which was at once friendly and compelling. As statuesque and commanding as my German grandmother was, I never remember a moment in which I felt uncomfortable around her, though nearly every other adult made me uncomfortable. In whatever way she'd assimilated her childhood, it had produced an almost legendary steadiness and certainty in her, which she readily conveyed.

Once while she was vacationing in Florida, she sensed, correctly, that something was wrong back home. Without so much as a phone call or a telegram, she got on a plane and returned to Chicago, where she arrived to find her son, Jack, gravely ill with a burst appendix. He survived, a rare occurrence in those days, and Eva Mae was there when they rolled him out of the operating room.

Eva Mae saw in Tom Heaney a person who was ambitious and willing to learn, and who, finding himself faced with her father's Germanic rigidity, could adapt. When they moved into her family's home in 1900, Tom began to change, much as she surely expected, and by the time her father died in 1925, they had moulded their own children, Irish named, into quintessential Americans. Significantly, their first son was not named Michael after Tom Heaney's father. Nor was he called Tom Jr., but instead he was named for Charles Konning. This act of obeisance to the head of his adoptive household was one of many accommodations Tom Heaney made to the world to which he aspired.

Over time he would loosen the ties with most of his six brothers, substituting instead the fraternal ties of Holy Family Court #1. Parish funds had evolved into the Catholic Order of Foresters. And the men of the Catholic Order of Foresters, who felt the need to care for their own community just as foresters looked after the woods and other natural resources, had brought together the fraternal and charitable needs of the Irish community and soon other ethnic communities in burgeoning courts associated with parishes, first in the Midwest and then nationally and in Canada. Tom may have worked for the post office, but his allegiance steadily moved to these extended communities and to the professional relationships approved by his father-in-law, Grandpa Konning.

To be sure, Tom's own connections and prospects had grown along with those of the Irish American community. Irish names had risen through the ranks. Chicago now had an Irish bishop, soon to be cardinal, and an Irish mayor in City Hall. Meanwhile, German Americans, grown prosperous but bedevilled by the First World War, had retreated to the financial districts to which their accumulated wealth had introduced them.

It was in this multigenerational household that my mother formed her earliest memories. "There was a song playing on a Victrola near our house on Central Park Boulevard. What was it?" Leaning on the stone windowsill in a blueing sunset, Kathryn listened as the lamplighters passed from gas lamp to gas lamp with their ladders. The flames flickered yellow, lighting up the autumn trees. *In the Blue Ridge Mountains of Virginia/On the trail of the lonesome pine.*

In that Blue Ridge Mountain evening, as the young Kathryn listened to a distant Victrola from her graystone window, her father, Tom Heaney, was well into the second decade of his career at the post office. Life was bright before them. Kathryn's oldest brother, Charles, was thirteen. Tom Jr. was ten, and Jack, Eva Mae's youngest child, was about to be born. The family had come to share what Eva Mae must surely have sensed had been missing in her life before Tom Heaney. It was what she would always sustain in him, a bright and even-tempered optimism, an ability "to look on the bright side," as Kathryn liked to put it.

Then in 1924, on the way back to Chicago from a holiday in Delavan, Wisconsin, Charles caught a cold. They'd had a good weekend. Most of the Heaneys and Charles's young bride, Alice Campbell, rode in a little Model A Roadster, while Grandpa Konning and Tom Heaney brought up the rear in an EMF, which as they said, stood for "Every Minute Fixing." In the elegant touring car, Tom and Grandpa Konning flowed along majestically behind the bouncy little Roadster.

During the next few days, Charles's cold grew worse. By midweek the doctors diagnosed it as strep throat, and to better care for him, Charles and Alice moved back home to Eva Mae's. In 1924, there were no antibiotics and so little they could do. Charles died on October 29 at the age of twenty-three.

The death of his namesake must have been more than Grandpa Konning could bear. "He hardly spoke a word," Kathryn said. "He'd go in his room where he'd speak to my mother, but he hardly said a word." Indescribable as Charles's death must have been for Eva Mae, grief upon grief was driven upon her with the death of her father a year later.

The death of her firstborn led to one of the bitterest moments of Eva Mae's life. Charles had long had life insurance, but since he and Alice had been married only a short time, he had not yet gotten around to making her his beneficiary. In the heat of grief, ever her frugal father's daughter, Eva Mae refused to turn the policy over to the family newcomer. Anger and bitter words followed, and none of the Heaneys were to see Alice for years to come. Then in 1941, she suddenly reappeared at Our Lady of Mt. Carmel Church for my mother and father's wedding. Kathryn didn't see her until she and Gerald Grieco were walking triumphantly down the aisle, and when their eyes met, my mother began to cry. Alice Campbell disappeared out the side door, and they never met again.

No one could have predicted or prepared for the death of Charles. What's more, the loss of the future he'd outlined for them, his talent, training, and wit, the profound companionship he shared with his father, must have shaken them to the core. Hardship, even economic hardship can be overcome, repaired, somehow remedied. But for Tom and Eva Mae, these existential losses opened old and deep wounds. Wounds that only long grieving might suture.

"Dad cried," were Kathryn's only words to describe Tom Heaney's grief.

———•———

Tom Heaney could dampen his grief through his work. A few years before Charles died, he had turned down the offer of the position of postmaster general of Chicago, left the post office, and become vice president of Garfield State Bank, where he stayed until the Roaring Twenties were coming to an end. In those days bank officers were held responsible for the losses when a bank failed, but with "the luck of the Irish" and not a little foresight, Tom Heaney managed to resign a few months before the bank collapsed. Then he found a passionate outlet in the Foresters, where he could serve God and man, and he did so, expecting sacrifice of everyone in the family to his fraternal ideals.

For Tom Heaney, the bonds of trust in the fraternal insurance business were based on more profound relationships than those in banking, and in this sense his was a more conservative and communal view. The family courts or local chapters of the Foresters were tied to parish life—to values of religious loyalty, early education, and cultural events. Consequently, even when money was tight, people had several good reasons to keep up their court dues and their life insurance policies too. So while the rest of the country was in a state of collapse during the Depression, the Catholic Order of Foresters, though it saw difficult times, remained reasonably solvent.

Eva Mae had no such direct outlet for her grief. She had only her husband and remaining children to which to devote herself. Perhaps it made sense that she constantly remade, rebuilt, removed, and re-adorned their homes. She moved her family from one apartment to another over the next ten years, five apartments in all.

Though comfortable, they were living through the 1930s, the Great Depression. Kathryn remembered it vividly. "People came to the back door asking for food, and you gave it to them because you knew it was real. They were hungry." For Kathryn and the Heaneys, the long tragedy of the 1930s had begun in the 1920s. They had been doing well, but with the unexpected death of Charles and soon after of Grandpa Konning, a restlessness and ancient uncertainty set in. Death reshaped the Heaneys before the Depression in America reshaped nearly everyone else.

Even into the 1950s, Tom's and Eva Mae's characteristic modes of being in the world could be glimpsed in the simplest of correspondences. Kathryn showed me two letters written to her from their apartment in the Belden Stratford Hotel in Lincoln Park, one from her mother and one from her father. In one letter Eva Mae takes responsibility for her husband's health and emotional life, even if it requires covert action and a dose of subterfuge. Tom Heaney's self-presentation in his letter is managerial. At home and at work, he assumes that whatever he's doing, it's important enough to enlist the allegiance of everyone—from Rose O'Donnell, his secretary, to his far-flung offspring.

Grandpa Heaney was buoyed in later life by several floors of corporate staff, his induction as a knight of St. Gregory by Pope Pius XII, and recognition by several hundred fraternal courts strung across the United States and Canada.

For Eva Mae, the role she assumed arose from a visceral, almost muscular response to grief. Ill health and contagion had surrounded her from childhood. And what's more, her intimations of precariousness would prove prophetic. Tom eventually died of pulmonary thrombosis, and his son Tom Jr., also a heavy smoker, died of lung cancer. Infections and lung problems, including her mother's tuberculosis and her husband's and sons' deaths, plagued her.

Late in life Kathryn still bristled at her father's executive presumptions. "We were supposed to eat, sleep, and dream everything Foresters." She paused to lick her lips. "You got sick of it after awhile."

As for the grandchildren, we had differing responses to Grandpa's success. My cousin Topper and I took considerable pride in Grandpa Heaney. My sister Regina, who grew up in jeans and in those days would rather tear a dress than wear it, tended to take Mother's side, probably because the life in the Foresters led to too many formalities.

CHAPTER 6

KATHRYN

In 1929, Eva Mae moved her family to 110 North Long, not far from the Boulevard in the most desirable part of Austin. It was a neighborhood of substantial two-story homes with large yards that were part gardens, part menageries, yards so large some people called them farmettes. This move would forever change Kathryn. The next year, the Cooneys, whose daughters would be her lifelong friends, confidants, and traveling companions, moved to Long Avenue.

Even before they arrived, everybody knew about poor Matt Cooney, chiefly from the nuns. His wife and infant son, gone on a company picnic, had drowned in the *Eastland* disaster. The disaster occurred when the crowd on board the *Eastland*, a large lake excursion boat berthed in the Chicago River, ran to one side of the vessel as it slipped from the dock, and in that sudden rush of people, the vessel capsized. Matt Cooney's wife and infant son drowned along with hundreds of others before helpless eyes. For Matt Cooney, his young daughters, Loretta, Marcella, Lucille, and Isabelle, and his post at the Bridewell (the county jail) were all that was left him.

Loretta Cooney and Kathryn were the same age, and once on Long Avenue, they quickly became friends. Indeed, the two families were to grow so close that Thomas Heaney would one day be consulted when Marcella Cooney and Harold Prendergast married. As young women in the 1920s, Marcella, Loretta, and Kathryn were taken on a visit to Bridewell together just "so they'd get the hang of it," Mr. Cooney used to say, implying that a close-up look at the realities of incarceration might be salutory for Loretta and Kathryn, who were a couple of terrors in those days. Kathryn often admitted in later years that he was probably right.

She herself, Kathryn told me, was full of the devil. Prohibition, the last attempt of their WASP overlords to contain the Irish, was in full swing, and she and the Cooney girls revelled in the ingenuity with which they could sneak a bottle into every possible venue.

Kathryn's friends finished high school and found jobs, or they took jobs after a two-year professional course. Kathryn went on to college. It was a mark of her independence and probably a way to one-up her brothers. Kathryn's degree was, in fact, a more impressive credential than the accomplishments of any of her brothers, whose success arose from familial position and burning the midnight oil, rather than from educational certificates. Kathryn, the only girl and physically less imposing than the rest, had always been determined to hold her own and keep her fire.

"I wanted to go to Rosary, which was the leading Catholic women's college at the time. But it was hard to get in," she told me. Her grandmother, Eva Mae, had been approached by people at Rosary for a donation, something she and Thomas Heaney could certainly have afforded, and though such a quid pro quo might be seen as inappropriate now, in those days it was a sure way of getting the attention of the admissions office. But Grandpa Konning cast a disparaging eye on the appeal. "He felt that you'd paid taxes for public school," Kathryn said, so "that's where you should go." He saw no reason to give to a special school when there were perfectly good public schools she could attend. For whatever reason, Eva Mae agreed, and as Kathryn told me, her mother "engineered the whole thing. She made me take the entrance exam, and I went to Chicago Normal College. A three-year course. Later I went to night school at Loyola and got a bachelor's degree in education."

In those days we would have said that Eva Mae and Grandpa Konning were *tightwads*, and that character trait did indeed cost them and those around them in personal relationships. Curiously, *being tight* was a quality that drew Kathryn to Gerald Grieco and his mother Marie, both of whom would hunt down the best bargain to be found, preferred the promise of bonds to speculation in stocks, and managed the family accounts down to phone calls, nickels and dimes. Despite what her mother's frugal ways might have cost her, Kathryn selected a husband and a family that reconfirmed those values.

It was Eva Mae's character, however, that was her lasting gift to her daughter. With only a high school education herself, she had been, like Canio, an autodidact. Perhaps most precious of all, she believed passionately in the equality of women, a principle that influenced Kathryn to be ambitious in her own right, outspoken, curious, and reflective— qualities that brought her to question for the rest of her life the inequalities imposed on her as well as on others.

The loss of prestige that came with having attended Normal did not prevent Kathryn and the Cooneys from meeting eligible men. They had charm and energy, and in Kathryn's case, the quick tongue of the Heaneys to encourage them. Mr. Cooney, now married to five daughters, bought them a beautiful Oldsmobile in a year when it had long, sleek running boards. It was a verdant green automobile that matched their extravagant flapper hats and their purple and yellow boa-feathered costumes. They would not be left behind.

The men they dated were well-trained and handsome, and they seemed to inhabit a world safe from the Great Depression, among them Ham Ridgeway, Major Ridgeway's son, Tom Dooley, the Cooney girls' cousin, and Norm Smith. With these admirers, nothing much was missed in Chicago. "The College Inn, tea dances at the Blackhawk on Sunday, the South Shore Country Club, the Edgewater Beach Hotel. I don't think there was a nightclub in Chicago we didn't go to," Kathryn confided.

Nearly their contemporaries, the Austin High Boys, of whom the renowned jazz trumpeter Jimmy McPartland was the best known, and other jazz musicians would go even further, frequenting Lincoln Gardens and the other all-Black nightclubs on Chicago's South Side. But if Kathryn and her friends were not quite that adventurous, they were drawn powerfully to the new hot music. "Louie Armstrong was among our favorites. No one even noticed that he was Black," Kathryn said. It was an interesting omission and something I found strange because in almost every other context of our lives, the race was always noted.

Kathryn found herself limited by other restrictions, however, ones that were more onerous than the choice of colleges. Her father, eager to impress his friends, was impatient with anyone she dated who wasn't Catholic.

———————•●•———————

After the sororities and bridge clubs of Normal, Kathryn moved out a bit, taking a job with John Casey at A. C. Allyn and Company. Casey was a vice president, a securities man who had handled substantial investments for the Catholic Order of Foresters, and despite the Depression, he watched the reserves grow. By the late 1930s, the Heaneys were prospering as well, living on Oakdale Avenue on Chicago's plush Near North Side. Kathryn was friends with Jane Bryne, whose family lived with the then CEO of the Foresters. "Jane and I would call the chauffeur and ride downtown to our little jobs in Mr. Cannon's limousine and call him back again when we were in a hurry to get home."

Long before the chauffeurs and speakeasies, however, Kathryn had begun to chart a rebellious course of her own. The cheerily optimistic Blue Ridge Mountain girl had a freedom and audacity to push the limits that extended from her years in Austin on into parenthood. When my sister and I were still little children, she told us how she and Loretta Cooney used to sneak out of Austin High for a smoke or ditch school altogether and go downtown. "Sometimes we'd hide out and smoke in Mr. Cooney's basement, where he kept a little kitchen to boil up some corned beef. Then when we heard him coming, we'd swirl wet towels around the room to clear out the smoke." At seven or eight, proper little sprites that Regina and I were, we knew that this was secret knowledge. It may have been questionable parenting to tell smoking stories and tales of "playing hooky" in front of little children. But Kathryn told that story for good reason. Just then, you see, Loretta Cooney was deeply on her mind.

That moment turned out to be one of my first and earliest clues to my mother's character, and it gave rise to my first thoughts about what human beings could be. Kathryn was telling us that story because Loretta was dying. There were times when life demanded more than its social limits proscribed. Throughout my childhood I would watch her test those limits with my father and with others in our extended household. Unwittingly, at seven or eight, then consciously as I grew older, I employed subterfuge much as she and Eva Mae did in adventures of my own. Kathryn knew how to negotiate the limits of life in Austin and wanted her children to have those skills and that permission too. Like Canio, she'd made a life for herself of them and meant that as a pattern for us as well.

CHAPTER 7

GERALD

The image of my father would change repeatedly in these years, and though these events shaped my vision of him, there are more objective circumstances and details that go some way to explain what happened and who he was, offsetting my narrower view. And of course, my image of him was quite different than Kathryn's understanding of him. It was her perception and willingness to sustain its contradictions that chiefly brought her children to maturity.

From birth my father seems to have occupied a position of privilege in his own household as he did in ours. Gerald was the first Grieco born in the New World, and as such, his status remained undiminished. Dad was christened Gerald, the American version of his grandfather's name, but so there could be no mistake, he was given a middle name, Gerardo, after the Italian form. In every respect he was a projection into history that the family had made for itself, a history meant to survive through him. By the summer of 1912, when my father was born, Canio was already an established illustrator in the exploding Chicago advertising scene. And by the time Gerald was a boy of seven or eight, trundling buckets of coal from the street to his parents' third-floor apartment, Canio had opened his own offices and an art studio that became a fixture of the Chicago advertising industry in the 1920s and 30s.

Until Aunt Rita was born in 1921, Gerald appears to have been the absolute center of attention and devotion of his grandparents, his aunt Celeste (Gussie), and his prospering parents. There's a photograph of him, a bit rotund, his hair cut in bangs suited to the occasion, leaning on a faux wall with his hand in his vest Napoleon-style. That picture still reminds me of an Irish folktale about a prince who accomplishes great feats, defeats tribes, and founds nations, all before he's twelve years old. Gerald looks like that prince, but he's only seven.

He was thought to be precocious and forthright, and he had an amazing temper that he honed firsthand at the knees of his grandmother Carolina, an Italian woman of an ancient school who appears to have absolutely dominated life around him. "Ruled the roost," as Kathryn and Marie used to say. Grandma Marie went further. "That temper of his! He'd better be careful. Someday it's going to get him in trouble." It did.

There is another striking photograph from that time. It's of Canio, Carolina, and the infant Gerald. I always thought my dad had taken it because it was lit with the same delicate shading and angles that he used for photographing shoes in his basement studio. The trouble was he was the baby in the photo at the age of one. That photo had been taken by yet another anonymous illustrator who nevertheless captured some of Carolina's more remarkable features. Kathryn, however, caught more than the photograph did in just a few words. "Carolina," she said simply, "was a screamer."

I came to understand what Kathryn meant years later in the early 70s while working for a ten-film editing house. Over lunch one day, someone had brought eggplant parmesan from home, and Johnny Sasso, one of the lead editors, told me a story about an Italian widow from the old country. It seemed to fit Carolina perfectly. Sasso's widow lived on the third or fourth floor of an apartment building with gardens along the side, the kind that could then still be seen in the Grand and Noble neighborhood. She had made a small gift to one of her Italian neighbors in the apartment below her. The woman, a new mother in her twenties, was a particularly good gardener and raised wonderful tomatoes, peppers, squash, and eggplant on the stony little patch of ground below their windows. After a few days, having found her young neighbor's thanks insufficient or out of some additional slight not easily remembered, something set the old widow off. Believing her gift had gone unrecognized and recompensed, she began to growl and curse at the garden below. "May the poisons come up from the earth into your rocky, little heap. May they rise into the tiny, delicate roots from the bowels of the earth and into the stems and the leaves. May they pass into the seeds of your plants and spread through the ripe tomatoes and red peppers and out into the skins. May the poisons grow and pass into your house and onto your table and crawl into the stomachs of your children."

And that was just the beginning. She went on to curse her innocent and unsuspecting neighbor in larger and larger circles and through each generation of offspring until the poor mother, old and shrivelled, was made to die from her plants and her stunted offspring. These were terrifying curses in those days, and they would have been echoed far and wide in the gossip around Santa Maria Addolorata. They would have spread north through the ranks of parishioners in the old Polish parish of St. Stanislaus Kostka to be heard as gossip and further in Saturday afternoon confessions. Food, you might say, for Jesuits mumbling Agnus Deis for their penitents and the greater honor and glory of God.

Carolina was fully capable of this kind of shrill, demonic condemnation, and she appears to have used it to silence everyone around her. Silenced everyone, that is, except her son Gerald, who by all accounts, went off and practiced her technique.

———— • ————

There is every indication that Gerald's life went forward without hesitation or contradiction well into his twenties. While Canio was building his business with a studio full of engravers and illustrators who could barely speak English, Gerald was becoming wholly American in the school yards and play lots around Carpenter Elementary. By the time he was twelve or thirteen, he'd convinced Canio to buy him a car, and on weekend afternoons the family would take rides to the North and West Sides of Chicago. Canio, resigned to this new age, allowed Gerald to drive the family out to the prairie's edges in Austin, Oak Park, River Forest, and suburbs West, places that would become a symbol of achievement for his younger sister, Rita, and for the rest of us. Austin was growing rapidly and would soon be annexed by Chicago, but most of suburbia would remain a patchwork of villages for another fifty years, isolated from the dust, industry, and disconnected ethnicity that defined Chicago.

Gerald graduated cum laude from DePaul University in 1934. A president of the prestigious Mu Beta Chi Honor Scholastic Fraternity and member of the Blue Key Club, he was as popular as he had been in high school. He had a prodigious memory for names and events and a remarkable ability to recognize the fundamental features of a face. At his thirtieth class reunion, out of seventy-some classmates, there were only two he didn't recognize or whose names he couldn't remember. He was an athlete of reasonable proportion, a ferocious tennis player and a luxurious swimmer. Though not particularly tall, his body grew sleek when he swam, and he seemed to stretch more than crawl as he slid through the water.

His college yearbook confirms much of this. It's filled with handwritten notes, compliments of all sorts, and invitations from friends. Yet between 1934 when he graduated from DePaul University and the start of the Second World War, the world collapsed utterly around him, or so he believed. The 1930s struck hard and left an indelible mark on two generations. Despite all the promise of his graduation yearbook, Gerald wasn't able to find a job—not "so much as sweeping the floor in a chem lab." He had long thought of becoming a doctor, but the terrible economic pressures that trying decade put on families swept that dream away from him. After DePaul, he continued to live at home at 50-0-7, working at Featherstone's Pharmacy without hope of accumulating the financial resources to continue school.

There were difficulties on other fronts as well. On Marie's side, their twelve Navigato cousins, once proudly secure in the wealth generated by their father Joe's flourishing enterprise, were suddenly stripped of resources when his bank failed. Over the course of these years, Marie broke ties with most of her siblings as one after another was lured into some association or another with the mob. It became a mantra for her, one that left her and us feeling increasingly isolated. By 1950, only three of her sisters—Flo, Lou, and Louise—were spoken of, and of the twelve children of Joe Navigato, they were the only ones I would ever know.

Canio's business, too, which had thrived on advertising throughout the 1920s, slowed considerably. In an age of intense unionization and with enlarged families of their own, the artists working for him began to press for higher wages. Canio, who, according to his wife and to son Gerald, "could care less about the business" and "only wanted to draw," was inclined to give them what they wanted. That probably worked for a while, but Marie, whose father's bank had just collapsed and who had a keen eye for the bottom line, began to worry. She started to spend more time downtown at her husband's studio and slowly took a firm hand with the bookkeeping. Meanwhile, her husband had been pressed to hire his nephew Danny Canadeo, the son of his oldest sister, Annantonia, and though Danny knew almost nothing about the business, Grandpa took him in.

Danny hadn't been trained as an artist. However, he was a cheerful guy who enjoyed a good time, and Canio liked having him around. He became a kind of agent for Grandpa, making sure the drawings met his clients' specifications, and seeing to it that corrections (in the advertising business there are always corrections!) were done quickly and accurately. In the midst of Canio's labor troubles, however, Danny's naturally talkative and open nature had the effect of undermining the confidence some of his clients had in Canio. In the sequel, it's unclear whether Danny took some of Canio's business to other art houses maliciously or whether he was simply trying to sustain hesitant clients. Whatever the circumstance, Danny's loose words of reassurance to their clients were seen as a betrayal. These events cast further doubt on the studio's future and further strengthened Grandma Marie's hold on the business.

In response to a work stoppage in the late 1930s, Gerald and Aunt Rita and what few artists remained loyal to the family were pressed into service, working late into the night. Dad learned some basic retouching and pen and ink skills about that time, and he was particularly aggressive about taking over his cousin Danny's role, reassuring what few clients remained. He was good at this, but he was said to have been a bear to work with, explosive within the family, charming beyond recognition outside of it. In fact, the unexpected fate of Grieco Commercial Art Company only fueled his own disappointments. Had Canio managed the business better, had Danny not betrayed them, had men to whom "his Dad had been loyal" for two decades not walked out, he, Gerald, might now be in medical school. But it was not to be. And in the late years of the 1930s, his bitterness, fed by memories of his first job, rankled him. (He was still after all only a "soda jerk and pill-pourer at Featherstone's.")

———●———

It was the genius of the Roosevelt Democrats, strong union supporters, to win the votes of people like Grandma Marie. It may also have had to do with the fact that their ethnic identity meant more when they lined up with their neighbors to vote than their commercial business sense did. What's more, they saw themselves as small people, as part of a neighborhood, steering their little boat by the stars in a sea of small stores and the families they served rather than as big business types, professional, career-minded, and suburban. Consequently, they were more comfortable thinking of themselves as Democrats than as entrepreneurs, a term that, though apt, would have surprised them.

As they would say often, they had found work, and like their émigré parents before them, they were glad of it. Their businesses were just names on the door. "You'd hang your shingle out and wait to see what happened," they'd say. If you were good at what you did, priced fairly, and if there were customers around, you made a living. Yet you didn't expect to grow much or even much want to. As any shopkeeper in Austin would say, you didn't want the headaches, the taxes, the accounting. You ran your business out of your pocket. It was left to others, the big shots, to create the franchises, open branches, and find investors. For you, an investor was a relative who'd accept a promissory note and often scribbled on a piece of paper at the kitchen table, or in the case of the Griecos, a mortgage filed with the family lawyer, who collected regularly, and in time dutifully returned the document simply stamped "paid in full." In this way the small apartment bulding at 13-48 Ohio Street and the interests of Gerardo's children in it was constantly mortgaged and remortgaged among family members throughout Gerald's life. It became their bank.

But Gerald, who admired his uncle Joe, the state senator, and often told stories of his travels, wanted more than this, and the course of his life was frustrated by an inability to move beyond the family business. Curiously, in Chicago in the mid-1950s, Gerald and several other artists founded a commercial artists union, of which he was secretary treasurer for a number of years. The question must have arisen, probably from Marie. "A union?" followed by a *harrumpf* and a rolling of eyes from earth to heaven and back again. "What do you want to go and start a union for? I'd thought we'd had enough of those around here already!"

Dad had responded in words inscrutable to me at the time but memorable, "Yeah, yeah, Rocco and Danny and those guys, what did they know? This is gonna be a real union with bylaws and a set of books, not some ragtag bunch of artists. They didn't know what they wanted from one minute to the next. The ol' man would have been better off with a real union like this, where the policies are clear and you know what you're dealing with." But policy is a difficult creation, not readily built on the experience of small shopkeepers or even a studio full of artists, high in the Garrick Theatre Building.

As he worked the farm he and Kathryn had bought in Reeseville, Wisconsin, in 1950, in part as a refuge in case the Russians bombed Chicago, Gerald allied himself first with bankers and tradesmen and then with dairy farmers in attempts to start a union in the hopes of establishing a fair price for what to all seemed an infinite labor. That effort at cooperative action no doubt seemed the natural way to go for a person with a certain standing, charm, and character. But in the end it was mostly talk. No one really knew how to get the kind of cooperation among farmers a union required. Gerald, true to form, took these failures personally or personally blamed others for not following through. So throughout his life, allegiance eluded him, and he swore and wept bitterly at its demise.

In the end, attempts at forming both unions and cooperatives defied and frustrated my father.

Irony of ironies, it was in the bitter final years of the 1930s, America's Great Depression, that Gerald wooed and proposed to Kathryn Heaney. Perhaps it wasn't so much irony as relief. Kathryn remembered going to meet him after work when she was still a secretary at A. C. Allen and Co. She would walk the few blocks from LaSalle Street (Chicago's financial district) to the Garrick Theatre Building. In the studio, Dad, Uncle Rocco, and the few artists still loyal to Canio were furiously trying to get out one job or another, not leaving for dinner until nine in the evening or perhaps just sending out for an order of chop suey. Kathryn put up with an interrupted courtship and set a pattern of loyalty that Gerald presumed upon ever after. Something about him, though, had already captivated her. It would take fifty years for her to reflect on it openly with us and finally reveal how her heart had turned.

In Austin in those days, women often made their own clothes, and they were good at it. Sewing machines were still usually the trundle type or had a small motor attached. I can remember Kathryn sewing, darning, and knitting, working for hours to make Easter and Christmas outfits for us. I asked her a few times, somewhat incredulously, if she enjoyed it. The answer varied depending on whether the task at hand involved new clothes or darning. "Sure, when it turns out right," she'd say in the case of the former. But when it came to darning, she shrugged and said, "It's got to be done." There wouldn't be a hint of resentment from her toward the confining chores of domesticity for years to come until well after our younger brother Tom was born. By then it seemed she wanted to go back to teaching as much to get out of this preindustrial, feudally organized household as to reacquire a career.

The story of how my parents had met is an interesting one and perhaps typical of the times. And ironically, clothes and a sewing machine had played a central part. Kathryn was still at teacher's college then. There lived a woman in the neighborhood by the name of Mary Mack, whom everyone admired for the clothes she made. When people had a little extra money, as Kathryn and the Heaneys did in the 1930s, they would take a pattern to Mary Mack or even just a picture from a magazine, and she would custom fit the outfit for you. Gerald had been asking around about the auburn-haired woman he'd seen now and then at Featherstone's, at Sunday mass, or walking home past his house on Washington Boulevard. The Heaneys at that time lived just a block beyond the Griecos on the way home from church. So religious observance, whether he was keen on it or not, fueled his interest in the mysterious redhead. And it developed that Mary Mack knew her.

In his front parlor, Canio had a Victrola. In those days people still dropped in unannounced of an evening and took a seat in the parlor, or on slightly more formal occasions, they might be invited over for cocktails. Within a few years and the arrival of television, this kind of habitual home entertainment would virtually disappear as the people increasingly found themselves not wanting to interrupt someone's favorite program or miss one of your own because you got tied up talking to a too comfortably repetitive or even an amusing neighbor. Gerald's DePaul yearbook has several entries that suggest these parlor gatherings were at the heart of his social life, much more than events at DePaul or entertainment downtown, a pattern that was very different from that of his parents.

So eager to meet Kathryn, he invited Mary Mack to one of these evenings around the Victrola and asked her if she'd bring "that redhead" along. I'm not sure if it worked the first time, but through Mary's good offices, flowers hidden in a package from Featherstone's now and then, and ice cream deliveries to the Heaneys, Gerald managed to attract Kathryn's attention.

In those days, until we moved away from Austin, Featherstone's Drug Store with its ice cream counter along with the Bier Garten at the other end of the block were the social centers of the neighborhood. At the German end of the block, the Biergarten was a more private place, ethnically defined, and still a sore spot after the First World War. But sooner or later everyone slipped in and out of the side door at Featherstone's. So whether Gerald advanced his cause at the pharmaceutical or the soda counters, he also made sure that he personally bicycled over to the Heaneys with their orders.

Up until then, most of Kathryn's friendships had centered around her three brothers, although Charles was now deceased, and she was particularly attracted to a relative of the Cooneys, who had been her closest friends since grade school. Tom Dooley, the oldest son of Matt Cooney's sister Bridget, had a flare of his own, and Kathryn said more than once she considered marrying him. But Gerald had a restless energy—a "tingle" about him was the word she used—an excitement that drew her to him. Little did she know.

Thomas Heaney's fortuitous move to the Catholic Order of Foresters and the combined failures of the Navigato Bank and Canio's business created the circumstances that led Kathryn Heaney to marry beneath her. This was, in any case, an economic fact if not an educational or religious one, though in Austin in the early 1940s, the alliance no doubt raised eyebrows for its shameless disregard of class and ethnic allegiances. A half century after the wedding, my mother told me that her father was ashen as he escorted her down the aisle.

CHAPTER 8

50-0-7 WASHINGTON BOULEVARD

After the First World War, as urban racism was increasingly directed at African Americans, Italians were moving up and out of the old neighborhoods and into middle-class American life. And so in 1923, my grandmother Marie moved her family out of the Italian neighborhood around Ohio Street to an expansive two-flat in Austin on Chicago's West Side at 50-0-7 Washington Boulevard. She moved west to escape the legacy of being Italian with eleven brothers and sisters. But most of all, she hoped to escape the association of Italians with the mob in these Johnny Torrio-Al Capone years.

It was a building complete with a yard, a garage, and perhaps most important of all to my father, a stoker that loaded coal into the furnace under the boiler, which would heat the house without his hourly intervention. Gerald could now attend St. Mel's High School for Boys, and there his wit, charm, and incredible memory for detail continued the family promise of successful transition into the New World.

Once moved to Austin, Canio, though prosperous with a studio full of graphic artists in the Garrick Theatre Building downtown, was instructed by his no-nonsense, business-oriented wife to never speak Italian, not even at home. Yet unlike my grandmother, he saw his Italian roots in a longer perspective, dating back to the Italian Renaissance, about which he avidly continued to educate himself from sources as diverse as Leonardo and Ruskin and the other great books, which stretched from one end of his living room bookshelf to the other. As for his Italy, its language and its heritage, these became a kind of *terra humana*, as well as a ground of defiance for him. Italian was the language he used freely when the heat of the Risorgimento infected his conversations with other Italians, when he argued with Marie, and especially in conversations with our uncle Enzo.

———— • ————

Twenty-five years later in 1948, when I was almost six and watching *Howdy Doody*, wondering why Clarabelle wore a horn and Captain Bob had oily hair and trying to talk with my lower lip set like a box on the end of a string just like Howdy Doody did, my parents announced we were moving to Grandma and Grandpa's. I expected to move right away, only to discover that the upstairs apartment, which is what we called our new house, was rented to the Schaffers, and they wouldn't leave. So Grandma and Grandpa would have to evict them. I hoped that they'd evict them in a hurry. Everybody in the family kept coming up with excuses for why the Schaffers should be thrown out. They didn't sweep the back steps. They made too much noise over Grandpa's desk. They were Irish and couldn't get along with Italians. But none of these would work because, among other things, Mom was Irish, and no Irish judge would believe the charge anyway. This went on and on like the adventures of Howdy Doody and Clarabelle until one day Dad paid the Schaffers some money and they moved away. So that's when we moved to 50-0-7.

The movers came early, and Dad and Regina and Scottie, our fox terrier, and I all drove to Grandpa's house before breakfast. Dad parked the Plymouth in the alley and let me hold onto Scottie's red leash. But as soon as Scottie saw the backyard, he took off running through the gangway and along the porches next door, his yelping echoing through the courtyards, making more noise than the Schaffers ever did. I held him back as much as I could, but it didn't do any good. Scottie just kept pulling me along. Finally, Dad ran down the courtyard to tell me I'd gone the wrong way, damn it! And what was wrong with me? Why didn't I stop that damn dog? I couldn't. Then Dad's hat flew off as he tried to catch Scottie. By the time we got back to the alley and around the fence and into Grandpa's yard, we'd woken the Buckleys and the Flynns and the Conboys and the Donaldsons across the way.

I have only one memory of the yard at 50-0-7 once before that, although we had gone there nearly every week to visit my grandparents. It was a warm, sunny afternoon, and we were waiting for Grandma to call us in for Sunday dinner. Regina and I were playing hide-and-seek in the cool brick passageways beside the house and in the narrow spaces between the garage fence and along the lilacs. Someone came out of Frank McMann's house next door. Whoever it was scared me because somebody had told us the ghost lady lived there. But this was a man, and when he came over to the fence where we were hiding and giggling, I thought he would try to squish us between the garage and the fence. Maybe we were having too much fun or making too much noise or doing something the ghost lady didn't like, and she had sent him to chase us away. So when I saw him coming, I jumped out of my hiding place by the fence and ran out in the middle of the yard.

Frank came down the walk along the fence and hung something over it, something white, dangling at the end of his arm, and he mumbled something. I didn't know what he wanted, but Mother, who must have been reading on the porch (and was still wearing a chartreuse dress with a wide, black patent leather belt from church that morning), told me to go ahead and take it. By that time Regina had arrived on the scene, but Frank, with his white hair and low voice, still seemed to be gesturing to me. Then I realized he was holding an old alarm clock with a bell on it and the back half missing. It was something he thought I might like to fix. That seemed like a pretty stupid idea to me since I didn't know how clocks worked, and anyway, who cared what time it was? But he jiggled some of the gears and made the hands move. They were brass and shone golden in the sunlight, so I took it, even though I was afraid the old lady's ghost goo would be dripping out of the inside and would stick to me. Somewhere I've still got the pieces of that clock.

My experience of childhood up until that time—or at least my earliest memories of it—had consisted of pure, specific instances. Bright, colorfully clear events in which words and actions were perfectly recorded, even if ambiguous in their meaning. When we moved to Canio's house in 1948, life became muddled and complex. The sudden immersion into a system of authority with five more or less contentious adults—Canio and Marie, Kathryn and Gerald, and Aunt Rita—now made life dramatically different than it had been when it had been shaped by Kathryn at 104 South Menard. At 50-0-7, life moved by indirection. Events occurred from which no easy lessons emerged. At 50-0-7, Kathryn and the Heaney world with which she had surrounded us were eclipsed. And it's probably accurate to say that intrigues developed that Kathryn could no longer encompass. There were now only conflicting explanations, whereas on Menard, our daily living had been open and defined by events our mother easily characterized.

At 50-0-7, the four of us lived upstairs in an apartment identical to that of my grandparents and Aunt Rita, who was about to graduate from Rosary College and who still lived at home. Between floors there were a lot of unanswerable questions and "unanswerable questioners," as Kathryn put it. We all lived around my father's and my grandfather's studios, which were south-facing rooms that overlooked the backyard. From all these intimacies, my sister and I carried away mythologies of our own, part Grieco, part Chicago Italian, part Heaney success, part middle-class Austin.

In the deepest childhood I remember, life was filled with brilliant, distinguished epiphanies too. I may have asked why Jack had given me the hat with the red and bronze insignia on it and why he didn't wear it himself, even if it was scratchy. But the hat and the question it contained remained open and explicable. An answer came as expected, one easily understood. At 50-0-7, that trust in coherence and logic broke down. Our life there would be filled with robust and passionate people who were often governing us, but much of their governance remained inexplicable.

We were thus introduced into a world of secrets. Nothing was more emblematic of the reign of secrets than the basement with its locked rooms, coal bins, and dank cobwebbed cellar that rumbled and growled with the buses moving along Washington Boulevard or with ghosts of the dead who came before us. Even in the brightest parts, it felt strange and alien as they sprang to life with the grinding and sloshing of various machinery. Adding to the eeriness of this basement, the florescent lights flickered and lingered, not coming on the way you expected them to do, startling the shadows.

The fact of such sudden, disturbing reversals in my daily experience and the subsequent years of self-reflection they required no doubt shaped the stories I tell myself now about my childhood and the terms in which I remember them, through to their consequences. In the last analysis, while these reshapings often made these stories bearable or joyous, sometimes they also made these disturbing memories worth obliterating.

◆

So now we lived in Austin and at the center of my coming-of-age story was Canio, whose name, he told us, meant "the clown." He had a trick up his sleeve or a card or a coin, and he had the mysterious escapades of Houdini in the back of his head. For a long while, it was Houdini's escapes I longed for, though they were truly inexplicable.

Yet my grandfather was not only the clown with whom we played. He was also a fierce autodidact and a subtle and engaging conversationalist. And through the days of passion and contention, he maintained his elegant style.

Occasionally, Canio would find me curled up in one of their French provincial couches, paging through his library of great books as the buses rumbled by on Washington Boulevard. "The great trick," he used to say, "is not just to learn what you read but to remember where you read it." For Canio, the history of thought was not a systematic, philosophic exercise as it was for the scholars at the University of Chicago who had compiled the contents that made up his bookshelf, but the deliberate effort of an autodidact in successive, repeated, and intermittent readings. The conviction that one is intelligent enough to be self-taught can be a dangerous one, but it was one that Canio readily embraced and that he balanced in his endless inquiries, be they with ideas, with practical people, and even occasionally, with the family around him. Though he might and often did feel their respect for him as an artist, the world of aesthetics and philosophy, he knew, was rarely one they would engage.

There is a photograph I remember, one that Dad took of Canio reading in his armchair. Behind him and in his hands are books from his hardbound set of the Harvard classics. That photograph was taken about the time Canio told me about Schopenhauer and other philosophers of the will. Occasionally, he spoke of Spinoza and Montesquieu. Or was it Montaigne? But how he spoke of them or to what purpose I can't remember. At the time I was too young, too ignorant of such things, and most of all, absolutely uninterested in his subversive learning.

Now, of course, his subversions fascinate me. Surely, it was subversive for the son of Catholic, immigrant Lucani to abandon his parents' peasant and materialist ambitions and to decide instead to steep himself in learning. Surely, it was subversive of him to take up the classics in opposition to his religious, pragmatic wife, to the church's dire warnings about "dangerous freethinkers," and to nearly everyone in the neighborhood. And in that photograph, with the bemused smile he directs at his son behind the camera, you can see the dawn of a larger subversion, of a man who sees himself as nothing less than the artist of Austin.

I have shards of memory of Canio in conversation, with his brother-in-law Enzo, with the shopkeepers, and in social gatherings. And I vividly remember observing him during one of the rare occasions when our parents hosted a dinner for *both sides* of the family, probably for cocktails and a light supper of the kind we would have on Christmas Eve. Kathryn had given Regina and me lines to recite for entertainment and instructed us to buy gifts for our grandparents. With our allowances, we picked out toothbrushes, shoelaces, and matches for cigars, but when we wrapped them in Christmas paper, they ended up looking more like crinkled lunch bags with nametags.

Forgetting about his dentures, I gave Canio a toothbrush. But I got through the nativity story in the gospel according to St. Luke all right and so sat back relaxed and quiet as a church mouse for the rest of the evening, relieved beyond words that I had made it through the reading without embarrassing flubs. In that heightened adrenaline state, I watched the rest of the evening unfold.

In those days the person at the head of the table was expected to introduce a topic of general if sometimes controversial interest. Once the conversation was set in motion, we would all join in, children included, until the dessert came or the world was won, and then we'd move on to new worlds to conquer or at least a game of cards. For some reason Grandpa Heaney sat at one end of the table, the head. Canio, who had come upstairs for the occasion, wasn't seated so much at the other head of the table as along one side close to the kitchen. It seemed to me he deserved more respect than to be seated on a chair brought in from the kitchen, though I don't know that that would have made any difference to him. Still, it was his son's dinner table.

As the evening wore on, Grandpa Heaney, who was clearly in command at the head and to whom my father demurred, never offered more than small talk. I remember the inviting glances Canio sent Grandpa Heaney's way. And I wondered what this man of Montaigne and Garibaldi and Verdi was thinking. His son had married well. But Thomas Heaney wouldn't even start a serious conversation at his son-in-law's table. I cannot but think that as he looked at Thomas Heaney, vastly more successful, tall with waving white hair, and high churched, such as the church was, Catholicism being the state religion in Chicago at the time, Canio felt a certain disappointment in his apparent lack of interest in ideas.

Grandpa Heaney certainly couldn't have missed what my uncle Tom saw clearly—the elegance and humanity that Canio exuded. While Dad was given to more emphatic displays and might at times have seemed avid, even patronizing in his enthusiasm, Canio's manner was restrained, cost-conscious as it were, but open to comedic opportunity. He knew how to live, people said of him, and he knew how to tell others about it. And although his favorite comics were Al Jolson as well as Amos and Andy and even though he would have loved to possess their comedic wit, he knew the greater virtues of attentiveness and a listening restraint.

So far as I remember, that Christmas Eve dinner was the last attempt my parents made to marry the two cultures they'd come from.

———•———

With Canio, Regina and I explored our Austin neighborhood on the far western edge of Chicago, which during and after World War II, we called the West Side, as distinct from the other two-thirds of Chicago, the North and South Sides. For us, it was a sense of place that hovered around a few dozen shops and churches, consisting of maybe 2,500 people out of the hundreds of thousands who lived in enclaves different than ours on the West Side. Unlike those Italians who still lived in Chicago's old Italian neighborhoods, we were brightly, perhaps naively American. We didn't think of ourselves as hyphenated, not Irish-Americans, not Italian-Americans, not Norwegian-Americans, although Mrs. Johnson across the gangway spoke with one accent, Johnny Mulkerin's father with another, and some relatives of mine in yet another argot. Many thought it was impolite to mention these differences, and once mentioned, such observations lay one open to a similar, disparaging dismissal.

As children growing up among these diverse voices, we held the belief, naïvely perhaps, that we were just Americans. For us, the laws that bound each of us were the same that bound all of us, governing people from whom we expected the same courtesy, and from whom we exacted similar benefits. So while a kitchen in one house might smell of potatoes different than ours or while certain holidays weren't celebrated by some families, we nevertheless believed we were all pretty much the same in the end. The Rosenbergs might have been Jewish, but they had a television set. And we'd all go there to ooh and aah at *Kukla, Fran and Ollie* and sing along with *Howdy Doody*. And in the evening we laughed with Gracie Burns, Red Skelton, and Jack Benny, who were beneficiaries of being *just American* much as we were.

Austin janitors were liminal figures. While not the most respectable of residents, they commanded respect as custodians who, along with shopkeepers, weren't afraid to turn a broom or handy rake into a cudgel if you were slow to yield. Some of them were responsible for two or three buildings and had lots of money to play the horses. Tony, the janitor who lived next door to 50-0-7, had sixteen units and maybe sixty more across the alley as well as some along Madison Street. He stoked the furnace and did minor maintenance, rounding the corner on wintry days with his Allen Bradley plow roaring, ice clumping his long hair and wrapping around his moustache. He was a peculiarity, but he was respected, a presence that made the neighborhood safe since troublemakers knew that he and his kind were likely to appear suddenly in any gangway and were alert to even the slightest trouble taking place around a corner. Janitors along with the priests and nuns stood in an orderly patrol that made the neighborhood safe and more or less predictable. They were symbols on several levels of an established order of which the police and fire department were the last and least used line of defense.

Vandella Dickson, our black house cleaner, lived on the West Side, but not in Austin. Nor did the organ grinders, the coal men, and the peddlers in the alleys who simply brought music, coal, newly sharpened scissors, and Good Humor ice cream bars to us in whatever language they preferred just as Van brought the gossip of another world along with rumors from the homes of our aunts and uncles.

What our parents thought of those outside the neighborhood and the prejudices they held about them was mostly spoken in bedrooms in those days. Those thoughts were part of another world, an older one kept from us when we were very young. It only gradually informed our prejudices as we grew up. It was only as teenagers that we were introduced to such things explicitly. The dawning of those differences on us and the scars they produced, the intimacies, often unspoken assumptions, and ways of thinking that surrounded them remain difficult to grasp, even at this distance.

CHAPTER 9

RIDING THE L

One chill March Sunday soon after we'd moved to 50-0-7 and Regina and I were six or seven, Kathryn bundled us onto the L train for a ride downtown. We were going to see our cousin Margie, but downtown we changed for the South Side L instead. Mom said something about maybe we'd go to the Museum of Science and Industry. It was a salt-and-pepper day, and Regina and I were in a good mood. We didn't care where we were going. After we'd ridden south for a while, I realized that Kathryn wasn't paying much attention to us, and then after a while as we pointed and laughed at whatever we thought was silly out the window, we noticed she seemed to be crying. When we got to 63rd Street, we changed cars and came back north across town. In late afternoon as the long shadows cut blue and yellow panels on the elevated platforms, we took the train back home. So far as I remember, Kathryn never told us what all that traveling and changing trains had been about that day or why she was crying.

I often think of my extended family arrayed in that two flat on Washington Boulevard—Kathryn, her auburn hair wrapped stylishy in a turban, sewing in the chartruse TV room; Marie in her kitchen downstairs, making crystalies with the tapered rolling pin I made for her; Grandpa Canio at his desk, the Sox on the radio behind him and the Cubs on television from Wrigley Field; and my father, Gerald, pouring chemicals in his darkroom in a cubby of the basement. Regina, Aunt Rita until she married, and I floated through these mythic stations, winning cases and currying favor where we could. They had constituencies and worlds of their own, these four. And the rest of us were left to negotiate our identities among them.

But perhaps the most mysterious identity of all was Kathryn's. She was at least as inquisitive as Canio, as independent as Marie, and as determined as Gerald, but without his furious temper. How someone with the dignity, wit, and reserve that Kathryn commanded had come to live in a house gushing with Italian emotions was long a mystery to me. She seemed completely different than the rest of the household in effect, style, and demeanor. Most notable among these traits was the cordial laugh she had, which was the first malleable feature of personality I ever noticed. Somehow when I was six, I realized she would laugh just to be nice. It made me wonder about other people's reactions as well. I'd try the same childish jokes on my grandfather, and I soon noticed he seemed to laugh the same way. Actually, he would chuckle and then move on to a story of his own as if to say he'd heard all mine before. He probably had. But it was infuriating. Then I had to listen not only to his story but to the next and the next.

Kathryn presented an even more puzzling problem, however, because when she laughed cordially, there was almost always some hint of understanding or some reserve, some lesson to be learned. Later I watched—or mostly listened—to her when she was with the Heaneys, particularly with her brother Tom, who had a gentle, lilting diction and a sparkling way of speaking, at once acknowledging what he admired in others and engaging their responses. It seemed to me he always knew how to edge in and out of conversation and that Kathryn enjoyed watching him do that as much as I did. Whatever it was the Heaneys talked about, it seemed ever light and airy, devoid of anger, and free of the palpable hostility that often filled the rooms at home. Nobody here stalked out of the room. And discussions didn't swim in some ideological concoction of Italian Risorgimento, novenas, and the family business. Wherever it was that Kathryn came from, it was a world where words transformed realities and a brushstoke of optimism made magic possible.

A year or so after Gerald died, I asked her about these differences, the most salient part of which was my father's temper. Pausing in the midst of breakfast and pursing her lips, she glanced about the kitchen for a moment in an expression of judgment or disgust. I couldn't tell which. Perhaps it was no expression at all.

"I thought I could handle it," she said, ready to leave the topic.

"Well, how did you find out about— I mean, when did you realize he was that way?"

"Oh, I guess I knew. It wasn't something I suddenly discovered after we were married or anything like that."

A few months after they were engaged, she found out just how serious Dad's temper was. They were at a party in River Forest, probably then the most prestigious suburb west of Chicago, at the home of the Caseys. John Casey, for whom she had worked as a secretary, lived on the western edge of River Forest, where the houses were larger and grander, second only to the wealth in the Northern suburbs, Winnetka and Wilmette. The party was given as a celebration of their engagement, and though they didn't know it at the time, John and his wife were planning a lavish wedding gift for them, an ornate silver coffee and tea serving set that we as children would see unwrapped only rarely on special occasions. Silver coffee and tea vessels with matching sugar bowl and creamer would be set on a large silver tray, silver-leaved and hand-tooled, as each was drawn from the green flannel sacks that kept them from tarnishing through most of the year. Then they were meticulously polished and used briefly of an evening before they disappeared into the upper closet again only to reappear a year later.

Gerald and Kathryn had a pleasant evening at the Caseys, but Dad became more and more agitated as they left. Driving home, he slammed the gearshift of his prized Nash, swearing as he changed gears, jerking the car forward, grinding the gears harder and harder.

"I thought he was going to break the shifter off," Kathryn said. "He was furious. He kept shouting about them. What right did they have? Who were they with all that money? Who did they think they were anyway, living like that! He went on and on, swearing about the house, the Caseys, and their friends, swearing at them as though they were right there in the car, all the way home."

In a way it was understandable. In 1939 and 1940, Canio's business had collapsed, and with it had gone what hope Gerald had of going to medical school. Torn between his affection for the artists he had known as a child, the treachery of his cousin Danny, his cum laude degree in chemistry that had not gotten him so much as a job, and his disappointment with his father, he saw everything he'd hoped for seemingly crashing down around him.

But Kathryn would not accept this explanation. Looking back on it all late in life, she doubted his interest in medicine. "He couldn't stand the sight of blood," she said. "I don't think he was cut out to be a doctor." That may have been, but in the midst of the Depression, with a college degree, something not many Americans had and something that was even rarer among Italians, the fact was there lay in front of him no future he could yet specify.

I think she recognized many of these stark differences between them and their two families and had seen them before her quite clearly on that mournful L ride. I remember wanting to console her that day, to tell her we were okay, which we were, high up on a bouncing train, overlooking a sunny day in Chicago. But she wouldn't look at me. She refused to hold my gaze for more than an instant, not acknowledging it when she did. I was only six or seven years old at the time, but what had to be acknowledged had been fixed in place in her mother's generation and in a generation before that, in uncertain times during a war that had taken her brother, and in a past that was no longer readily explicable, if it ever had been. In a way, that past was becoming a mystery even to her, who so often tried to explain it to us in sensible terms. Worse, it was a mystery she had lived through, one that reached back to events, choices, and circumstances even her parents could barely comprehend.

Catholic women had an expression in those days. You would hear it whispered about among their friends and neighbors. Someone or other had "taken up her cross," they would say, whatever that meant. About the time of that L ride, Kathryn began going to Mass almost every morning. For my mother, religious devotion was a saving grace. It brought continuity to our household, though it would also exacerbate some of the conflicts to come.

CHAPTER 10

AT PLAY WITH CANIO

My father's studio remained off limits for Regina and me as a place to play. The picture I see before me in that space is of a young boy commanded to model shoes for his father's photographic orders. I would have to sit perfectly still in the studio, forbidden to move while we waited for the plates to develop, at which point Dad would return and take another shot of my propped-up feet or turn on the lights and release my toes from their duties. It was a kind of command and control center, though it may have taught me something of patience and of the photographic process.

Canio's studio was another matter. Since he lived downstairs, we always had someone to visit, and he was sure to have candy and colored pencils at the ready. He would be consumed in his paper, so it became standard practice to go up and bat at it, to announce our presence, or to crawl around his ankles until we drilled our way into adult absorptions.

Unlike in Dad's office, Regina and I could wander around in Grandpa's studio most of the time, except when he had large orders, which meant shoe boxes piled in pairs to the ceiling. Shoes in various stages of pose and conjuncture and other samples extended even into the dining room during "the season," as these periods were called, where they obscured every green wall and nearly all the windows. Next to the windows, Canio had his desk—he and Dad called it "the boards"—which was tall and positioned in full regard of the southern light, thought to be the most even and reliable for artwork, second only to north light, which would have been best of all.

As he sat, his back to the bookcase and the wall, his desk was close enough so that he could slide behind it with a view of the yard and the lilac trees on one side and a view of us on the other side when we came scrambling into the room. Situated that way, he could open the top drawer, our favorite, and also block the way to the shelves, the airbrushes, compressor valves, and his ever-rumbling radio as well as to the Nunn Bush and Crosby shoes and the other odds-and-ends objects he drew out of curiosity, all of which he kept along the window. The layout was a strategic one that worked well for Regina and me.

As it was, almost everything of interest at Grandpa's drawing board was in that first drawer with which he blocked passage to the rest. He had, in fact, long since dedicated it to his grandchildren, but in ways only he could associate. He had grassy brown twine there with which to wrap packages but also to string Cat's Cradle and perform a dozen other finger tricks for us. In the back of the drawer, there were old leather baseball gloves, flat and powdered, now gone earthy white with wear. He also wrapped packages from that drawer, so along with the twine, it was full of tape, labels, and stamps since the principle of order here was not categorical but functional—to have everything at hand that he needed on the way to the post office. And in delicious combination, it held everything close at hand that his grandchildren might have wanted as well. Chuckles, dried figs, Mounds bars, peppermint sticks, and at Christmas, nuts and hard candy.

Above the desk drawer, like a flag seen from afar, was a true mystery, namely a string of blue smoke that rose heavenward from his ashtray. To me, this was a fabulous occurrence like the genie rising from Aladdin's lamp, a thin column of smoke that held a magic carpet of blue above it, spread out across the ceiling. Sometimes that column was so thick I wanted to climb it all the way to heaven the way they did in *Jack and the Beanstalk*. But at the top, the ceiling put a cap on my dreams. No giant, no golden goose either. Still, it was a great mystery since every other object I'd seen, living or dead, seemed to stay mostly on the ground. What's more, this column of cigar smoke curled back in a knot and rose heavenward again at just one point. Why just there? It was even more mysterious. As for the blue smoke that came from Canio's mouth in donuts, I more or less understood that. It was like a first rule. Things people caused could be explained. He was doing it! But smoke that curls on its own, that was a mystery. That vertical column of blue carbon, curling and then rising again, was a barely calculable piece of work. And what about the cloud above, the blue-gray haze, thin as air itself, all seeming to rest on this gossamer column?

Canio's desk smelled like cedar pencils, and as he sharpened them, first a 2-B and then a 5-H, shavings would scatter around. The smell of fresh lead, dry leather, and blue-gray cigar smoke eventually permeated the room. This was neither a workplace safety issue nor secondhand smoke for us. It was, in fact, a kind of aura, in which he, his drawing board, and the blue-gray mist were inseparable in our expanding awareness of the world in which we found ourselves.

Regina and I reveled in our role as command audience for our grandfather's lavish, albeit self-absorbed attention.

If he hadn't time to take us out in the yard or if it was rainy, he'd often do hand tricks instead like rolling a tennis ball from behind his head. The ball would course down his shoulder and the length of his arm, where it settled like a limp bubble in the upturned palm of his hand. Mother said he was "extraordinarily ambidextrous," words chosen, no doubt, to teach us what they meant. We liked the words. They sounded funny to us, and they were kooky to say. So naturally, we took them for our own, knowing them only as what Canio could do. Ambidextrous never meant anything but Canio curling a tennis ball off his shoulder, over his elbow, and down into his hand.

Sometimes when one of the tricks really worked and the ball appeared as a bulge in his sleeve, he seemed to have added magic to art, performance to drawing, inventing a mysterious mixture of the visible and invisible. Occasionally, the ball would disappear altogether, only to come back as a nickel, a cold coin suddenly squeezed from behind my ear. For a while when I was three or four, his tricks were so numerous that I thought that was how baseball was actually played. This was before we had television. Instead baseball was on the radio, so I couldn't understand why the announcers didn't say how Luis Aparicio made the baseball disappear.

Then television came, big and gray one summer, and I began to see what Canio's magic was about and how large baseball really was.

When he tired of tricks, he would tell us jokes, jokes I won't tell again but which we were required to hear over and over. They were terrible. *Why did the chicken cross the road?* "To get to the other side." And another one that began in a jaunty rhythm. "I can *not eat* the *soup!*"

From the kitchen we could hear Grandma groan. Finally, all patience lost and thrown to the winds, she'd storm out of the kitchen, scowling. "Young children shouldn't hear such things!"

He would look up, perfectly aware of what she was about to say.

"That's enough now! You and your jokes, you should be ashamed of yourself!"

"Whaaa?" Canio's gaze would trail back to his enraptured grandchildren as though he'd never seen her before. "Aww, gowan."

"Teach them something important! Such nonsense. What's the use of that?"

Grandma usually tried to intervene before too many Chuckles were handed out or we created significant trouble, with orders to eat "solid food, not candy and sweets and all that stuff that's no good for you." Incensed but sure she'd made an impression, she would make these remarks and march back to the sizzling and popping double boiler from whence she'd come, wringing her hands of us all.

"Don't you want to grow up strong?" she would say, her words ringing in our ears.

I hadn't considered growing up at all yet, and Regina said that even if we wanted to, she didn't know how.

"What can we do about it?" she asked Canio. "People grow, whatever they eat, and no matter how old they are." She was right. Uncle Johnny was thirty but looked fifty. He was wider than the door every time he came through it, and he went out wider still.

I agreed. It made sense to stick with candy. That's what grown-ups ate when they came over, and they'd had no trouble at all growing up. Grandma herself, continually baking apple pies with a crust only she could make (until Regina figured it out), must have sensed her tenuous position.

There were parts of life that didn't make sense to any of us, but you followed orders and continued to observe them. But which parts? And how much was reasonable? It was a silly question. We were *told* what to do.

Perhaps Grandma was right to intervene in our play with Canio. His pen and ink illustrations were probably overdue Mandel Brothers orders, and there were few remaining clients. It began to appear to me then that she supervised most of the significant details of life—what time we ate, whether we stayed up late, who was important, who should or shouldn't be spoken of—as if the whole rise and fall of the world somehow ran through her. Being a boy, I resisted that view, believing that this was Canio's house and that he should be the boss. The fact was that things were much more complicated than my "father knows best" view. And there was also a kind of conspiracy. An unspoken arrangement between them. Grandma was there to be censorious, Canio to have fun.

Only later did I realize you could draw similar circles around Grandma Marie, my mother, and Mrs. Durnbach and their friends, the sisters of Mercy in grammar school, Mrs. Mulkerin, Mrs. Conboy, and maybe even crazy Mrs. Menardi. All of them moved in predictable circles and had opinions of their own, which kept a constant stream of status, class consciousness, and misfortune rolling through the neighborhood. Events and reputations lumbered by like the green- and cream-colored transit authority buses growling out along Washington Boulevard, their noisy shifting growing to a fever pitch and then receding gradually into the distance. I would wake from a nap on warm summer afternoons to their pounding, throttling diesels and to voices gossiping in innumerable kitchens, swimming in from gangways too distant to be understood ... or perhaps understood all too easily from porches next door—voices born up on the aromas of endive soup or Irish stew or sausage simmering below.

Sometimes you could hear whispers even from as far away as the corner, where my mother and Mary Dernbach would part on their way back from church. They had been at Normal together, and now they were here, prim, correct, solicitous, and professionally trained, taking reasonable responsibility for our education. And not only ours but that of other students as well, involved as they had become in the curricular choices of the nuns at St. Thomas Aquinas. So there was a kind of continuous oversight, weaving from hot summer afternoons to the cold days of the Feast of the Epiphany. A cool, professional oversight that held the mirror to us in many pertinent details, reaching far beyond Grandma's groans and Canio's joking solicitations.

For Regina and me, scrambling around Grandpa's legs was risky. But it was different for our cousins. When the Bold boys, Aunt Rita's sons, came to number three and then five, Regina and I watched them play tricks on Canio. Their guerrilla tactics were far more effective than ours had been. As Canio liked to say, "The Bolds aren't five boys. They're fifty fingers."

The Bolds were around far less often and were far more numerous, and being all boys, they knew safety in numbers. Besides, at their age they couldn't tell anger from disaster, so in most of the tricks we played on Canio, they were fearless and incorrigible, brazen in fact, and completely reliable. They would wait until one of them had distracted Grandpa. Then someone would crawl under his feet and make for the sample boxes just for the fuss it would generate. Regina and I, on the other hand, having been the first grandchildren, were long since cowed, and expected to set an example.

If things went very badly, we were all apt to run down the hallway. There we would hide in the bedrooms, the living room, or slip out onto the front porch. Or if things really got bad, we would circle down through the gangway between the buildings into the backyard and play there quietly, thereby proclaiming our innocence. Canio, having scattered us that far, went back to work and relied on Grandma to bring things back to normal.

Though we were no longer small children when we joined the Bolds in Canio's studio, Regina and I reveled in the renewed possibilities that their numbers brought. And with them we rediscovered Canio, or more accurately, we discovered how much fun it had been to have an adult who wanted to play with us.

CHAPTER 11

CANIO, ENZO, AND THE RISORGIMENTO

From the 1930s, Canio and Marie were Roosevelt Democrats despite the fact that *big labor* all but destroyed the family business. Canio's discussions with his brother-in-law Enzo Stasio were filled with the populist sentiments of Garibaldi and with their interpretation of the dreams of Verdi and Puccini for a reunified Italy. Ironically, it was only Enzo who got back to Rome in his own grand gesture of reunification. For the rest of his life, he sent love letters to his estranged wife, Gussie, who remained in Chicago.

In many respects, Canio and Enzo were typical Italian anticlerics whose anger at the church began with the papacy. Their anticlericalism was, in fact, as vehement as their wives' prayers, rosaries said for their salvation that droned on and on through morning Masses and afternoon novenas. You could see Canio and Enzo, the two of them of a Sunday evening, arguing some fine point of Italian politics or silent as stone in a game of checkers, while at the other end of the house, Grandma, her sister Louise or one of the others, and Aunt Gussie prayed novenas over the drone of buses along Washington Boulevard. Running down the hall and back again, your ear segued from one set of incantations to the other—aves and buses at one end, Garibaldi and checkers at the other, a punctuated cacophony of ideology. In the end, it was Marie who eventually won Grandpa's soul. We never learned who said the last rites for Enzo.

———•———

An Italian social democrat, Enzo had been a radio commentator for a while in the 1930s and 40s for one or another of Chicago's several ethnic Italian radio stations. And with all the authority of a reporter turned radio announcer, Enzo had a penchant for writing letters to highly placed officials, letters in which he represented not only his own views but putatively those of the entire Italian community.

This led to an interesting episode at the beginning of World War II. In an environment of rising suspicion of anyone of German or Italian descent, Canio's loyalty was questioned by the Immigration and Naturalization Service. This matter was eventually resolved when Canio hired a distinguished lawyer whose advice to Canio was simple—become a naturalized American. And they all did. Ironically, but for Aunt Gussie's document of naturalization, we would never have found my grandfather's actual birthplace and the Brindisini.

By the early 1950s, with the McCarthy era in full swing, Enzo's left leanings became a liability, and the Italian radio stations, once so relevant, abruptly became American. Enzo returned to Rome, by now a man in his sixties, and competed with the paparazzi so famously depicted in Fellini's *La Dolce Vita*. Surviving as best he could in a world as foreign to him as America had become, he wrote love letters to Gussie, who, knowing how he had threatened her and infuriated the family, kept both the letters and her grief close to her heart. "That old coot!" she would say of her estranged husband, and we would know she'd received another love letter. In one last, great gesture to his beloved and estranged wife, Enzo somehow traced the Grieco name through archives in Rome back to AD 1100 when, as he wrote in typically flowery terms, the name simply referred to "one boat load or another of misguided Greeks whose only explicit legacy was the name."

In love as in opera, Gussie was torn. And although she had a successful career as a buyer for Marshall Fields, her trips to New York on the Penn Central were not for appearances on the stage at the Met, her singing career never having flourished. In the end, she lived a quiet if operatic tragedy of her own.

My favorite memory of Enzo was the night he had some kind of attack or other, after an especially well-seasoned meal of antipasto, pasta, meatballs with Italian sausage, and a tossed salad. (We often had two salads with our meals—Italian antipasto, the appetizer typically consisting of olives, anchovies, sliced sausage or pepperoni and artichoke hearts, at the beginning and an American tossed salad at the end. The hyphen between the two, of course, was a bowl of pasta and meatballs, while a five-layered chocolate cake from Dressel's provided an exquisitely German-American coda.)

Enzo's *attack* occurred at about 7:30 one Sunday evening in February. It had been snowing all afternoon, and it was growing deep by nightfall. Suddenly, we heard screaming and crying from the living room as the women, preparing to say their novenas, were suddenly calling for an ambulance instead. Aunt Rita, richly perfumed and in a new suit, dressed for an evening out with her friends, was especially panicked, no doubt anticipating her date would arrive in the midst of this Old World chaos. She was young, sophisticated, and entitled. This was a mess.

To tell the truth, I was angry at her. I thought Enzo was interesting. He said complex things and made Canio say things so complex I couldn't understand them, so it seemed to me the only thing worth thinking about just now was helping him get better.

The Pulmonary Rescue Unit or "pulmotor," as the medics in Chicago were called then, responded to screams and a phone call in a matter of minutes. Perhaps more than the rest of us, Rita was relieved that the firemen arrived so quickly. With their masks, yellow oxygen tanks, and black boots with yellow stripes, sporting enormous red fire helmets, they transported snow and cheer into the middle of the living room. Once there, they stood like statues for a moment as though they had always been and always would be, the center of commanding attention. Finally, they spotted Enzo in the middle of the crowd, still agog at their arrival.

Leaning precariously on the thin arm of Grandma's French provincial sofa, gasping for breath, Enzo, normally ashen-faced, had a purple pallor. They soon got a rubbery yellow mask on him, and despite two days of stubble growth, they sealed it about his face well enough to give him the shot of oxygen he needed. And that was evidently all he required because in a minute he was up on his feet again. Whether to keep their place of commanding importance or to assure his recovery, we never knew, but the firemen demanded that he sit back down and take a bit more from the mask.

I don't know why, but at just that moment, Regina, looking out the window at the other end of the house, announced that the garage had fallen in. When I heard her, I ran down the hall, thinking, *She's just a girl. What does she know?* But there it was, the hip roof covered in snow and sinking into the garage just as she'd said. Soon enough, in similar disbelief, everyone came running down the hallway to the rear window to see for themselves, leaving the firemen and poor Enzo to recover as best they could, their glorious and shining moment eclipsed by a hip roof.

For Enzo, it was a brief moment of heroism that might easily have been extended. After all, on that particular night, he had just given each of us children a dollar, unlike the measly quarter for which he was famous on his visits. Considering this, Aunt Rita later opined that it must have been the shock to his pocketbook that brought on his attack of purple pallor, which though I hate to admit it, was a seasoned possibility.

The pulmotor squad, however, was undaunted. Convinced they had saved yet another life, they marched out as ceremoniously as they'd arrived, leaving Enzo alone in the living room to contemplate what he might. Around him the Harvard classics lined the bookshelves, and the operas of Verdi were nestled beneath the old Victrola. And in the armchair was the biography of Houdini that Canio was reading at the time. All about Enzo were all the accoutrements of glory, but he had neither the audience nor the lineage with which to meet it.

CHAPTER 12

BOUNDARIES

By 1950, I had begun to notice that everybody and everything in our neighborhood had a reputation of one kind or another, inside our house and out. Featherstone, the pharmacist, was famous for his Green Rivers and the marble-topped soda bar. Dad had once been a fancy-moves soda jerk there and then a promising young chemist. Schniederman, the baker, was famous for his apple slices and butter crust bread and for the thick-browed immigrant girls who worked behind his counter. Johnny B., whom at eight we thought was fun and tricky, diddled with his three-year-old cousin so often he was sent away, and his parents also disappeared shortly after. The Jewel, though a grocery chain, was famous for its meats and soon drove out the butcher shop. With a pair of monocles that flipped down over one oblate eye, the jeweler lived behind a store black as pitch but was known for the white marble of his watchmaker's table and the pewter-colored jeweler's lathe in his window. The Heitbommers, owners of the hardware store, had become famous because their son was a physicist, which evoked Einstein and meant genius to us in our tiny Austin neighborhood. Cousin Carms, Aunt Flo, the two Toms, Mulkerin and Menardi, each of them was a story. And next door across the gangway, Tom McMann was known for his mother, the recluse who wandered from floor to floor through the night. She was called the ghost and was deeply feared because, it was said, no one had ever heard her speak.

For the Griecos, the measure of it all was still my grandfather, the artist with the French beret who was in fact an illustrator, wasn't French, and would probably have preferred to be a pitcher for the Black Sox "except for the sellout." Canio still walked to the corner for a cigar dressed in his suit, his overcoat, and his scarf of perfect red in winter, and on summer days he would return home to a now air-conditioned porch that was still his studio. There he listened to two ball games at once, one on TV from Comiskey Park, the other on WGN radio with Jack Brickhouse on the road with the Cubs. Or was it the other way around, Cubs on TV and the White Sox on the road? All of it brought to you by Hamms, the beer refreshing— "*From the land of sky blue waters, Hamms … the beer refreshing.*"

It was as though it was all one team, and in our days we were as much a part of it as the players were.

At his desk Grandpa, who could draw in his sleep, penned Ross board into shoes of sparkling possibilities.

So you begin to see how we were multiplied and divided, taken up with urgent, charging opportunities, drawn by sometime dreams and possibilities. To us in those days, America was a land of opportunity, so that no life, no self was ever so small as to be encompassed or absorbed totally. Even if by some strange multiplication of selves, across space and time, in an engineering feat befitting a physicist like Einstein or Henry Heitbommer, even if you could somehow have become the people speeding around you, we remained words, fragments, and stories to one another and to ourselves. We were all just that—stories held in place by a neighborhood that was somehow both safe and sacred to its kids, and we moved through and around these people with varying degrees of reverence, a reverence in the end not unlike that reserved for the nuns.

And yet the circles of time and consequence that passed through Austin in those days of childhood became part of a collective tragedy, still unforgiven, unforgotten, having become a piece of the true bitterness of America. It's a bitterness none of us has adequately faced but one that nobody can actually escape. However, in Chicago today, that is exactly what many are still trying to do.

The year we moved to 50 0 7, Van appeared. She was the first black person I had ever seen except on the Aunt Jemima syrup bottle, and she was too trim, too soft-spoken, and carried too many bags, brooms, and buckets to be Aunt Jemima. She had cleaned for Grandma Grieco years ago, and now Marie thought she should clean for us too. Kathryn resisted at first, but then for no reason I could tell, she acquiesced.

At first, Van scared me. She was the first adult I ever saw who stepped aside when I came in, and there was a certainty about her, a confidence and a diffidence that was unlike the finger pushing that came from most adults, people who always had to let you know who the boss was and who poked at you and otherwise behaved too predictably. Van was wholly other, often solicitous, asking questions in a quavering, almost plaintive voice that in word or thought never seemed to find a bottom. There was a bottom, which you heard clearly when she shouted a question over the vacuum cleaner to "Mrs. Grieco?" but we never came within its sphere. Another voice was reserved for me and Regina. To us, she said, "How are you today, Children? How nice. Did you enjoy your day at school?" No one ever asked that, and certainly, no one ever waited for an answer. So not only did she step aside for us to pass through, pulling the vacuum or the broom with her, but she thought it her duty to make conversation, to elicit our stories and wait upon us for an outcome or until she came across some useful happiness. It was unaccountable. As far as I could tell, no other adult ever did that except to make a point. Van did it all the time, up to the day she died.

Through the 1960s when the West Side burned, through the indifference and racial hostility of the 1970s, through the constant rhetoric of racism in the 1980s, she remained solicitous of us, carrying news of cousins and friends from one household to another and awaiting that turn of phrase, the arrival of some detail that somehow assured her that life continued. And through her old age, the ravages of her daughter's ill health, a marriage come and gone, she remained an interpreter of us, always warm and firmly herself, and very clear about us.

Not that I had the slightest idea what to do with all this when I was seven at 50-0-7. Within a month after her arrival, her presence abated as

I hurried past, moving past her faster than with most adults, but within a year her interest in us had turned those passings into a strut. I can't recall anyone, except perhaps my uncle Tom Heaney, who ever had such a direct energizing effect on me before or since. We were still kids, meant to be seen and not heard, but like Canio, Van made us something human.

Outside the sphere of Van, other attitudes and injunctions applied. In our first years at 50-0-7, my sister Regina and I were creatures of only one long block marked off by the newsstand at one corner, the buildings between Madison Street and Washington Boulevard, and ending at St. Thomas Acquinas kitty-corner across from the newsstand. As children, we lived mostly in the alley in between. Beyond this ground was alien territory where you kept a close eye on the crowd, gave strangers a wide berth, and looked to your escape route home.

Johnny Mulkerin, Denny Dernbach, and others soon ranged farther and proved bolder, playing ball with the guys in the next block east of where the newsstand was and riding bikes far west of Laramie, the commercial street two blocks west. But for my sister and me, Laramie Avenue was the fringe of the unknown, the far edge of the world. For a long time none of us were allowed to cross it. On Sunday mornings when traffic was light and it was quiet out along Madison Street, Regina and I sometimes rode our bikes out to the Laramie railroad bridge, the world's edge. Cycling south along our side of the deserted street, we would reach the top of the bridge, itself two blocks long and spanning the switch yards below. Then roaring down from the top, brakes off, feet far from the peddles, we would race back as fast as we could and come to a screeching finish at the bottom or head toward home when fear got hold of us.

But Laramie Avenue remained the limit. And not until nearly sixth grade did we venture across it or even more than a couple of blocks from home in any direction. Even then, when we did go farther, it was with permission and strict instructions about when to return and also with loose change set aside for a phone call in case something happened. But what if we were kidnapped? How could we call? It was too scary to ask, an unthinkable question, and one likely to throw Dad into a rage. We were rational enough not to think the unthinkable. So whether *phone money* came from Grandma Marie or one of our aunts, we ran down the back steps and pocketed the change. Regina, segregating accounts, kept phone money in one pocket, her own money in another. I just pocketed it with the rest.

East of us it was different. By the time we were old enough to travel off the block, we seldom went as far east as Crawford Avenue, except to go all the way downtown or to see the dentist, Dr. Bailey. Crawford Avenue, eight blocks east of Pulaski Road, was a busy intersection on Madison Street, a cluster of clothing stores, professional offices, and even a couple of small hotels. Conversant with ethnic slurs, we had another, less friendly term for his neighborhood. There was a Madigan's Department Store there, where my mother had worked during high school, but by now the area was said to have *changed*, mostly as a result of the battles between rival neighborhoods that raged across Garfield Park in the late 1940s.

From the dentist chair on the seventh floor, you could see out across Madison Street to the dust and smoke tailings that define Chicago's South Side and to the major buildings on Crawford. Sometimes Kathryn would shop at Madigan's while we went for a checkup. But most often she was glad we were free of the whirring dental drill, and she took us straight home. So we never really learned much about Pulaski Road or even the rooms beyond Dr. Bailey's office, except for the hints around us.

Dr. Bailey had a waiting room so hollow it boomed with conversation from the dentist chair inside. It was tiled like a bathroom floor, but instead of a bathtub, it had brown leather armchairs set around the edge, chairs that clicked like railroad cars when they slid over the tiles. Patterns of small, white, hexagonal tiles with black ones in the middle made rows of diamonds and hexagons around the edge. And all around the room there was a dim, even light that came from high up on the wall, from troughs that ran along the ceiling, and it made the room an eerie pink and blue. If you talked, your voice echoed through the crinkled glass door that read, "Dr. Robert Bailey, DDS," backward, and your words also came back, reverberating down the hallway. Loud as we usually were, Regina and I would try to kill that echo, whispering ever more softly and distinctly. It was no use. Some part of it always remained. We were never sure, whispering as softly as could be, that secrets weren't seeping down the hall, under some door, and into the ears of a thousand dentists next door.

When you whispered, you could pick up the smell of this place, a constant smell, of Spic and Span, of pine cones, and of dental floss. In and out of Dr. Bailey's chair, wherever you were, you never escaped those odors. Even if blood shot out of your mouth, somehow you could still smell pine and Spic and Span and dental floss somewhere.

On one particular visit, Kathryn had gotten into some conversation or other in the dental chair, and she and Dr. Bailey continued to talk as he escorted her out into the waiting room. Regina and I, obedient and anxious to go, sat shuffling our feet, and when addressed, answering politely. At one point, Mother asked Dr. Bailey if he thought he should be worried. I had no idea what she was talking about.

"I really haven't been affected," he said, his voice, mild and modulated like Grandma Heaney's. It came from a face that was soft and pale, almost colorless, except for the pink and blue florescent lights in the troughs above, that trimmed his white smock. If there was something to worry about, you'd never find it in that poker face.

"To tell you the truth, Kathryn," he said and waited to be sure she was following him, "I don't expect to be affected this high up."

"You hear so many stories," she said. "There are more rumors now than ever."

"Yes, Kathryn, you're right. It's not like the days when Tom was at Garfield National. You know your dad got to know nearly all the merchants along Crawford Avenue."

"Wasn't that something!" Kathryn said. Her voice would rise to a kind of partial quaver in moments of admiration for her father, someone whom she often genuinely and unhesitatingly admired. "Mother and I used to marvel. I don't know how he did it!"

"Well, your dad was always the kind of man who made it his business to get to know people, and to his credit, he has kept in touch with a number of them since, even after he left the bank. I've always admired Tom for that. But you're right, though," he continued. "There are people here who've been affected by the change."

His voice trailed off as he made it his doctorly business to grip Regina's chin, having a look at her new front teeth. He reaffirmed that he would probably not recommend orthodontia. Regina smiled happily as he let her jaw slip from his firm but fluid hand.

That conversation was all, the only hint. Why Dr. Bailey should be worried or why he wasn't worried "this high up" or what was affected remained a mystery to us. When I was thirteen, Dr. Bailey retired, and we found a new dentist farther West. By then, all of Austin had been affected.

In 1919, when Kathryn and Gerald were nine and seven, America had experienced the Red Scare, the first of many to come. From that point forward, American politics, which hadn't experienced a significant challenge from abroad for two generations, not since the British entered the Civil War, suddenly found an enemy worthy of its self-annointed and self-aggrandizing Monroe Doctrine. Also in 1919, whether by accident or design, America experienced the worst summer of racially motivated lynchings in its history.

Reds and race would, in fact, dominate most of my parents' political lives, would help define Kathryn's choice of education as a career, and in part would lead them to buy the farm in central Wisconsin in 1950. By the mid-1950s, the divide over race and Reds had reached such depths in our household that Gerald was cheering on Senator McCarthy's radio witch hunts from his drawing board, while Kathryn, holding her own, usually at the other end of the dining room table, inveighed against every implication of racism in one long paean to education and against the failure to provide it. In her passionate view, what African Americans lacked in skills, housing, and financial resources could all be explained by poor teaching, inferior schools, and a white culture that assumed its intellectual superiority.

CHAPTER 13
THE AGE OF REASON AND THE APOSTATE

In the spring of 1949 before I made my first confession at the end of April, I went up and down the list of sins until I was pretty sure I couldn't find any I was guilty of—nothing mortal anyway. The worst was wanting to kill my sister. But I never really did. I knew I couldn't have meant it because it would have been too bloody. So I went to confession and got three "Our Fathers," three "Hail Marys," and three "Glory Bes" for penance. That was a lot to say but "normal," Sister Mary Eunice said. I knelt down and did them right away like you were supposed to, but I didn't feel any better. Sister Eunice told us we might not feel any different after we went to confession. I couldn't tell whether she meant our class was especially bad or pretty special, but whatever she meant, she told us that after confession we would all be pure and lovely and clean in God's eyes, no matter how we felt, and that was all that mattered. Since I'd expected a little more after going through all those sins and into the whole examination of conscience thing, not to mention the effort it took not to think of any really mortal sins, I naturally felt lousy. But at least in confession I did say the "Bless me, Father" part right, which was pretty long and hard to memorize. So even though I didn't feel any different, I was glad the first part was over. The penance wasn't so hard if you didn't doze off or get distracted and kept count. So I was all set.

What I had to do now was get through first Communion and not embarrass my aunts, uncles, parents, and grandparents in front of the whole church. It was a big deal because Uncle Enzo was an agnostic, whatever that was, and so was Grandpa Canio. If anything went wrong at church, he and Enzo would take my side because they thought all this "hocus pocus" stuff was too much for a little kid. If that happened, there'd be a big row with aunts screaming "Heretic!" at them and wrapping themselves in their shawls and marching down the hallway in a fury. And then they might not speak to Enzo all night and the whole next day, or they might pick a fight with him about something else like what he'd said on one of his radio talks. Then the whole history of Italy from Napoleon to Garibaldi as well as the French popes would come up, and all this shouting had nothing to do with me except it hurt somewhere over my head. So anyway, it was a good idea not to be an embarrassment to my family.

Then there were Grandma and Grandpa Heaney, who were supposed to come on Communion Sunday. He was the high chief ranger, and he knew Bishop Stritch personally. And people at the Catholic Order of Foresters where he worked said he might be made a knight of Saint Gregory someday. So if they came to church and I screwed up, he'd be embarrassed, and who knew what might happen? But as it turned out, I was lucky, sort of. They called the Friday before and said they wouldn't be coming. Maybe they'd heard about my falling asleep at the altar rail during Communion practice a few weeks earlier. I don't know. Anyway, I was relieved a little, but then too, I might miss out on some pretty big presents.

At first Communion, there wasn't a lot to do. Stand when everybody else did and kneel and stick your tongue out at the priest when he came to you, but not before. Some girls had their tongues out way before and were squinting at God with their eyes closed when the priest was still three kids away. I would have laughed. I did laugh to myself, but their tongues looked prickly and really disgusting, so it stopped me from laughing right out. Their tongues were so round they made you think of chopped-up hot dogs, and I thought the host would fall off before they caught it. But that didn't happen, and now the priest was so close I could hear his cassock brushing along the floor and see the gold threads in his stole. What was really weird was that I could smell the altar boy. I think it was Pete Conboy or Tommy Mulkerin. I forget which, but I knew I could smell one of them. But not like they were out in the alley because they were covered in dusty vestments and Vitalis.

For weeks I had had these scary feelings that I might not like the host and that when I tasted it, I would want to spit it out. One of the guys in Terry Murphy's gang said there was a kid at Resurrection who had done that, and when he turned around to leave the communion rail, he blew up like a ball of fire. When the smoke cleared, the guy said, his parents rushed up, but there was nothing left of him, not even ashes. But I didn't believe it. It was sacrilege to believe God made special miracles. That's what the nuns said. And Canio said miracles were just a bunch of stories they made up so the priests could get away with murder. Still, I was scared I wouldn't like the host and would want to spit it out, so scared I wouldn't let myself think it. I was determined to just swallow it quickly but not too quickly because I didn't want to choke and make a lot of noise either.

That spring I had some practice eating things I didn't like, including asparagus and peas and other green stuff that looked pretty spooky to me. During Lent that year, I made a sacrifice and ate that stuff when it was served. So I had had practice. I tried not to breathe when I chewed these disgusting things, or I thought of Hopalong Cassidy chasing Indians across the western prairie so that I wouldn't have to think about the asparagus. But the host was made of some kind of strange bread that was real flat. So I practiced for first communion by eating crackers without actually chewing them and keeping my mind on the High Sierra and other beautiful cowboy places. After a while, I got pretty good at this, and I was sure I could do it, whatever the host was, even if it tasted like Jesus.

The Saturday before the big day, my mom took me for a haircut. I think it was the last time she ever took me. I sat in the big iron chair near the window. The other two were empty, and that didn't make sense because there was only ever one barber and there were always three porcelain and black leather chairs. The place felt like a hospital. The barber talked to Mom like they always knew each other, and I wished she'd stop because all I wanted to do was get out and go home. Then on the way back, she stopped at this little candy shop on that end of the block.

I asked her how she knew the barber as though she hadn't lived in the neighborhood for many years, and she said that she didn't but that she'd seen him around. I don't think she much cared for my butting into her discussions with people, and after a few more of these incidents, I learned to keep my mouth shut, especially if I wanted to be nosy.

The next day, Communion Sunday, I got up early and put on my almost white pants and all white shirt and a new tie and a real belt, not a cloth one like the ones on little kids' pants but one made of real leather like cowboys wear. Mom inspected me and combed my hair a lot, enough to knock down the colic, and she pulled my shirt down snug on my shoulders before she said I looked sharp, whatever that meant, and sent me off to school. We all lined up in the church vestibule, and after a long wait, when nobody even talked, we marched piously past the baptismal fount, past the hundreds of candles the old ladies had lit for something or other, and down the main aisle, our hands pointed heavenward in prayer and thumbs locked together in nervous exhaustion.

Four or five years later, I remember going through the whole thing all over again when I made my confirmation, only this time the bishop did it. He slapped you on the cheeks, and maybe he would slug you if you were bad. But a lot of us were bold and cynical by then. The nuns said Tommy Duggan was bad because he had long, greasy hair swept over his ears and a ducktail haircut. By then I had a job, and the girls hated us. But they giggled and stared at the high school guys. Most of us didn't believe the cardinal ever hit anybody. Besides, how would he know which one of us to hit? So the story was a lot of bull. I saw what happened. He slapped Duggan, but not so hard it knocked him over. So what's the big deal? It wasn't like he turned around and blew up in a ball of fire. Besides, Archbishop Cardinal Stritch was almost a saint. When he died, people lined Jackson Boulevard all the way from downtown to Austin just to see his motorcade pass. Whatever happened to Duggan, Cardinal Stritch wouldn't have done it.

So first Communion came and went, and as it turned out, nobody noticed me more than anyone else. We had a party on the cement porch out front overlooking Washington Boulevard with a warm May breeze and a blue sky over us and startling red and white petunias waving from the big cement urns on the corners of the porch. Regina and I passed around hors d'oeuvres, which I'd never had before and were pretty good, and everybody gave me gifts, lots of them in envelopes, which meant money, though you weren't supposed to count. I also got a couple of shirts and socks. I felt pretty good like I'd pulled it off and could relax if I could just get out of those perfect white pants.

That night and every night from then on, I tallied up my sins for the day before going to sleep because ever since the last of April, I'd reached the age of reason, they said. But it never hit me, not for a long time, what had happened. That spring as the age of reason dawned, the age of my self-loathing began.

Weeks before my seventh Christmas later that year, while waiting to have my tonsils out, I was given the task of repairing strings of Christmas lights. Those were "lonely days of sin and sorrow," as Hank Williams put it, spent stuck in a living room chair, wires and sockets tangled in my lap, spilling down onto the floor and caught around my ankles. It remains my first memory of Christmas vacation. Laboriously, I cross-wrapped the light sockets with friction tape. I hated the tarred and sticky tape, the smell of camphor when you tore it, the black gum it forced under your fingernails. And I despised it more when Dad came in, swearing at this and that, inspecting my work imperiously, or worse, saying, "Hurry up. How many have you finished?" and barking other requests for ever more efficiency and progress. It was bad enough to be forced to wrap tarred cloth in figure eights around the sockets. It was worse that the black gum covered my fingers and the smell of camphor itched my runny nose. But to be punished further by having to give an account? With each twist of the friction tape, I began to believe adults were evil, that I'd been enslaved, that I'd been sent off on some brutal, despicable mission by all of them. Well, all of them except my mother.

My fingers were nimble at this task, however, more graceful than my curve ball, and when at last the plugged-in strings of lights brightened around my ankles, I began to marvel at the color of electricity. Of course, I had to be careful about plugging them in. Dad had insistently raised the possibility of my being electrocuted by *the juice* in a string of faulty lights, so if I was to get any fun out of this at all, I had to turn them on and off furtively. My first idea was that I could feel the color and then see the electricity there running through my fingers. I tried that, wrapping pink and black-smudged fists around the wires and then around the blue and azure lamps. But it didn't work. The bulbs grew hot quickly. That was okay, but there was no juice in them. Why was it supposed to be dangerous? They were just warm. That's all.

I decided to find out. The tape, he said, was insulation, which kept the electricity inside somehow, kept it confined in the bare copper strands and brass recepticles I was so carefully wrapping. I decided that since it was dangerous, I would start small, trying to feel what the juice was like. Wetting my fingers, I found a battery and held the metal ends of it, but I couldn't feel a thing. Somehow I knew more batteries meant more juice, so I tried a bunch of them together. But it was no use. It was as though I could feel the colors of the Christmas lights, but there was nothing, no tingle of juice in the batteries. Maybe I had the words wrong, was looking for the wrong thing. What was *city* about electricity, and if the city was all around me, why couldn't I feel juice in something that big? In the end, I gave up on the words, and though it was dangerous, I decided to dive my finger right into one of the light sockets.

People said touching the sockets could kill you. But all that taping had armed me with a newfound coordination. I was fast now, my fingers nimble. So I practiced. Unscrewing a bulb from one of the living room lamps, I slowly sunk my fingers down, drawing them out quickly, and then down again, reaching deeper and deeper into where the juice was supposed to be. Each time I slipped in, I retreated more rapidly as my fingers sank deeper and deeper, reaching for the bottom of the live socket.

As I think of it now, my hands were enabled by more than practice. In those days being seven or eight and Catholic placed one in impressionable circumstances, and I was impressionable indeed. I was eight months into in the age of reason. Never mind that the rest of the world, as I later discovered, had attained it in the eighteenth century or that for extended periods thereafter, the European psyche had collapsed in paroxysms of its own rarefied, rational air. The age of reason of which the nuns spoke was not eighteenth-century rationalism. It was a time that made us morally responsible for our own spiritual survival. And the emphasis here was on our eternal survival. No mere temporary salvation would do. So as subversive as it sounds, we were admonished to obey the commandments, even if it meant disobeying our parents. And if they asked us to commit sin, we must disobey even then. According to the catechism, which we had been memorizing for our first Communion, should anything go wrong when we disobeyed our parents, our superior morality would be rewarded by a swift, immediate, and uninterrupted ascent into heaven. All of which must have played a small part in the sensation I sought, one hand still clutching the light bulb, the other's fingers dipping slowly downward into the lamp socket. Off stage or closer, ringing in my ears, I could still hear my father swearing.

Or was it just ringing in my ears? Just what were these sins that our parents might ask of us? And how could my parents, good and true Catholics, ask us to do such things? It was never explained. Worse, it seemed to me that my parents, who had moved to this house so mother could attend novenas on Fridays and Mass in the morning, how could they do such things? But then there was my grandfather, the apostate, the anticleric, the artist of vaudeville and showgirls. And then, too, at the other end of the hallway was my father, bellowing, forcing me to do things I didn't want to do. Who was wrong … or right? I hardly knew.

Suddenly, I was faced with painful, problematic questions. Here was apostasy, a mortal sin at its core, thrust on my newfound, reasonable being. The beginnings of responsibility, which I thought, which I hoped, would come at twenty-one, were suddenly mine at the ripe age of seven. It was all too much to think about, my fingers stuck halfway down a light socket, legs wrapped in wires, my nose dripping snot, and the disgusting burn of camphor in the air. Why was he doing this to me?

As it happened, I was saved not so much by theological insight as by high skin resistance. Those fingers, reaching lower and lower, never quite encountered the cruelty of the world. I was, however, learning to take risks, and too much risk would come of this. I've been enamored of calculable risk ever since. This time I was also lucky. Dry fingers and high skin resistance were not among the hygienic details taught in Catholic school. But I eventually felt the sharp jolt of the juice, and the sudden thrill got my fingers out of there in a hurry. Or perhaps the real thrill had been in the defiance. Perhaps it was that I'd managed to do what my father was most afraid of.

Touching electricity and living to tell about it had somehow changed me. But whatever had made me want to do that forbidden thing now made for rebellion. Rebellion in small phases perhaps, but these small phases would be mine.

———•·•———

Caught between church and family, my frail catechization tried to retain the best of both worlds. And true to deeper instincts, it did so in a way that pressed my own advantage. When I felt guilty about being in Grandpa's way, about taking over his billiard table, or a dozen other slights, I decided it must be part of his punishment for his rabid anticlericalism, for his *not going to church*, and though I didn't admit it or maybe even realize it at the time, my revenge for his failure to defend me against my father. As the church taught, this was my error, and a cleric somewhere might reasonably take some pride in the fact that I took its canons so seriously.

So just what was Canio's sin? In Roman Catholic terms, he was an apostate, an agnostic philosophe whose cosmopolitan anticlericism played out in the midst of Catholic women telling their beads, intoning novenas, and meting out judgments on many if not all who passed through the prism of Catholic doctrine. His sin was a lack of faith. But every religion sees this in every other and in unaffiliated worship as well. So what were his sins? To be sure, I didn't know. Only he and perhaps Marie did, and after his death, when anger and bitterness were ripe, her accusations, aside from his missing Mass, and his occasional attacks on the benighted clergy were few, the usual Roman litany of faithlessness.

Of course, Canio was full of pride, that all-encompassing Catholic sin. The accusation of pride was often leveled irrespective of content, identity, or the canonical standards imposed by a jurisprudent priesthood, itself bent on buttressing its own pride and authority. But aside from these legalistic issues, what Canio ultimately found was Christianity on its own terms, untainted by its tragic rationales and founded in absolution and forgiveness. His sins in his eyes were many, and to his great credit, he was confused by some of them.

In fact, I believe my grandfather was a man more sinned against than sinning. Marie, her eyes bulging, her head shaking, her brows pinched up to heaven, prayed for his soul. Or was she reading answers inscribed in the ceiling, the way clerics directed the faithful to the mysteries inscribed in the far reaches of stained glass windows? Who knows? But telling her beads at the octagonal table in the living room, where each night she took her novena, she looked up to heaven.

Throughout the family, people believed that Canio *could see things*, that despite his apostasy, his artistry somehow included a kind of spiritual power. And so his eyes were permitted, even expected to linger beyond modesty or discretion on whoever or whatever came before him. So although we didn't always agree with his perceptions, we had to acknowledge his insight. It was not easily overcome. Over against this intuitive and nearly unquestionable authority, there were always those who played the religious trump card. He was the apostate. One could always hold up the cross in judgment. For a long time, I fell for that one too.

I would have preferred to have loved Canio more and sooner and to have been less confused. Absent love, Christianity makes none of us the better. It dissolves into legalism and accusations, formalities that Christ himself recognized as merely human, and thus of God least likely and earthly institutions most common.

CHAPTER 14

TOMMY MORRIS'S PITCH

Eventually, I acquired a reputation for haughtiness in the neighborhood. It was a reputation become a given, cultivated in fact and gossip, one that had begun to take hold when I was around eight, probably because of Tommy Morris's mother. She used to tell Tommy, a particularly clever friend of mine, what a good boy Gregory was and to ask him things like, "Why can't you be more like Gregory?" Though I certainly didn't think of myself as superior or above the rest of my family or friends, this and similar utterances, which irritated the hell out of Tommy, over time had the effect of redefining our relationship. I always knew when he'd heard something like that from his mother or from one of her acquaintances. When I wanted to talk to him about something important, that praise made it hard to catch his eye.

Tommy wasn't a bad kid as redheaded Irish boys go, as most of us came and went in Austin. He did nothing worse than setting off a book of matches in a hallway or flipping a glass bottle under a car as it passed just to hear it blow. He was capable, as we both were, of planting a cherry bomb in a garbage can when we found one with a lid, though it could be hard to get our hands on a good one, distinguished by a tight red ball and long green fuse. Like twenty or thirty other kids, we played the neighborhood games in the alley—running bases, hide-and-seek, kick the can—and we played with an understanding that anywhere we could run to was fair territory, at least until some janitor or the sisters of Mercy shooed us off the property.

Don't misunderstand. We didn't venture near school when we played. But the nuns and janitors always seemed to turn up where we were in the midst of a game. Suddenly, a pair of nuns would appear in the alley on the way to visiting the sick or on some other errand, or they'd turn up in Schneiderman's bakery or the meat market. They'd also come upon us hiding in the recess of one of the glass storefronts one block south on Madison Street. And you knew you were in for a chastening. So you learned to give them a wide berth when you spotted a pair of them coming along the broad sidewalk, walking slowly, even devoutly, being sure not to splash anybody from the puddles, keeping your eyes down as you passed as far from them as the sidewalks permitted. It was a source of enormous humiliation to be singled out in one of these accidental encounters, and being boys with pockets full of cherry bombs or other surely punishable booty, you were in terror of being stopped. Even if they were friendly, to have the nuns speak to you on the street suggested you were somehow a serious sinner and in great need of spiritual renewal.

So if one of the nuns did stop you, you stood very still, your heels together at attention, looking directly up into her eyes. You stood that way, not so much listening as praying for the end of the dreaded inquisition or hoping that some cousin or aunt wouldn't happen by and witness your humiliation. Worse, you were sure that your sister or one of her friends would come along, and someone would blab the whole thing that night at the dinner table. Most of all, you prayed that your bulging pants pockets would appear to contain only the fists you'd formed there and not the marbles, caps, six shooters, or clothespins that by now were digging holes in your thighs. If you were lucky, Sister would dispense some brief moral counsel, and you would be sent on your way. You were unlucky if she asked why your hands were in your pockets.

Some of the bigger guys, though very few, had become scoffers, perhaps under the same influence as my agnostic grandfather, and occasionally, they made jokes of the nuns' attention. The sisters seemed to know this, so in their turn, they steered clear of those fellows, preferring to teach the irreligious by modesty and example rather than risk an affront to their authority and demeanor. As young boys faced with navigating this complex moral landscape, we quickly learned to ferret out every possible secret passage and every basement window suitable for transit and to perfect the high art of leaping from porch rail to porch rail, no matter the chasm that yawned below. There were also safe spots and certain occasions where the nuns would rarely appear. You seldom found them on Featherstone's corner of a summer evening among the bookies and fun-loving girls, for instance, or near the Bier Garden at the other end of the block. And you were safe almost anywhere in a snowstorm, as it was believed that the nuns' habits would stiffen with ice and that their starched bibs and mantles would melt.

In all these territories, Tommy Morris and I were alike, no worse on any given evening than intent on setting off a big bang that would make the aunts sitting at their kitchen tables spit up a sip of tea or freeze in the middle of a bite of almond-pecan coffee cake. "What in heaven's name was that?" one would say, ever ladylike, swearing without seeming to swear. Then eyes would roll in the circle of knowledge among them, all too familiar with our shenanigans. There would be no shouts. No running feet of somebody coming after us. The civilized conversation would resume, a bread plate quietly passed, and the doings of young boys quickly forgotten.

<hr />

As it happened, there were other opinions than those of Tommy's mother, most notably Canio's. He took the opposite view of Tommy and me. Unlike Mrs. Morris, Canio regarded Tommy as the model. He saw me as the noodle.

I had realized early on that Canio would have preferred a wiry, circumspect base runner like Luis Aparicio for a grandson or someone who could put "a little English on his fastball," as he said, using terms that were clearly applicable to Tommy's pitches but barely put a spin on mine. Canio loved nearly everything about baseball. If truth be told, he would have loved being a ball player even more than an artist.

By third grade I had the clear sense that Tommy was more like my grandfather's boy than I was, even though his bright red Irish head of hair was far from Italian and he was no artiste. (Not that I knew more than three words from all of Italy then, but some intuitive inconsistency in the whole thing had come to annoy me. It just didn't fit!) Not only could Tommy hurl a competent fastball, but by the time we were eight, he had taken charge of the newsstand at Madison and Lavergne. So as a pitcher and a newsboy as well, he had followed Canio's bold example. What didn't fit was me. But what good would it do to admit it?

It was in the summer before third grade that it happened. I remember one salt-and-pepper day when I was playing catch in the backyard by myself. Canio came out and made me come along with him to pick up the evening papers. These daily trips had begun to eat into my summer, not to mention my self-esteem—him dragging me to the corner, Tommy running the newsstand. There was no point in my coming along at all, only to walk back home with my grandfather feeling useless. To make matters worse, I'd have to wait for Canio at the newsstand while he slipped across the street for a chat with Featherstone, and eventually, I'd find myself helping Tommy, often out of just plain boredom. By late summer Tommy would sometimes pay me, especially if the traffic was heavy along Madison Street or if it was raining and he wanted to stay inside the ramshackle newsstand. So I made a little money as I stood under the battered green canopy, leaning in from the splash of passing cars, feet soaking from the wet planks and spray. And soon I'd become a regular newsboy. More often than not, as autumn came on, it seemed Grandpa would be heading up to the corner later, nearer to dinnertime. And he'd always buy his paper from Tommy and tip him, even though it was me who had saved the *Chicago American* for him or the *Daily News*. Worse, he'd tip Tommy even if I ran it over to him. Though I'm sure he saw my resentment, he refused to acknowledge it.

Then one day, he did. "It's fair," he said, chuckling at my dour expression, implying I didn't need the money. "Your dad takes care of your supper," he said. And he continued in this line, smiling, keeping me in his eyes, trying to kid me in his way, though mercifully out of earshot of Tommy. At first blush I was so struck by the unfairness of it all and blind with my bambino Italian rage that I just wanted to hit him. When I finally realized his point, I turned away, making clear I would have none of it, too furious for words.

But however much anger I felt, I knew in my heart that times had changed and that Canio had gotten his way. I was a committed newsboy now, riding out the fall at Lavergne and Madison, handling my customers, and giving Canio no satisfaction for his chuckles. The fact that he'd created the opportunity, gotten me out of the yard, and even brought Tommy and me a candy bar now and then escaped me. So by winter, in quite practical ways, he'd managed to transfer his admiration of Tommy to something he knew his grandson needed.

There are few times in life when someone takes the effort to plan an identity for us. For some of us, it never happens at all. Canio had no sure guidance in these matters, no help from the Heaneys, and no help from the crowd of artists he once employed, now dispersed to other studios. Just how he thought of all this is difficult to imagine. Perhaps he knew of my will to rebellion. Certainly, he could see my unspeakable anger. But like good teachers everywhere, he knew enough to work with what he had. What he had was a distant grandson, a Tommy Morris, and the charm and subtlety to set me off without the slightest hint he'd done anything at all. Canio rescued me that summer from the backyard, from a poor fastball, and from my peculiar, silent isolation. That accomplished, he had made of me a new person, not the impossible cowboy figure I imagined myself or the angry and unsuccessful wretch glued to a crystal radio but a person in some ways like himself, the newsboy he had once been.

And in his insistence that day on the fairness of his tipping, he revealed to me his response to my view of Tommy's missing dad, to the shape of gossip, and to the reigning fears and hypocrisies that sheltered us.

<hr />

One week Mrs. Morris and Tommy disappeared from the neighborhood, and I never found them again. So Tommy and I were never really able to straighten out how he felt about his mother's injunction to be more like Gregory.

On the way to Tommy's birthday party that year of third grade, I asked Mom if Tommy's dad would be there. Suddenly in the silence, I could hear our footsteps crunching through the alley as though there were rocks in our shoes or our feet were tin cans crushing the concrete. I must have said something terrible, I thought, but I couldn't even guess what it was. When she finally answered, Kathryn said she didn't know if his dad would come, and then in a low voice, almost a whisper, she leaned down to me. "I think they're getting divorced." Then after a moment more of rocks and pinched feet, she continued, "You shouldn't say anything about that."

It was 1950. It was not just divorce that was taboo in our German, Irish Catholic, and a little bit Italian neighborhood, but even the word *divorce*. People thought of divorce as a disgrace, a sin, an event born of scandal, or one shortly to become a scandal. Even speaking the word aloud was a bad example to children. Once spoken, it was a kind of permanent stain on the air. In fact, my mother hadn't known what to say. Torn between the prospect of hurting Tommy or Mrs. Morris by even raising the speculation and hurting me with the facts, she must have chosen the role for which she'd been trained, speaking now as a teacher. It was a role in which she was used to carefully persevering in a short and uncomfortable lesson. And as for me, walking along, taking in my mother's lesson, I think I experienced the first moment of a self-consciousness that there were topics so painful as to create a barrier between myself and my mother, between myself and one of my best friends at the time, Tommy. "Divorce," uttered *sotto voce*, entered my lexicon and my imagination as an unspeakable taboo.

Tommy's mother was a perfectly bright, redheaded woman with large curls falling over her modest brown print or surprising daisy dresses. Her eyes were slow blue, and even when cautious or reflective, her mouth remained warm. What was most surprising was that if you looked close through all that was keen or censorious about her, you could see freckles as though she was still a little kid. It seemed to me that Tommy's father would have had to have been crazy drunk to get divorced from her.

I never met Tommy's father, but I imagined him looking like Hank Williams in a gray ten-gallon hat, just out of the rain in some hotel bar, with nothing better to do than flick ashes from his cigarette and watch it and himself glowing in the brown whiskey bottles and the bar mirror. I wanted to ask him why he'd left her. His mouth, I imagined, would just kinda droop. He'd have nothing to say. It was an image, I'm sure, out of the country and western music on WJJD that I listened to on my crystal radio. WJJD was, in fact, the domain of my own emerging self-image. To me, Tommy's father was the forsworn cowboy, having walked out, leaving behind every commitment in his life to live as a rugged loner. Which involved being speechless, I guessed, except for repeating the equivalent of some sad, old song. But whatever he was, forsworn was something I swore I'd never be. Forlorn perhaps, but never someone who broke a vow, who abandoned someone like Mrs. Morris. Not me.

Somewhere there is a picture of me in my cowboy salad days, a smiling Italian bambino in a piped green cowboy shirt with satin scalloped pockets. I'm holding a ukulele, thinking it's a guitar, and smiling up with a set chin, held as high as Gene Autry's. Cowboys—good cowboys— were happy. They rode the range, brushed down their horses, cooked on campfires, and sang songs on WJJD. That's what I'd be. Certainly not some dissolute sitting in a bar somewhere, served up bourbon by my cousin Carms, the bartender, and leaving Mrs. Morris behind. It all made perfect sense, and it made me pretty sad for Tommy. Sitting there that way, I was convinced his dad was a jerk, even though I never saw him. So although Mrs. Morris was noisy at times, putting this good-boy stuff on Tommy, I still liked her.

And that was how my dreamy cowboy days with WJJD would come to an end.

***

By Christmastime of 1950, there were a lot of other third-graders at the newsstand, and all of us had a keen eye for the good tippers. We would see a blue Oldsmobile or a Willys or a certain truck through the rain and mist along Madison Street and scramble out of the shack for it. It was tough now that Johnny Mulkerin, Tommy Collins, and some of the other guys had discovered the newsstand. On rainy days it was getting crowded, so I decided it was time to look around for new opportunities. *Something else in the news business*, I thought. *Maybe a paper route.* Tommy Mulkerin, Johnny's brother, had one, but he was older and taller. When I tried to talk to him about it, he just kept walking. But Billy Buckley's dad knew someone, and he'd gotten a route, so I spent a few days riding along behind Billy on Maypole, Lamon, and West End Avenue, knotting papers as we rode and flinging them from our bikes. It was tricky work, getting *The Chicago American* to skim a porch and land at the foot of the front door while keeping close enough behind Billy's wind-blown, curling hair as he pointed and shouted out what porches to hit.

"They give better tips if you get it right to the door," he said. The drizzle, spraying up from the bicycle spokes, soaked our knees, and as he shouted over his shoulder, the wet air rose and made a halo of his breath. But in addition to the obvious discomforts, I really didn't like the neighborhood, and most of all, I hated making collections. Before long, I went back to the newstand, still resolved to find something better.

CHAPTER 15
BETRAYAL AT THE BILLIARD TABLE

In the 1930s, Canio would walk across the Loop from his studio, skipping lunch to watch professionals play billiards. Through some intricate calculus, visually defined, he would there try to perfect his own game. To him, billiards was a kind of mathematical artistry. He marveled at the combination of geometry and judgment that went into a three-cushion billiard shot. It was the perfect synthesis of art, Newtonian physics, and the science of perspective. In the twentieth century when the physical world seemed to be changing from the natural and reasonable to the atom, the quantum, and the invisible and unreasonable, the geometry of billiards must have been a lucid comfort to him.

It was a point Canio sometimes made obliquely with a joke about relativity. "Einstein," he said, "was asked, 'Why does the chicken cross the road?' to which he replied, 'To get to the other side.'" For some reason, what humor there was in this quip served to diminish the unfathomable complexity of special relativity. And Einstein, who was both a politician and an eggheaded academic to much of that generation, was thereby reduced to theory and impracticalities. In the end, of course, the "greatest physicist since Newton" (as others had dubbed him) had the last word, encompassing even this kind of thinking. "It's important to make things as simple as possible," Einstein said. "But not too simple."

So much did Canio love billiards that in 1939, when he moved Grieco Commercial Art Company from its offices downtown to his studio at home, he purchased a billiard table of his own. Three feet thick, it was long enough to fill one end of the basement. In fact, it was mammoth. It had to be brought in in pieces, and it took three weeks to assemble. When he wanted to play billiards, Canio had my dad remove the planks that protected the table, and in the low and glowing light, the basement turned hunter green. Canio would bring down a glass of his favorite Chianti, and to the smell of cigars and slate, the room resounded with the crack and knuckle of cream and red billiard balls.

Canio knew the game. Twisting in crescents or in long, slow arcs, the Bakelite balls would kiss and brush against one another, the only sound in an otherwise echoing and noisy room. At other times, they would mysteriously come to a sudden halt as if struck by the vivid French names for the shots that maneuvered them—carom, kiss, massé (a shot made by hitting the cue ball with the cue stick held nearly vertically). As for the subtle maneuvers of his own cue stick, he liked to refer to them as "English." The exquisite game may have been made up of Newtonian physics, but it seemed to be driven more by exotic French words than the blue chalk tips of his cue stick. For me, it was billiard words that brushed and crackled across the glowing felt.

Unwittingly and then maliciously, when I was in third grade, I played a small but despicable role in Canio's ongoing displacement in the family.

It was Christmastime in 1950. I was now eight. The billiard table had been there ten or eleven years, and Dad let me set up my electric trains on the planks that covered it. From one corner I engineered an American Flyer freight train as it streamed along the tracks, whistle roaring, smoke rising in thin curls like tender incense curling upward toward Grandpa's studio. From that Christmas on, Canio had to compete with two of his offspring for the billiard table. And before long I had other projects there as well, a vise at one end, endless sawings and pieces of metal and projects in various stages, such as an ice boat, a radio chassis, a motorcycle.

I was in the basement sawing a piece of iron. Footsteps intruded on my concentration. At first, I thought it was Lenny Donaldson or one of Dad's friends.

"Heesaw! Hizsaw! Pishaw!"

It was Canio, imitating the hacksaw as he made his way to the billiard room. No one else would think that was funny.

"What are you doing?" he asked.

"Cutting off a piece of angle iron." If I said any more, then I'd have to explain the whole project.

"What for?"

I gulped a bit. When he found out, he was really going to think it was stupid. I shrugged toward some timbers in the corner. "For my ice boat. To hold up the sail."

He looked at me, at the wood, at the hacksaw. "Sounds like *huhzah, huhzah* to me."

He chuckled, hoping I'd get the joke. "Whadaya want that for?"

I refused to be amused. I wouldn't even look at him. Seeing how hopeless I was, he padded back up to the studio, weary of his grandson, his son, and all those eminently practical men of the world who did things but didn't know why.

He surely resented my refusal to engage him. And worse, I felt some foolish victory in it all, a successful trespass on his table, the cold rejection of a joke, of which neither of us would thereafter speak. But my defiance of him that day had changed something between us.

For a long time, I secretly justified my victory by reminding myself of the weakness with which he deferred to my father. Somehow I had gotten the idea that since Canio was the oldest person in the household, he should be my defender. But when it came to Dad, Grandpa Canio seemed to run from his temper as much as I did. Surely, he, too, must have been terrified by the son who had grown up to become my father. Canio had become powerless to control him, and so in Gerald's eyes had fallen in stature from his position as the enabling *paterfamilias*. Now he was *the old man* not only in private conversations with my mother or with me but sometimes in the heat of an argument he had with Canio himself. In many ways, Canio had become as much a victim as I was.

This realization came to me slowly, not as a shock but with a grieving, spinal dread as though my last hope and strength lay in Canio for some reason. In fact, it was a lost hope. But I was a young boy, and true to biology, young boys never lose hope. Absent any other possibility, I refused to admit the failure of this childhood trust, and I held onto it in defiance of all evidence to the contrary. I refused its passing.

There was more to it, I'm sure. There is always more to these relationships. But whatever happened between Canio and me that day in the billiard room, whatever prayer I might have had for his protection, whatever satisfaction I derived from the idea of Canio's defeat—even while the circles of gossip sustained his reputation—neither that victory nor the kind of Catholic self-righteousness that defined it ever gave me any real cover in that house. There was, in fact, no cover, succor, or protection whatsoever from my father's unpredictable and relentless temper. Although I may have won some strangely Catholic moral high ground in my small act of rebellion, the fearful wolf remained at the door. Abandoning Grandpa was a pharisaical triumph, a pyrrhic victory.

By the time of Tommy Morris's birthday party, the billiard table was most often boarded over, covered with boxes of shoe samples that Dad photographed for his clients or that Canio drew in airbrush, pen, and ink for his customers. Thus, what had begun for Canio as the rhythmic lunchtime crossings of the Chicago Loop in the 1920s and 30s—and in the other pleasures of working downtown, including the lunches at Henrichy's, Vaudeville, and the showgirls at the Erlanger—were long gone, and not to be resurrected. Only the billiard table, silent, then explosive, remained.

In his three-piece suit, Canio still waited for the downtown bus, but more often than not in the late afternoon rather than the morning, now as the western sun turned green trees to bright yellow along Washington Boulevard. The rays that pierced the dappled shade lit his shoe boxes wrapped in twine, water tape, and brown paper. He would carry the parcel of shoes and his finished renderings, which he would hand deliver or drop off at the downtown post office for clients now far away, often somewhere in Tennessee or Wisconsin. So what in the 1920s and 1930s had been a bustling business conducted by nearly two dozen artists for the commercial houses within a few blocks of one another had become by the 1950s the lonely, private work of a father and son on Washington Boulevard, surrounded by their families and what manly distractions they could retain. They had been domesticated, and they took up certain domestic issues in proportion to the degrees of freedom to which they'd been reduced.

Among my childhood idols, Uncle Jack was now long gone, and in his way, Grandpa Heaney himself, who though alive, had by now become too remote to live up to and a visitation for rare Sundays. I was seven and then eight and then nine, and I had come to the precarious ground on which Canio stood only to find myself narrowly, fearfully constricted.

Living in the time that was my father's, I was running hard to be free.

CHAPTER 16

THE END OF CHILDHOOD

The circles of reputation and personality in Austin were easier to see, being at somewhat of a distance, than were those closest to you. Canio, by way of example, was the complex product of public and familial impressions, but after all, he was a generation removed, whereas my father, being much closer, was more difficult to bring into focus and therefore a far more ambiguous figure. It might have been possible for some of the neighbors, I suppose, to sum up his reputation in a word or two, but to me he was a complex presence—and a constant challenge on so many levels—in my daily life.

The decision to have not one but two photography businesses in the household put us well out of step with the neighborhood. It meant that Regina and I were confined, unlike our peers, to the farther regions of the house and that friends could be brought home with permission only and then only if they behaved. In fact, our friendships were lived out elsewhere, seldom coming nearer than the backyard and then only if we "kept quiet."

After the summer of 1950, we began to work the farm. For the next six years, Regina and I would spend late spring, the summer, and early fall at the farm, attending a one-room schoolhouse when school was in session, working the fields and barns in the summer months. And then we would climb into the back of the car for the drive home to Chicago where we'd take up our seats in Catholic school. So in summers, there was some respite from the regimen of permission. But we were out of step at the farm as well since everyone in Reeseville, Wisconsin, was related to someone else, and Italians, especially Italians from Chicago, were unheard of in Dodge County. To the locals, we were city people, naive about Oliver or Allis Chalmers tractors, unfamiliar with farm animals, and at best a curiosity. Seemingly wealthy, urban, and elite, we were also presumed to be inscrutable. Strangest of all, we were from a city no one ever really thought of since Milwaukee was closer, German, and thought of as Wisconsin, whereas Chicago was, as they say in New Zealand, "the back of beyond." What's more, perhaps most peculiarly, we were Italian and Catholic, an altogether foreign species to German Lutheran dairy farmers.

The amazing thing was that we were accepted at all, to the degree we were, although Dad's charm among strangers and his decision to cultivate friendships with the Catholics, particularly the Jakels and the Yaumans, leading families in Reeseville, went some distance toward positioning us favorably in the township. It was a difficult position. As in Chicago, circumstances had conspired to make us outsiders, even among our own.

At home in Chicago, Dad lived and worked mostly in his studio, actually a closed-in porch off the dining room directly above Canio's south-facing studio a floor below. Gerald was entirely at home. He entertained his clients. He processed film. He photographed samples. He canned tomatoes. Whatever the business required, he did in his studio off the dining room, and whatever had to be shipped, he wrapped and packaged on the billiard table in the basement. Whatever he photographed there, he processed in the darkroom opposite the boiler. Even our kitchen was drafted into the business—unexposed film was stored in the refrigerator for safekeeping. If he was *behind* in his work, he would be in his studio off the dining room until one or two in the morning. And if a client required the work to be shipped, he built packing crates in the basement, running his Craftsman table saw in the middle of the night. During the season, he sometimes would end his day at the beginning of ours with an early morning trip to the main post office downtown. Since Grandpa Heaney had once been postmaster in Garfield Park, I imagined them meeting downtown, my white-haired, distinguished grandfather personally handing my father's packages across the counter for him. *That's a grand way to treat your postal clients,* I thought. But by that time, Grandpa Heaney was long since otherwise engaged.

Dad's clients were elegant people. They were taller and better dressed than most of our neighbors, and for the most part, they spoke softly, circumspectly, and colorfully like my uncle Tom. I was struck by the fact that my dad could be so charming when his clients were around and would graciously do whatever it took to please them.

It was understood that it was our duty to please Dad. It was as though the industrial revolution, already a hundred years old, stopped at the doorstep of our extended household. Our two-flat was an old-fashioned cottage industry.

In the rooms of this cottage industry, I continually scrambled to escape my father's rage whenever I imagined his ears catching the noises my basement projects sent up to his studio, when his impatience suddenly focused on the mess I had made on the billiard table, when the tautness of his body registered his rising temper, when that temper reached the point of explosion and his arms and hands and upper body gathered in the energy to throw whatever was at hand. Of course, *whatever was at hand* was too often whatever I happened to be building or wiring at the time. Destruction swiftly and inevitably followed, and my fear intensified because I knew I was also *at hand.*

I've told already of the time he destroyed my proudly constructed telegraph with its keys and sounders. About how I ran to my closet, struggled fumblingly to lock the closet door, and then waited to be discovered, trembling, snotty, exhausted by anticipation. About feeling alone and abandoned. About retreating deep into my head ... and finding myself becoming, like him, increasingly angry.

Let me pick up where I left off in the opening chapter, namely with a young boy conjuring a world in a closet.

Huddling there in the stillness, I thought I heard someone coming. Footsteps downstairs? If I listened hard enough, I could recognize them, even that far away. They were Canio's. He represented relief at last. I was sure. But how could he help me up here when he was so far away downstairs? My head was spinning, still screwing me up. What good could he do? Even my ears were lying. I had to see what was going on. I had to get control of myself. No help was coming. I had to concentrate. I must have gone on like this—screaming silently, breathing hard, talking now frantically and now reassuringly to myself for half an hour.

Most of my gear, the things I didn't want Regina or anybody else to fool with, was in the back of the closet. There was a wide, white enamel counter anchored to three walls. Under it were drawers as wide as the closet, bigger than I was and creaky too. You could never get them to come straight out. I looked at my stuff in disgust. My communication system in progress wouldn't do any good, not now. It still couldn't talk to anybody. I wondered if I could shut off the light, crawl into a drawer, and hide. I wouldn't be scared then, and he couldn't get it open. I'd shut the light off, but there would still be the reassurance of daylight. There was a little blue glow that came from the crinkled glass high up in the vent window. But I couldn't think. Nowhere was safe. Besides, if I was inside the drawer, who would push it closed? Maybe I could kick it closed, but what if it wouldn't open? So what! I'd be safe there. But then he'd get it open.

Trying to find words to swear with, at myself and at him if I dared, even if it was a sin, I still couldn't stop my internal screaming, the voiceless swearing. Then I was swearing that I would never swear. But even that was a sin. With all of this racing back and forth in my mind—wanting to disappear into the coats and then imagining myself suspended from a coat hanger among them or climbing into the drawer or breaking for it and running or in my imagination, simply flying away like Superman did on the radio—I finally calmed down.

I had to decide what was important. What *was* important was retrieving the rest of my telegraph set from the dining room table. No one else was home. There was no protection. I began to plot my trip back down the hall. I knew most of the places where the floor creaked, but sometimes it was impossible to get by them. Still, his radio was on. It might have been the *Arthur Godfrey Show*. No, it couldn't be. That came on earlier. I had to plan ahead. Almost the whole telegraph set was on a pine board. If I got there, I'd try for the batteries and wires or the pliers and other stuff on the table until I heard him make a move. If I was really quiet, and I squeezed my fingernails under the board until I got one hand on it, I'd be ready to run. No, with one hand under, I would then slip the board to the edge of the table and then grab it all and run.

It would have been easier to wait, but I couldn't. He might walk by and throw something at my stuff, and it'd be even more messed up than it was already. Between planning that and shouting silently at myself and wanting to crawl up and disappear into the clothes, I must have hidden out there for an hour or more.

After that day I knew I had come to the end of something. There was no going back.

There had been other incidents like this—chairs swung over his head, nearly touching the ceiling, shouts from other rooms, terrors that made you freeze as if your face, denying what you had heard or seen, could make the sounds stop, make everything that was wrong with the world disappear forever.

I'd even tried throwing things myself like the time I tried to slam a playmate with a hoe. It finally occurred to me that I was becoming complicit in all of this violence. By the time I was eight, I heard myself shouting at myself, "Control yourself! You *must* control yourself!" Words learned from my mother, the same ones she used when he threw things.

But on that day I swore to myself something new and determined, "I'm never gonna be like him!"

Hopeless and stupified as I was, I yet knew how to internalize repression. Wherever I'd learned it, it was a useful lesson in a dangerous situation, a lesson underscored or revealed to me by the Sisters of Mercy and by Kathryn too. But there was yet another law. There could be no revenge. No revenge meant no sin, and that's what you were supposed to do if you didn't want to go to hell or confession. You had to avoid sin. The instructions in the Baltimore catechism were worded somewhat differently, of course, but they produced the same psychic conclusion.

By the time I was eight, this and the terrors on Menard Avenue, rolling back as far as the growling faces in my dreams, had become an accumulation of acts and responsibilities that made most contact with Dad difficult for me. Whatever the old explanations I'd provided myself for my father's rage had been, they no longer held. When I broke the lamp chasing my sister, I'd learned that I couldn't lie and that I wasn't much of a runner either since she got across the lamp cord without tripping but I didn't. Then the violence and screaming I heard proved to be not just my father's craziness because I got whipped up in it too. So by now I was not only complicit but also somehow partly to blame for the rage that stormed through our house. I was becoming dangerously out of control.

A while back just after we moved to 50-0-7, Dad had decided I might run into some trouble at school and that it was time to teach me how to box "so you can defend yourself." It had been humiliating. While I stood in the bathroom, where the tile floor always made me dizzy and where I now thought I might bounce off the radiator as I was trying to dodge a punch or slip on the tiles and hit my head, he sat on the closed toilet cover and showed me how to make a fist. I wasn't much good at it. He kept barking at me to keep my guard up, but it guarded nothing because every time he jabbed at me, I fell against the wall or the radiator. Or worse, he grabbed me and yanked me back toward him, where I had to endure further thrusts of his fists, which were big enough to clobber both my guarding arms and my entire face. Much as I wanted to believe he was on my side, I couldn't. But I kept reminding myself that he made the money that fed us, so I shouldn't think such ungrateful things. Caught between fear and ingratitude, I struggled to make sense of violence and bullying directed at me.

In fact, the incident with the telegraph fit a persistent pattern. From my earliest memories, I had learned to live in a kind of fail-safe mode. Every move I made had to be checked and double-checked. And I had to be ready at all times to get out of harm's way. I was learning how fast shoes could fly, but I hadn't yet figured out which way to jump to avoid them. Protecting myself became an obsessive and all-consuming task. Worse, it was a task that made trust impossible. If someone came home drunk, you'd see it coming and hightail it outta there. But my father's temper was "unpredictable," as Mom said, so I couldn't have known it. If she was around, I could take the cue from her when to hide out. That day, though, she wasn't around.

So by the time the telegraph had been turned into a slurry of wires and wood scraps under his slamming fist, trust (if I'd even thought of such a thing) was out of the question. The only safety lay in the fail-safe mode. I needed to get out of there—fast! But it still needed a lot of perfecting.

It would become a permanent way of life. In the car, working in the garage, riding in elevators, playing with Grandpa, going to the doctor, it became a skin I wore, a new identity. And when friends were around, I would have to gather them under my skin too. Since that was almost impossible and I wasn't sure I could trust them to keep their heads down, I decided to stick with the old friends I had but not chance bringing any new ones into the house.

The next summer I tried to talk some of my pals into helping me build a fort in the yard, but no one else in the neighborhood seemed to feel the need of a hideout, so I spent a lot of time building it myself—that is, until it collapsed. Actually, I was trapped inside when the roof came down. The roof was so heavy I couldn't get a deep breath. Nor did I have the strength to get out from under it. Somehow, Tony, the ill-shaven janitor next door, heard my gasping screams and came running around the fence between the yards to pull me out. As kids, we always hated the janitors, so my rescue was pretty humiliating. Once freed, I ran straight into the house as if I hadn't even seen him. So what had begun as a hideout became just one more humiliating complicity with the enemy. Tony, who knew and understood all this, no doubt having himself been swept from gangways by the brooms and water hoses of an earlier generation of janitors, had (as I broke free of my prison) a worried look in his eyes. But when I glanced back from the doorway, I saw his grizzly face wide with laughter. That quick look backward was to be his only thanks for rescuing me as it turned out.

From this humiliation I might have taken two lessons. I took only one at the time. I didn't take the lesson Tony taught me that if I tried hard enough to make myself heard, help could usually be found, even in the most unlikely placess. The one I took away from that near disaster was that I needed better engineering skills. Controlling events and circumstances became for me an overweening preoccupation, and since adults had a lot more to offer in that regard and were more reliable in these realms than schoolkids, I decided the time had come to leave childhood behind. Got up and out like a rocket. There was no help for me around there anymore.

In the next few years, Henry Heitbommer, Lenny Donaldson, Louie Esposito, and Rocky Marotta would become my secret guides to a new world. I couldn't tell anyone what had happened. I'd just get beaten up for being a sissy, I figured, and if Dad found out I was trying to escape the dangerous realm of childhood, who knew what he'd do. I couldn't even think of it. There was no telling anybody. Around Austin, word traveled too fast.

Henry, Lenny, Lou, and Rocky may not have known it, but I was memorizing every word they said, reading what they read in the drugstore, looking up what they talked about in the library. If I could have figured out a way, I'd have dreamed what they dreamed about. At the time, of course, I didn't understand any of this. I quickly forgot my father's hands flying, my own voice screaming, out of breath and words. Sometimes I could still see me shouting at myself as though my forehead was a mirror, but I soon decided not to look, never again. I gave it up. It was no use peering into mirrors.

That scattered telegraph set and the collapsing hideout were the end of childhood for me.

Grandpa Canio, Grandma Marie, and Greg, c. 1956

Kathryn Heaney, c. 1930

Gerald Grieco, c. 1930

Uncle Jack Heaney, 1940

Greg and Gerald, 1944

The Griecos, c. 1950 (left to right back row: Gerald, Canio, Kathryn, Marie, Gussie, Enzo; in front Regina and Greg)

The Heaneys, 50ᵗʰ wedding anniversary, 1950 (from left around table: Greg, Topper, Regina, Uncle Tom, Thomas Sr., Eva Mae, Kathryn, Aunt Rae)

Greg, Regina, and Tommy, 1952

Sugarbush, the Farm, 1950

Linden Avenue, Oak Park, 1960

chapter 17

APOTHEOSIS OF
THE GIMP

Pete Schaffer. "The gimp." "The cripple." "That poor boy next door," as people called him. When he went out, you could hear him coming down the back stairs like loose bolts and slapping shoe leather. His brown hair flying one way and his head the other, his bad leg followed him like a tail, and his coat, even more uncertain, billowed like an unmoored cape.

Pete symbolized for us the satisfaction of our own sense of goodwill. When he did well, we were especially proud of ourselves. Not that anybody gave him much help or an ounce more consideration than he won on his own. To me, Johnny Mulkerin, and Tommy Collins, he was one of the big guys. We had to respect him or at least his friends, or else we'd get beat up. We had no choice, no matter what the rest of the neighborhood said.

When we had change for the candy store or went to Featherstone's for a Green River, we often had to get by Pete and his buddies on Lavergne Avenue first. They mostly ignored us, occasionally sneering at "those punks" without looking our way. But when he and his buddies were pitching pennies, it was a different matter. If they wanted to slow us up, they dawdled, and we stopped. And if we were pitching pennies ourselves, they muscled in and took over the game. After a while we pretty much stopped playing on that part of Lavergne, or if we did, it was when we were sure the big guys wouldn't be around.

Tommy Collins liked to start games north of the alley, where there was less traffic and where Kathleen Conboy and her friends hung out. But for the most part, pitching pennies was a game for the big guys. Among the best of them, Pete Schaffer, with his rangy out-of-balance body, could hike a penny lower and skim closer to the cement than anybody in the neighborhood. It was amazing to watch him. The copper in anybody else's hands would skip two, three times along the pavement. But when Pete flipped it, a penny landed dead on the crack … or bounced from one side to the other as though it and the crack were magnetized.

For the most part, people walked around the game out into the mud and grass. If there was a crowd, women with shopping bags and babushkas would take the other side of the street. This was the big guys' spot and their game. It was understood. And when the stakes went to nickels and quarters, we were told it was "gambling," and that was "a sin, so stay away." Once in a while somebody we didn't know or a cousin visiting the neighborhood would walk up Lavergne right between the big guys as though there wasn't a game in progress.

The big guys had a way of dealing with this. They would just stare at the intruders or make faces or mimick them but continue the game, usually not saying much of anything, for fear somebody's dad would come out of some alleyway and box their ears for sassing a cousin or for leaning on a car that was simonized. ("Yeah, probably *two weeks ago*! So what's the big deal?") But the fact was that if you were a stranger, you could walk right through the game as if it wasn't there, and they wouldn't say a thing, at least not anything you could hear. Or they'd just mutter the word *asshole* at a decibel level known only to themselves.

What would eventually become of Pete had long been the subject of some discussion in the large apartment buildings that lined Lavergne. His father was dead or *missing*, one of the divorce euphemisms in Austin. If a man wasn't around, you didn't ask, or you directed the question to Mrs. Olsen across the porch rail in a whisper. She was an authority on the courtyard building next door and much of what went on along Lavergne Avenue. In fact, she was such an authority that if she happened to be wrong about something as occasionally was the case, none of us would admit it because she liked Mom and told her everything that was going on over there. Actually, it was what she didn't say that was most often the object of discussion. In the midst of a sentence she would suddenly step back into her kitchen with a knowing finger to her lips and an unspoken *goodbye*. That was all the news for this day. The families she wouldn't speak of and the husbands out of work or in disrepute were pronounced upon with a knowing eye or a vague smile.

Kathryn would borrow things from her—a darning ball, a carrot, or a cup of sugar passed across the porch rail from two stories up. And the next day Regina or I would trot down the yard and into the courtyard, where Scotty had run away with me, and up the steps, chipped like the scars of pimples on Pete Schaffer's face, to Mrs. Olson's door. Sometimes I'd bring back the carrot or some sugar or a pie tin, or I'd return the favor she'd done us with a piece of cake. Occasionally, I'd try to ask her questions, the sort my mother would, to which she would just laugh and say, "Shouldn't you be off to school?" Even if I asked about Pete Schaffer, who wasn't that much older than me, she'd keep her silence, her eyes letting me know with great certainty that my question was out of place.

In this web of neighborhood idioms, we all had valued places, situated in our activities, our roles, and what was expected of us, clearly defined from childhood to old age. Consequently, Pete Schaffer's mother was always "poor Mrs. Schaffer," who, as they described her, should have worn torn house dresses and had a dirty face, though she didn't. And Pete, who had no father and had had polio when he was six, had no future anybody could see.

When Pete was eighteen and I was about eight, I learned to ride a bike, a girl's bike from Sears, not a boy's bike, because it was Regina's bike too and because girls' bikes were supposed to be easier to ride. I felt like a real jerk. Before I'd learned to really stay on it, some guys from Emmet (the public school kids, not the Catholics) tried to steal it from me. I was never sure why they didn't just grab it and run since they were bigger and I was obviously scared. But I think it was because they realized it wasn't a Schwinn, or maybe they thought a boy riding a girl's bike was so far beneath contempt that it wasn't worth stealing anyway.

That spring while I rode up and down in front of the house, Pete Schaffer went off to technical school. For a long time, no one knew what that meant. Then one day, with obvious pride, Grandma announced that

Pete had finished his training to become a court stenographer. Now with his long hair trimmed and a black wool coat that somehow didn't flare so wide as his old one and with a satchel the shape of a bowling ball but thinner, he slipped out in the morning mist and took the bus downtown.

I was amazed. From how people talked about Pete's stunning accomplishment, you'd have thought Grandma Marie or Mrs. Buckley had paid his college tuition. Mrs. Olsen now said, "See! I always knew he was a smart boy," and, "It's a good job for him." This collective pride also appeared among men in the neighborhood, some of whom seemed to think they might now have a friend in court. "With a little luck, maybe we can get a parking ticket fixed." And soon the stories began. How they'd all helped Pete along the way one way or another.

———————•·•———————

Pete had done well, but somehow Canio seemed oblivious to all this. Or he knew it and had decided to pretend not to notice. That Saturday—or perhaps it was the next—when Pete brought home his first paycheck and was playing pitch penny with the big guys on Lavergne, Grandpa and I walked back from Featherstone's, where he'd gone to buy a handful of cigars for the weekend. I remember because he gave me the shiny metal tube from one of them, which I alternatively thought of as the Lone Ranger's silver bullet, a missile, or a monstrous finger growing from the corner of my hand. Suddenly, we were standing smack in the middle of the pitch penny game before I realized what Grandpa was doing.

"Hey, come on now!" one of the big guys barked. Then mostly just startled, he turned suddenly polite. "Oh, hello, Mr. Grieco!" Canio bent down at one end of the game. The big guys moved over, half out of respect and half in disbelief. I'd heard change rattling in Grandpa's pocket, and now I realized he'd drawn half a dozen pennies from his suit trousers. His hands were fast and nimble. He could roll coins up his sleeve and shake them down the back of his hand or bring them out from your earlobes without you ever seeing how they got there. Now suddenly, low and sleek, his leg swinging back for balance like a kangaroo's tail, he was pitching right under Pete's arm, the pennies slapping down on the crack like mud on a brick wall.

"God, Grandpa," I wanted to say. "You're not even in the game." But he *was* in the game and faster than Pete, outpitching everyone there.

"You can't gamble with an officer of the court, can you?" he said.

There was a nervous burst of titters because suddenly nobody knew whether in his new role as court stenographer, Pete was supposed to be gambling or whether Grandpa knew something that might get them in trouble. Pete thought it was hysterically funny, and he stopped in midpitch to laugh with Grandpa.

"Let 'em arrest me!" he said, and pitched another one, a nickel, right on the line.

"See! What'd I tell you?" Canio said to me. And just as suddenly, he walked right on through the game, the fellas parting on the other side. "These guys can pitch wisecracks, but they can't pitch pennies." I thought he was going to sweep up his winnings from Pete, and I started to tell him not to.

"No, no," he said. "Let 'em have it. He's a big shot now." So we walked on through and headed home for dinner. And with a wink over his shoulder, Canio looked back at Pete, who stood there in the midst of all the big guys, grinning.

After that, when Canio passed the guys out along Lavergne, they'd part in the middle of the game to say hello and pause in case he wanted to join in. They may just have thought it an easy way to up the ante. But that wasn't all. They liked the way he had put the crown on Pete. He was a man now in Canio's eyes and in theirs, and that aura had attached to them too.

CHAPTER 18

EXPLOSIONS

Robert LoGerardo didn't have a father. Maybe he was killed in Korea or something, we didn't know. All we heard came from Robert saying his father was "mixing in action." We were in fourth grade, and he was from the northside part of Terry Murphy's gang. But we weren't playing marbles anymore, and Terry wasn't picking fights like he used to. Robert liked guns and chemistry, stuff like that, and brass shells he got when members of the American Legion marched around Peanut Park on Memorial Day with their medals and made their rifles snap to and shot blanks in the sky.

The park was actually called Leamington Square, but that didn't fit because it was just a triangle with a war monument on it. It was too small to play ball in, so we called it Peanut Park, like everyone else had when they were kids. But on Memorial Day, it got respect. It wasn't much of a memorial, no dead bodies or anything, just some kinda tall cement with bronze plaques and lists of battalions or regiments or something and plastic flowers with ribbons hanging off, all stuck in red, white, and blue targets. Some of the targets even had soldiers' names written in the middle on them, names that the old ladies or somebody had left there.

Even though I couldn't find my uncle Jack's name on the bronze plaques, Peanut Park was still our memorial, so after we'd collected all the spent cartridges the Legion guys left, we'd cross Laramie to look at the new Fords. Or if it was hot, we'd cross back to the church and get a drink at the fountain or maybe mess around with the candles. We had to be quiet there though because there were always old ladies around, mumbling prayers for dead victims or something. We had to sneak up to the St. Jude altar or Theresa of Avila when their backs were turned so that we could grab the tapers. The long ones were in cups way up over the candles, so we couldn't reach them, but sometimes there'd be big ones in the sand trough in front of the candles. They'd be left there, still smoking, so we'd grab them and keep going. If there weren't too many old ladies around, we'd light candles all over church, going from saint to saint until somebody got spooked because you were supposed to put a dime in the tin box for each candle. After that, we'd have to confess because it was stealing from the saints. Sometimes some girl would be there with her grandmother, and she'd try to snitch on you. That spooked us too.

"I'm telling Sister Mary Annette if you light more candles without putting in money!" She'd whisper so loud half the church could hear. It was a trick sissies had learned from the nuns, who whispered at us like that during Mass. "Sit up straight, young man!" And when you were supposed to be kneeling straight, they'd say, "Get your bottom off that seat!" We'd shape up for the nuns, but mostly shrugged off the grandmas and the snitches.

"So tell her! What do I care!"

———————•———————

Everybody in the neighborhood had a story about Peanut Park. But Robert LoGerardo was the only one I knew who tried making a science out of it. He had this *theory* that we could make the rifle shells work again, maybe with a taper and some powder from his chemistry set. Nobody believed him, but then no one knew exactly what blew the shells up either. Along with his chemistry set, he had a book with 127 formulas, so I had a hunch making the shells go off was worth a try. Besides, if anybody could explain what made them bang, he probably could. We had cap guns and red rolls of caps you could scratch with a nail to make the whole roll fizzle. Then the red paper that held the gunpowder would burn up too in a ball of black smoke out in the alley. But nobody explained how gunpowder killed anybody, except that the shells the American Legion had were supposed to be blanks and real shells had bullets in them.

The best we could figure was that it was like the Masked Man and Tonto. The Lone Ranger always handed people a silver bullet from his gun belt so they would know who he was. You could see the bullet in the shell then, real plain. But that still left out one thing. If you killed them, where'd the ghosts come from?

We were going to Robert's house that Memorial Day, but I was scared off somehow or had something to do. Or maybe I was just thinking about Uncle Jack, who gave me my middle name because everybody said I was his favorite. Whatever it was that spooked me, I didn't go to LoGerardo's house for a couple of weeks. Actually, I rode halfway there once on my new bike. I got as far as the Simpson Electric Instrument factory. There were all these meters and gauges out back in the trash with shining red and amber coils and parts polished so bright you could see your fingers reflected when you picked them up, and you could even see your fingerprints on them when it was cold. But the day I got there, they were mostly smashed parts scattered around the alley. It seemed pretty stupid.

Anyway, by that time it was pretty late. Even though I didn't know what time it was, the shadows were really long, so I went back home. The next day at school, I asked Robert if he ever got stuff from the Simpson factory. He said that it was all junk and that you couldn't make bombs out of it anyway. But he was going to run his trains in the back yard that day if it was sunny. He wanted me to bring one of the accessories from my American Flyer.

"So we can have two whistles," he said.

He had a Lionel set with three tracks. All the Lionel engines had whistles inside them. But American Flyer engines didn't have whistles. They just made real smoke instead. So American Flyer put the whistle in this scale model Barnum and Bailey billboard with a Clarabelle clown face on it. It was pretty silly, a Clarabelle whistle, but it sounded really good like a real train. Robert thought it would be neat to blow the clown whistle when his train went by and then start a war of the whistles. First, Clarabelle would whistle. Then his train would whistle, and then Clarabelle would go again. That would go on for a while, Robert said, "till all the trains were mad at each other and the cars and shells and everything blew up."

It all sounded pretty good to me, so I got home after school as quickly as I could. But when I headed for the basement, my heart dropped. The door was open. That meant Dad or Grandma or somebody was down there working, and I'd have to find a way to sneak the whistle out. It was Dad, and he was being friendly as though he wanted me to help him with the shoes he was photographing. I knew he wouldn't want me to load the stoker or take the clinkers out this early because the dust would settle on his negatives, which were drying in frames up over the washtubs. I was trying to get back to the billiard table where my train set was, but he kept asking questions about school and what Johnny Mulkerin was doing and other stuff. Mostly things I didn't want to tell him.

Anyway, I was standing by the door, waiting for the quiz to finish. It seemed like it was just about over because he was swirling prints around in the wash tank with his big tweezers and didn't seem to be watching me much. I still didn't know how I could get the Clarabelle whistle out because it was fat and green and had such a strange shape anybody could spot it stuffed under your coat.

Regina and I had our own keys to the basement then so that we could lock our bikes up. I liked to sneak down there when no one was around and work on my trains or read Grandpa's old magazines. He'd shown them to me once, pointing out the shoes on the women and how in some magazines the skirts were long and at other times they were really short.

"That was during the war," he said. "And all these women are wearing nylons to get their legs shaped that way." I used to get out those magazines so I could see if they had fighter planes or soldiers in them smoking cigarettes like Uncle Tom. But mostly, they were just women dressed up in vacuum cleaner ads.

Anyway, when you locked up the basement, you had to shut off all the lights and then let your eyes get used to the dark till you could see the cracks of light around the door coming from outside. But before your eyes were used to the dark, the house would start to get creaky with people walking around upstairs. It sounded like the ghosts of the people we figured must have lived there once. Sometimes I'd just get the lights turned off, and Grandpa would start the air compressor in the basement darkroom. It would bang and blast and rattle so much I couldn't find the door. The compressor was next to the door actually, and sometimes in the dark, I'd walk right into it. The basement had some good stuff though, even though the coal cellar and under the stairs were kinda scary.

So that day when I was standing at the door trying to figure out how to sneak Clarabelle past Dad, the compressor blew into action. Well, it didn't actually blow up. It just started right behind me, but I was so busy imagining the Clarabelle whistle stuffed under my jacket or wrapped in a bag or in a box of junk I could pretend to carry out, I'd forgotten all about the compressor. It made me jump right into the middle of the room!

"Stay away from that goddamn thing!" Dad said as if I'd been about to stick my hands in the pulleys. The compressor stopped almost as quickly as it started. I could hear footsteps overhead as someone came from Grandpa's studio to the upstairs doorway.

"Gerald?" There was a pause. "Gerald!" Grandpa couldn't hear us, I guess. He must have thought we'd left the lights on. "Gerald, is that you down there?"

"Who the hell else would it be?" Dad said.

Canio ignored this.

"I'm going to run the compressor, okay?" said Dad.

"Well, you started the goddamn thing. What the hell'd you stop for?"

Grandpa's footsteps crossed quickly overhead toward his studio and then disappeared. I thought maybe he was in the kitchen. Wherever he was, it was a good break, so I took advantage of it and headed for my trains in the billiard room. When I got there, I hurried up and unscrewed the wires from the Clarabelle whistle. It was stuck. Dad had hammered brads into the base because when it blew, it vibrated and slid around the train board. It must have taken me fifteen minutes to get it all apart. I could hear the buses droning by on Washington Boulevard, one after another now, which meant it was late, and I'd never get to Robert LoGerardo's in time. Just as I was about to stuff the Clarabelle sign in a paper bag, Dad poked his head into the room.

"I'm leaving now. Be sure to lock up when you go. Okay?"

I tried to hide the bag, but I think he saw it. Anyway, I wasn't sure, so I just moved Clarabelle over near the transformer like I was working on it or something. *It's perfect*, I thought. *I'll go now and just tell Mom they asked me to stay for dinner. Aw, shoot! She'll know it's phony because Mrs. LoGerardo won't call.* Dad was still fussing around in the darkroom. Precious minutes ticked by. I could hear the buses wheezing along, one after another, dropping crowds at Lavergne Avenue.

The next day it was the same story. Dad was in his darkroom, printing. This time I went straight back to the trains, stuffed Clarabelle in my school bag, and headed out the back door.

"Where're you going?" he said.

"Oh, I think I'll ride my bike around the neighborhood."

"You can leave your bag here then. I'll take it up," he said.

Just then the compressor blew again. Spew. Bang! I could smell oil blow out the ports as it sputtered, lurching backward and forward, and then chugged up to speed. I still jumped, even though I knew it was coming.

"What's in the bag?" Dad shouted over the noise.

"Just stuff I'm taking to Johnny's."

"Let me see," he shouted over the din.

"Forget it," I said, flipping the bag on the table and running out.

"You're not taking your American Flyer whistle to Johnny's, are you?"

I didn't even look at him. How could I take it, if it was lying there in the bag? I bounced the bike up the five cement stairs, jumped on, and took off.

"Don't be late for dinner," he shouted after me.

In the most conciliatory voice I could fake, I shouted back, "I won't," and then I rode hard out of the yard, so he wouldn't stop me. I got to LoGerardo's by four.

Robert had most of his tracks set up and was chasing a coal car around, his arms dipping and swooping like the wings of a fighter plane dropping, one by one, the tiny bombs he'd made out of the rifle shells. Every time he released one, he made all the sounds. "Click, clunk, swish, swzzz, long whistle, pikush!" Then *Ba-BOOMM!* He'd figured out just what the bomb bay doors sounded like when they opened and the sound of smoke and dust blowing up from the railroad tracks, thousands of feet below. When the shells landed in one of the cars, he'd scream, "Direct hit! *Kaboom!*" And his arms would fly up as if his whole body had exploded.

That went on for a little while. Then he stopped the train, and we got down to business. He had some old firecrackers and some punk. We mixed them with some kind of white stuff from his chemistry set and filled the shells. Then he started the train, and we were bombers again, gliding with our arms out over the tracks. But none of the shells blew up like we'd hoped. Mostly they just tinkled onto the sidewalk or fell on the tracks and shorted them out. Then the train stopped. That was about all there was to it. So we decided we'd fill a whole coal car with firecrackers and shells and tallow and bits of punk and make it really blow up. We were doing that just as the sun set and the long shadows slipped out across the yards.

Down the block you could hear tired, weary mothers calling their children and their neighbors' children as people headed home for dinner. "Oh, Charlieeee!" some woman called from her back porch like an old, forgotten song, some worn-out tune as though all that was left of a sweet remembered evening was that forlorn pair of notes.

"*Chaaar-leeeey!*"

Hearing the women cry that way told time as well as the church bells, and soon enough, Mrs. LoGerardo called us in too. Robert still had two or three more shells to stuff into the coal car, and he was working furiously to get it done.

"Stay for dinner," he whispered. "We can blow the trains up after." But that woman calling *Charlie* reminded me how Grandma Heaney had flown all the way back from Florida because she had an intuition that something was wrong with her son, and how she'd been right because he was in the hospital with appendicitis and he almost died. But that wasn't Charles, it turns out. It was Uncle Jack, and he got killed in France, though I had it all mixed up at the time.

"Come on, Greg. We can even take some firecrackers in the house and put 'em in the spaghetti. *Kablooey!* That'll be funny! Spaghetti all over the place."

But I began to think the coal hopper he was stuffing would blow up in Robert's face, and that's why we'd been kept from seeing Uncle Jack's face at his funeral because the dirty Nazi mortar shell that had hit his jeep had shredded his face and body. I couldn't have explained it, but everything around there seemed to be on the verge of blowing up. All I wanted to do was head home.

"*Rob-berrt!* Spa-ghet-ti time." Mrs. LoGerardo's voice sang from her first-floor kitchen in drawn-out harmony with the mothers down the block. Robert was a good kid and didn't need to be told to wash his hands twice. He jumped up and went in. I made some excuse about having to get home and took off on my bike down the alley. Heading out like the Lone Ranger on Silver, I figured I'd ride past the Simpson factory to see if there was something in the pile of junk that wasn't smashed. But when I got there, the place was blue with shadows and my heart wasn't in it. I just headed home.

That was near the end of fourth grade. I never saw Robert LoGerardo again. Some people said he had moved away, but they didn't know where. And somebody trying to be funny, probably Lawrence Walsh, said Robert said he was "mixing in action." But eventually, a story went around that he had blown himself up with his chemistry set and some old batteries. I always told myself that story was a lot of hooey, but like ghosts and things that go bump in the night, *mixing in action* outlived all other explanations.

CHAPTER 19

ELECTRICITY AND FATHERS

Robert LoGerardo was my last playmate. It was the end of fourth grade, and I still played ball with guys in the neighborhood, but then I got a job and all that kid stuff was over.

At the farm in Reeseville, it was different. Farm kids all worked, and there was fierce competition as to who was best at it, all of which came down to who got to drive the tractor. In Wisconsin, work and play weren't separated into parts of the day, except at school during recess, which was mostly competition too, this time athletic.

Farm work was—and is now—filled with backbreaking toil and unpredictably idle moments, and even though the rhythm of the city was most familiar to me, I learned another sense of comfort there. Occasionally, you stopped long enough to sit down and stretch out, finding a patch of shade off an open field, playing mumbly peg, or sitting just below a hillock to catch a tiny breeze, an updraft of air as it flowed from the valley below. Usually, it was because you were stuck while somebody went back to the barn for a clevis pin or bailing wire, or you were waiting for a wagon to come back for another load or for the dogs to bring the cows up the lane. So you found a piece of grass to chew or simply sat silent, your eyes looking around for entertainment. There were usually a couple of bugs skittering around in the grass to watch or a hawk far off on the rolling horizon. If it was August or September, you began to watch for a pheasant and to tune your ear to the rustle of corn leaves so you could hear the slightest variation in their sound.

"There's something, over there," somebody would whisper suddenly. Hunting season would soon be here. But for the most part, you didn't talk. What was there to talk about? Girls talked. Talked and chattered. Sometimes you could hear them near the milk house or where they'd been pulling thistle in an oat field. They always sounded goofy! You didn't want to sound goofy. Not guys. You didn't want to sound like that, so you didn't talk.

It wasn't like the city. In Chicago, play was almost nothing but talk.

But now that was over. By the summer before fourth grade, I had decided to grow up.

———◆———

Back in the neighborhood that autumn, I went from store to store searching for anything to do with electricity. There were a couple of radio shops on Madison Street, and there was Heitbommer's.

At the other end of the alley, Heitbommer's had been the standard stop. By third grade I was allowed to enter the store under the back porch, the way parents with gloves on came from their gardens, the way the janitors and big guys did. You'd stop outside the back door, take a deep breath, grab the doorknob, and rush in. It smelled like dead cats back there or rose powder, or maybe it was creosote from the barrels next door. Once inside the store, though, things were clean and well-organized and smelled of nothing at all. Heitbommer's had lots of parts out in the aisles to look at, and it was assumed that young boys rummaging through hardware were trouble. Coming down the aisle, their son, Henry, would be on me in a minute.

But what I really listened for, even more than him, was the sound of the long stick and the crawl of the ladder, which meant one of the drawers high up near the ceiling, the oak and brass drawers filled with boxes and with sets of five dovetail sides was about to be opened. The rows of drawers, sorted out and arranged in Henry's mind and reaching almost to the ceiling, opened out as long as his arms did from the ladder rail. Henry's customer might want roll pins and butt hinges or chrome-plated brass shower rings that were one inch by five-eighths of an inch or stove bolts and eight-penny nails. I had come for batteries and bell wire.

Once inside, I was usually impatient. Often there were too many customers, so Henry didn't have time to explain things like how buzzers worked or why telegraphs clicked—important issues if you had to reach Johnny Mulkerin overnight and you couldn't use the telephone.

Henry was wire thin and seemed seven feet tall, though he often wore red and black lumberjack shirts that made him look thicker. And his face was thin as a braid of hair, and his hair had curls in lots of extra places. I thought he was a little strange and some other people did too, but that's why I liked him, especially since we could talk business—buzzers and batteries, bell wire and things, real man talk like the janitors and butchers who came by now and then to see the German-made knives. Sometimes I wondered what was on top of his head, and I hoped he'd bend down so I could see it. Could he really be related to fat, squat old Mr. Heitbommer and to Mrs. Heitbommer, who seemed to sit out back all day, adding up figures in German?

About that time Henry got a summer job at Argonne National Laboratories, which even impressed him. It impressed me too after I told Dad this. He smiled with his easy laugh, encouraged to hear that his son was finally taking up with the right people. I thought Argonne was a gas, so the place was probably just a lot of stinking chemicals, bags of fertilizer, and bubbling bottles out there where they probably made orange neon lights for Miller beer signs, but I kept my mouth shut and didn't say anything about that. But when Henry got going and there weren't too many customers, he wanted to talk about nuclear reactors. I just wanted to know how many batteries it would take to run a telegraph and why there had to be one at Johnny's house and one at mine. Why couldn't there be just one?

"It likely depends on whether you're going to have full duplex transmission."

That stopped me cold. Here I was trying to be an engineer. What was full duplex?

"Hmmm," Henry reflected. "There might be a way, but you'd probably have to have three wires, not just two between your houses."

That was out. *Too expensive*, I thought. But what was *full duplex*? I had to figure a way to trick him into an answer.

I'd already let him in by this time on the secret telegraph plan. Johnny and I were sworn to secrecy, but I figured, *Heck, Henry lives way down at the other end of the block and won't tell the grown-ups anyway because, you know, he has a girlfriend and kept that a secret.* Anyway, the only way I knew how to get help—besides from *Boy's Life*—was from the scratchy ladies in the library. So I had to tell someone! Henry was the best. He said we'd need some beryllium copper for the springs, but we could also use that for making motors for the next project, which sounded okay to me.

This all ended abruptly when Mrs. Majory's son-in-law pulled down the wire to Johnny's and Dad got impatient with my keying and destroyed my telegraph. I tried to go back to Heitbommer after that and start again, but my heart wasn't in it. Then Henry went away when school started, so for sure no one was there to help me.

———◆———

All of which led to the autumn of *Elements of Radio*. I poured over that book, repeating whole sentences inside of whole other sentences until I could see electrons attracted, repelled, biased, oscillating, and bouncing, until I figured out what one relationship and then another meant, until sentence after sentence exploded out the whole meaning. The book had been my cousin Lenny's, and he must have stored it in the basement somewhere when he went to work for Motorola or in Grandpa's closet. Somehow I got hold of it. Just in time too.

Here's how it went. Electrons came from cathodes if plate voltages were high enough to attract them. Grids slowed them down or sped them up. Around grids there were bias circuits.

I had decided I wanted to make a radio. It was a challenge, but I figured that if I could figure it out from a book when I was eight, it would sort of prove I might be an inventor just starting out like Morse before the telegraph or Eli Whitney, whom I hadn't read about yet but would. Figuring this out would confirm I was significant and important beyond, you know, just my own suspicions.

I was determined to do it, but with Henry gone and my father busting up projects, it was pretty clear I'd have to find someone to teach me. Lenny had brought the book back from the navy, so I thought about joining up. But Johnny Mulkerin told me you had to be eighteen, and he knew because his brother had tried to join once and had gotten turned down. Meanwhile, I'd gotten the parts I needed, ordered from catalogs at Allied Radio. I'd even gotten the 67.5 volt B battery. I wired it furiously in the closet, barely mounting the parts. The #30 tube glowed, and that radio started up, music I remembered from my crystal radio on WJJD and other stations, which came squealing in as you turned the variable condenser. Then in a flash it was over. The tube glowed bright and then went suddenly dark, having shorted out against the B battery.

Character had once again defeated my well-laid plans. I felt stupid and idiotic for rushing headlong into playing with the thing instead of wiring and mounting the parts properly. Thank God no one knew. What an idiot! But that made it worse. I couldn't tell anybody either. I would suffer grief and defeat at my own hands, and there was no one else who gave a damn.

Dad was always buying things used. He would take me along sometimes when he'd found a bargain in the want ads. He wasn't the best one in the family at this. Grandma Marie was a legend for the deals she'd make in Chicago's department stores, returning things three and four times as items were marked down. But Dad was pretty good at negotiations too. So in my remorse and with at least six weeks of paper sales and allowances ahead before I could buy a new vacuum tube, I thought I'd look around the television and radio repair shops for a used one.

"Whaddya want a used one for?" the man at the counter asked me. "You just gonna short it out again?"

"Tell 'em we got enough of 'em already, broken in the alley!" said his partner.

"It wasn't my fault. Menardi did it," I said, thinking to myself, *Now they're blaming me.* I opened my mouth to blow them off. But then I remembered that Dad had told me he always had a plan when he made a deal, and blowing them off wasn't part of my plan. Besides, my new watchword was *control*. My dad might blow up, but I wasn't going to. And then, too, I was scared. These were wise guys like the big guys in the apartment buildings, only bigger. I just wanted to get out of there.

"Not to break," I said. "I'm building a radio."

"You want a radio! Get your grandpa to buy you one like that one over there."

"The kid thinks he's David Sarnoff."

I didn't know who that was. "It's a triode. Like a DeForest tube," I said, beginning to wonder if they knew what I was talking about.

"Yeah, yeah, I know. We got a new one," he said, still talking about the radio. Then about the #30 tube. "That's pretty old, though, not much use for them anymore. I might have to order."

What really hurt was the part about Sarnoff because I figured he was some kind of inventor. I blushed as though they'd heard me talking to myself in the closet or something. How'd he know I was going to be an inventor?

At last I got out of there with a price far more expensive than the mail order price from Allied Radio would be.

There was another store on the block with some small appliances, but when the guys there finally asked what I wanted, they told me they didn't have tubes. I was down to the last store on my list now.

———◆●●———

The third radio shop on the block wasn't even a radio shop. The sign said E-Z Washing Machine Company, and it was full of big white washing machines, pails of laundry soap, and strange signs that wiggled when you passed. But there was a radio there too, and I was running out of options. So one day I squeezed along the entryway and peeked in at the door. There was someone inside with his back to the counter and a bench full of radio and TV test equipment behind him. I walked by a couple more times on the way to and from Schneiderman's Bakery and even looked in early one morning when the store wasn't even open yet. But I still wasn't ready. I decided to read some more *Elements of Radio*. I had to be sure I could ask good questions.

I didn't know it at the time, but the man leaning over the test bench was Louie Esposito. He entered my life that day, and he remains in it even long after his death.

Louie had had a black-and-white picture of himself taken on the day of the shop's grand opening. The date had been written on it, probably by the E-Z Washing Machine Company publicity agent who was no doubt glad to get a shop named after the company. I could never figure out why I had never heard about any grand opening—Louie said quite a few people had been there—so complete were my family's contacts in the neighborhood. But I didn't know anybody who'd been to the grand opening, so I assumed it couldn't have been much. Louie, who had strong opinions about almost everything (a quality I admired in Grandpa and Grandma and was glad to see in him), remained strangely silent on the details of the event and seemed unwilling to talk about them. On almost every other topic, however, he liked to argue.

Louie, who ran the TV part of the shop, was a bachelor. Rocky, who was responsible for washing machine repairs, had a girlfriend and never ceased to tease Louie about his lonely life. "For his remorse," Rocky said, "Louie has his violin." I was never sure whether it was a real violin or just a figure of speech.

From this moment in fourth grade on, I would work for E-Z Washing Machine Company a few afternoons and every Saturday, except for the months when I was at the farm. In the early days, I felt lucky to wash the store windows, enjoying the smooth brown smell of the rubber squeegee as it stripped Chicago's grit and grime from the sun-heated glass. We'd move aside the odd cardboard displays with eyes made to look as though they followed you as you walked by, a ploy to lure women in for a sale or at the least remind neighbors where to come for repairs. But I soon became an old hand there, spending most of the time cleaning and rebuilding water pumps. I became familiar with every tool and machine and with every part or attachment in the bins that lined the walls. I learned to deal with customers on the phone and to take parts orders when Rocky and Louie were out on service calls.

Usually, Louie was impossible to talk to before ten in the morning. He'd come in unshaven, stamping the snow and sleet from enormous thick-souled shoes during the winter, and then trudge from the front door to the mirror in the little bathroom at the rear of the shop. He'd strip back his shirt, letting it hang like Raphael's drapery around his waist, and proceed to his shaving. I soon learned that anything said before or during that ritual was sure to annoy and even offend, no matter how innocent.

He sounded like a grunting old grampus, pulling at his thick jowls in disgust in the flourescent light. The mirror relentlessly reminded him of the wear time had taken on him, the angst of life's passing by, the unsatisfied relationships he longed to put from his head. But there it was, confronting him in the mirror each morning, and none too pretty at that. However, I thought he was beautiful—the way old mountains are rugged, quick to brighten, stormy and thoughtful, and in the end serene.

If I got more than a grunt out of him as he shaved, there was the chance of a comical day before noon. Rarely did it take much longer.

Late in the afternoon, he would often put one big saddle-soaped leather shoe on the silver radiator that hissed and clattered along the length of the storefront window and lean in my direction as he talked.

For his part, Rocky was quiet and appreciative, as taciturn as Louie was loquacious. But they both spoke freely when they were together and pretty much treated me as though I was just another adult. I wasn't, of course, and sometimes comments about the opposite sex went uncensored, but that was about all. Thus, by fifth grade, I'd achieved my goal: I was a man among men, and I expected to be one.

Saturday mornings with both of them out on calls to customers' homes, I became public relations man, confidant, and dispatcher for the two of them. In the afternoon, with a great deal accomplished, we'd talk about the eccentricities of the clients—the TVs full of cat hair so thick you had to vacuum your way in to see the tubes, the husbands sitting forlorn and frustrated in the midst of a pile of parts, the shade-tree engineers, the kindly nuns.

Selling parts gradually became my responsibility. If my hand was
squeezed behind a crankcase or if I was in the middle of taking a customer's
phone call, I had earned the right to use direct language with adults, a
right that needed to be respected because you were getting paid.

With my newfound wealth, I consumed endless Vienna hot dogs with
the works—pickles, onions, mustard, tomatoes.

"Cukes?"

"Hold the cukes."

"Peppers?"

"Hold the cukes. Hold the peppers."

I had earned the right to give orders, I discovered, in the sandwich
shop too because I was paying for the hot dog. In short, these were heady
times for a boy of nine. And Canio and his newsstand and, ironically, Dad
and his fury had been the catalysts that had made this new independence
possible. Though not yet really free, I was out on my own—and more my
own man—than I had ever been. If ever one had believed in the Greek
idea of fate, one generation's frustrated quest for happiness dooming the
hopes of the next generation, this would have been the time to abandon
such beliefs.

It was a time of sixteen-ounce Pepsis and empty pop bottles piling up
in the red pine cases in the rear of the shop. It was a time of menus off
the charts of traditional Italian dietary limits, whether of Canio's Lucani
or Marie's Neapolitan traditions. In the shops we were men together. We
found what we liked, liked what we ate, and ate what we wanted. There
was little language off limits, and collegiality and care for one another's
travails prevailed. But of course, sexuality was still a cautionary tale. In
this, Louis and Rocky were still my fathers.

At times a gentle tension simmered between me and Louie. He would
want to talk about philosophy, values, belief, the roots of guilt, and the
sources of redemptive reassurance. What you knew for sure and what
you thought was sure but wasn't. His science went beyond Maxwell's
equations, beyond radio and radar, beyond the navy textbooks or the
rules of magnetism. It cut to the mystery at the heart of things. I was too
young, and I was eager to be doing things, making things. Like Rocky,

I was convinced that where no answers were, you'd crossed a line too far, had raised a question too suspicious, or were trying to construct a framework of ideas too impractical. My only interest in those days, besides building a motorcycle, was sine waves because sinusoidal waveforms on the oscilliscope made me dizzy. Canio, who stopped in at the shop more often now, was more to Louie's liking in this regard as he loved to talk and argue about such things.

Canio, either confident that I'd earned a responsible place in the running of the shop or curious about what had become of me, stopped by regularly, though it was more often to engage with Louie than to see me. The two men had become frequent conversationalists as I became less absorbed in radio and theoretical discussions and more in washing machine pumps and the generally practical affairs of the service business, which Louie, by turns, loathed, attended to compulsively, disregarded, or held in contempt. His attitude toward the business was no small source of friction between him and Rocky. Being an opportunist where business was concerned, as a result no doubt of the influence of Canio and my father, I quickly shifted my allegiance to Rocky and away from my true benefactor. But like Canio, Louie didn't seem to mind.

Canio always respected the counter, even if the passageway was open, never crossing through the gate into the shop. Although if he and Louie were having a particularly animated conversation, he might lean in a bit. He always respected the proprieties, the rhythms of the place. But his look was sometimes one of longing or of worry. My ear, just out of sight, cocked in their direction as they spoke, hoping for some piece of domestic intelligence, such as a clue to my parents' connivances or plans, or for some useful information to bring to new arguments or to an understanding of the world of adults with all its enviable freedom.

When Canio came looking for me now, I was often inaccessible in the rear of the shop, hands covered in grease, and on a path that was no doubt as distasteful to my grandfather as it was remote from him. And though he and Louie talked about opera and took justifiable pride in the Italian contribution to it, my own musical tastes were changing. Other melodies bounced through my head as Canio, caught up in the glories of Verdi and

Puccini in the showroom on the other side of the counter, looked back almost wistfully toward where I sat working intently.

Louie once told me about a conversation he had had with my grandfather not long before he died. "Canio said to me, 'If you see a beautiful woman and it doesn't happen for you, life just isn't worth living anymore.'" And years later I learned from Louie that Canio had come down to the store to meet him when I told my grandfather I wanted to work for E-Z Washing Machine Company. He wanted to know in whose care and mentorship his lonely, introverted first grandson would find himself.

CHAPTER 20
THE PRECINCT OF DOUBT AND PRECISION

Comical as it may seem and as much as I had to revise and sometimes reverse what I learned from them, I wouldn't be writing this now were it not for the Sisters of Mercy. Remarkably, not once in the eight years of grade school did I ever detect a hint of prejudice in their words, in their discipline, or their demeanor. We were quite simply all *children of God* in their eyes, and though they grew up in times far more prejudiced than ours, somehow through prayer and religious zeal, they had transformed themselves and their own ethnic origins so that in most instances they were persistent, unclouded examples to us.

That was no easy task. We had come to school with a lot of cultural baggage, which they cast aside, making us children of God first, which is to say, something like human. At first Communion, the boys in creamy white suits and the girls in pure white dresses, we received the sacrament, but we were also consecrated therein to this other identity, one that was at once wholly human and as we thought, wholly American. That presumption for Catholic Americans would be crucially tested in the 1960s with the Vietnam War, abortion rights activism, and the evolving disarmament and antinuclear movements. Many of us had grown up anti-Communist to the core in the mold of Joe McCarthy, Father Coughlin, and television personality Bishop Fulton J. Sheehan. So it's important to credit the nuns who taught us our first global view and whose example a generation of Catholics experienced in parochial schools, often free from even these political prejudices, which the nuns at St. Thomas Aquinas generally avoided.

Lest we go too far, however, it's important to remember that we all had an easy out. There were no blacks in the neighborhood. Schools and neighborhoods in Chicago weren't integrated in those days, and one consequence of this very lack of exposure to black people in those early years was that our ethnic prejudices and contempt could later shift to blacks and others less spoken of, often in the most destructive words of all. What's more, as for our religious ideas, it took years to unlearn some of what we learned implicitly, entangled as we were in papal hierarchies and an unquestioned patriarchy—for example, in the sisters' humble deferral to the parish priests on every occasion—and of all things, a curious lack of moral nuance at the heart of American Catholic education.

———————•◦•———————

As children, we had been taught to believe in guardian angels, taught that they rested on our shoulders invisibly, that they spoke in our ears and thus accounted for the voices we heard telling us what we ought and ought not to do. And of course, we had been taught that the devil also hovered within earshot. This primitive psychology of social control divided consciousness into warring parts, good and evil, heaven and hell, in which the *you* instructs the *I* that is implicitly and perpetually listening in, one ear bent to its own shoulder, awaiting the counsel of its better angels. And since that counsel of better angels is always entering one's ears, as if externally, children become subjects of persistent admonishment, perceived as coming from without. This dynamic had made possible at age six our entry into the age of reason, and it later prepared us for the instructions of the Baltimore catechism and confirmation, which, it was believed, would train us to fit seamlessly into a church in which a voice that's speaking ex-cathedra from on high tells you in minute detail what to do. The persistence of this psychology also produced its own terrors and confusions.

For many of us, the problem began with a small dark blue, paperbound book with numbered sentences called *The Baltimore Catechism*. There the pages were black and white, and sins were imagined as spots on your soul, shown like black splotches in a milk bottle, and mortal sin turned the milk bottle entirely black. There was no elucidated moral message here, no nuance of God, of redemption. The Baltimore catechism was entirely one of guilt, conformity, and mortal fear.

Recited in class in preparation for Confirmation, the Baltimore catechism began this way: "I am the Lord Thy God. Thou shalt not have strange gods before me."

"Ask her, Tony!" Gertrude whispered.

Tony Manginardi's hand was up, way up already. He was squirming in his seat, trying to get taller so that Father McCauley would be sure to call on him. He *had* to! This was the third day of preparation for the sacrament of Confirmation, and everyone, except Father McAuley and Sister Mary, wanted to hear Tony Manginardi's questions.

"I tell you what, Sister. If you don't mind, let's skip ahead to 'Thou shalt not kill.'"

There was an audible groan from the anonymous rows at the back of the room. Fifty-four of us were squeezed into sixth grade alongside the cloakroom on the east side of St. Thomas Aquinas church, and all we could see out the window were brick walls and gray Chicago gloom. Our tepid chocolate milk and break time were still forty-seven and a half minutes away, forty-seven and one half exactly by the IBM clock that moved on a pulse from one in the office. It was connected to the time machine in Poughkeepsie, wherever that was, and the Bureau of Standards, and it radiated radium or something. It clicked again. Now it said forty-seven minutes exactly.

When Father skipped ahead to the fifth commandment, every arm in the room slumped downward. He looked around, wondering what had happened to all those questions. I was sitting next to Tony in the sixth row back, my head propped on my hand, my hand propped on my elbow, my elbow purple from leaning on the glass ink well stuck in a hole in the corner of my desk. I could see Tony was lost too, looking down at his desk for some reverie, some ineffable, long-lost consolation.

"Go ahead," I whispered. "Ask him anyway."

Tony's eyes flipped to one side. "Let Doogan do it," he whispered.

Gertrude looked at me looking at Tony and then followed my glance to Doogan, hulking in the back row. Like Doogan, she was big. I wasn't as big as her, and Kathleen McGinty, who'd sat in front of me ever since first grade, was even taller than I was, way taller. Something was wrong with this picture. I was supposed to be tall like Uncle Jack. Growing up around here wasn't working out the way I'd expected. Doogan's clenched fist scratched hard with a chrome pen, back and forth on his desk, but there wasn't any paper under it.

Still, nobody's hand went up.

"You all know about this one. No killing," said Father McAuley. "But that also means no fights or things that start fights like calling people names."

I could see Tony Manginardi's shoulder twitching, and I knew what he was going to ask. "Isn't calling names part of 'Thou shalt not bear false witness?'" But Father McAuley droned on.

Gertrude poked Tony in the shoulder again. She knew what that shoulder meant, and she was itching for some action. "Ask him!" she said, pushing him harder this time. Tony slumped forward pretending to fall off his elbow, and then slowly, laboriously, hand over hand like Sir Edmund Hillary climbing Mt. Everest, he propped himself up on his desk.

"You ask him!" Manginardi said out loud and then grumbled. "Let Doogan do it. He's the one who picks fights."

Doogan was the bitter end of Manginardi's existence. Snow or spring rain, he beat Tony mercilessly from school to home and back to school again. Like a punching bag or a burrow for books. Manginardi was his donkey, whipped along by the threat of Doogan's fist.

Fact was that there wasn't a question in the room. Tony and everybody else knew about the fifth commandment. All we did from morning to dusk was fight with somebody, our brothers and sisters, some kid on the block, the gangs at school, the sixth-graders in the other class who we thought were goody-goodies "because they got in line first when the bell rang." Every place you went, you were either fighting with someone or defending yourself from being beaten, and no one anywhere was about to confess it or ask a question about it or suggest that it was wrong, "Because it wasn't!" All we wanted to do was to kill someone or other, and we couldn't, so whatever it was we were doing didn't break the commandments.

There was another long pause. Everyone thought about the IBM clock's relentless ticking. "Click." It was finally ten seconds past ten to eleven.

"Well, Sister, I guess unless there're some questions about that, we can go on. Do you have any questions you think the class should ask?"

Sister Mary Cyril was a very thin, slight, and ashen-faced woman with pinched shoulders that even in her habit, made her impossibly narrow. Like Sister Eunice, our second-grade teacher, she was always roller-rubbing her permanently chapped hands in front of the huge white semicircle that covered her chest. And she was the quietest and most soft-spoken nun any of us had ever known. She was even quieter than Ellen Tufts, who had to sit up front so she could be heard and who sometimes wrote her answers on the board just to keep from having to speak out loud in class. Hard to believe, Sister Mary Cyril was even quieter than that. And in every way, meaner.

Tony Manginardi heard Father's question and let out an audible sigh and then collapsed on his desk. "Sister couldn't get in a fight if you punched her," he whispered, his words sliding from the side of his mouth as his head drooped and then slammed on the desk.

"Well, Doogan, we haven't heard from you today," said Father. "What do you think? Is fighting a venial or mortal sin?"

Doogan looked around at the floor, at Gertrude, at Terry Murphy, and at the floor again. He hated Terry Murphy more than anyone else in the world, except maybe for his older brother. Killing that worthless rat face would be a venial sin, he thought, so fighting with him must be *mortal*.

"Mortal? Got it backward, Doogan," said Father. Tony leered back at Doogan, murmuring something softly but loud enough for half the class to hear.

"No, young man. Killing is a mortal sin. Fighting is usually a venial sin, so long as no one really gets hurt."

Tony Manginardi's hand sprang up. "But what if you really wanted to kill him and you got in a fight? Maybe he hurt you, and you didn't hurt him, you know. Is it still a venial sin just because you wanted to kill him?"

"No, Tony. You're right. That's a mortal sin because your intention was to kill him."

Tony felt better. He figured he couldn't even hurt Doogan, so what was the use trying? Wanting to must only be a venial sin. But now there was a catch. We were all thinking about how Tony's smoldering heart yearned to kill Doogan, and every eye looked back to see his reaction. Doogan sat smugly, digging his chrome pen into the desk. Slowly, a grin etched its way over his face as he scratched deeper and deeper, salivating at the challenge.

"Who cares about that punk?" Doogan said and grunted, never looking up as though Manginardi were dead on a road, not worth the bother.

"But Father, what if your dad and your mom said that if he picked on you, you should kill him? Then what if he picked on you, so you fought back because you wanted to obey your parents? Would that still be a mortal sin? And what if—"

"As I said, Tony, God sees the intentions in your heart. So if your intention was to kill someone, then it's a mortal sin."

"But, but, but what if—" Tony's hand stretched up so high now he was standing with one knee on the fold-up seat. "What if your parents said to kill the Japs or the Germans or some rats like that, wouldn't that be a—"

"We'll get to that later, Tony, when we talk about honoring thy father and mother. Right now it's killing we're on. Doogan, do you understand the difference?"

Doogan nodded. Even in sixth grade, his hair was slicked back. By the time we were in seventh, he looked like Elvis Presley. Most of us were afraid of him, except that some of the girls in the other sixth thought he was *cool*, a really big word then, and they would giggle like jerks when he was around.

"Let's go on then, Sister," said Father McAuley.

"*Thou shalt not commit adultery*," Sister Mary Cyril said.

"We'll cover that with the ninth," said Father. Somehow we all knew we'd never get to the ninth. In years of parochial school, no one had ever got to the ninth, and some kids who had older brothers and sisters who graduated said they never got there either.

"Let's go on to the seventh commandment. *Thou shalt not steal.* When is stealing a mortal sin?" Father asked, looking over his confirmees.

"I don't know. A million dollars? Jeez!" sputtered Tony, half aloud, and then he slapped his hand over his mouth for swearing.

"What about that? A hundred dollars, a thousand dollars, or a million? Let's hear from someone new." His eyes scanned down the class list. "Kathleen McGinty. When is stealing a mortal sin?"

Kathleen was the tallest girl in the class, and she always stood up and pushed her ponytail or her curls behind her head and then pulled her skirt down and straightened it. Then she folded her hands in front of her and gulped before she answered. She was quiet and proper, and she would stand beside her desk for two minutes at least before she had anything to say. No one ever thought she was stalling, just that she needed time to think up an answer. But she might have been buying time. Sometimes when she got up, her curls would bounce like coiled springs, tumbling down her back as they uncoiled, and if you were lucky, you could catch hold of one of them and stretch it out so it would bounce off her head. But that day she was wearing a ponytail and a red ribbon, so I didn't chance it.

Just as she was about to speak, she glanced down at a page in the catechism. "It's a sin, Father, if you mean to do harm to someone and not just take it for yourself." Her voice was at once shrill and breathy as it ended, so it seemed to trail off and disappear in the nether reaches of the room.

"Goody-goody!" Terry Murphy said. He hated her guts, probably because she was tall and pretty with pale, translucent skin, and he was stubby with a duck face and freckles. Terry's entire enterprise consisted of thinking up ways to attack anything or anyone good. Kathleen probably didn't hear him, and if she did, she would have been too polite to react. Curling into the desk as best she could to hide her height, she sat down.

"Who said that?" The kids in front looked around. Sister Mary Cyril was already slipping down the aisle at a slow, menacing pace, one step at a time as only she could, a ruler clenched in her hand, glowering at us.

"I want the person who said that to stand up. Immediately." Her voice was almost as thin as Kathleen's now. She had a proven reputation for being mean, and we didn't want to see it.

Tony Manginardi's hand shot up.

"Yes, Tony. Was that you?" Father McAuley said.

"No, I just had a question, Father."

"Clever." Gertrude whispered, thinking Tony might just get us out of a jam.

"What if somebody said something bad but didn't mean to say something bad?"

"We'll come to that later, Tony. Just now it's the culprit we're after."

There was a long, dreadful pause while they stared at us. We stared at our desks, and our desks stared back at us. After what felt like ten minutes of clock clicks, there was a rustling. Terry Murphy's leg slid from his desk, and slowly, resolutely, he stood up. Suddenly, with a crack, his cast-iron seat snapped back behind him. In every grade and whatever classroom we were in, Terry always seemed to have a loose chair, one that creaked and slammed when he got out of it. And in that same instant, he would snap to attention.

"Just what did you mean by goody-goody, young man!" Sister Mary Cyril demanded. In anger, her voice was wholly other than usual, dense and guttural like the sound of a bone, a thigh bone being dragged across soggy ground.

She spun about and came back down the row to Terry, but she found herself standing on the opposite side of the desk from him. As she moved past him toward the front, it seemed for a moment as if she were retreating and he would get off. But he had no such luck. She came about the front row and sailed right up in front of Terry.

Terry stood with his knees locked, his chest out, his hands clutched tight behind him. What chin he had was thrust high in the air, David Niven-style. Whatever that chin might have meant, it seemed to be stuck there. Come what may, it would remain resolute as Terry stood, arms stiff at his side, fists locked hard into one another behind his back. Standing at attention like this, the whites of his hands told the whole story. He knew what was coming.

In a voice too low to be glowering, Sister Mary Cyril repeated, "Just *what* did you mean by that goody-goody, young man?"

"I just thought, Sister, that, you know, it was the right answer." For a moment we were sure he'd say more, and hoping against hope, we thought he might even get away with it. But Sister's eyes were closer now, glaring down at him, not six inches from his nose. He didn't dare utter another syllable.

Terry Murphy had been the leader of the toughest gang in our class since second grade, and he had a reputation for honor in the face of punishment that none of us could match. We were slow to stand and admit our offenses, whether a part of his gang or not. Terry always stood first, confessed his guilt and his leadership, and took what punishment was coming to him. It was a point of honor with him. And when he confessed, he made only one demand, specifically that the dramatic moment of admission be sanctified and him along with it. By sixth grade, however, these repeated spectacles and our declining interest had diminished his stature in our eyes. His influence had begun to wane. Nevertheless, he was this day as he had always been, gutsy and swift to act. And although we'd come to take him for granted, he hadn't lost his flair for the dramatic. We all knew he would own up to what he'd done, but not without a dramatic pause, a show of bravery, and a bit of a firefight.

"The right answer?" said Sister Mary Cyril. "It didn't sound like that to me, young man! What commandment does it break when you make fun of someone else? *Class?*" Neither her eyes, which were fixed on Terry's nose, nor the tip of the ruler left him for an instant.

"Fifth." "Seventh." "Fourth." "First and third."

"What's the ninth?" Gertrude Smith tried out loud to remember. She had a way of asking a question as though she was talking to everybody. "Wait! It's the sixth, isn't it, Sister?"

"Stop and *think!*" said Sister Mary Cyril, never for a moment taking her eyes off Terry, nor giving an inch to his upturned chin. "What does it mean to bear false witness against thy neighbor? What commandment is that?"

A chorus rang out, "Eight!" All the sixth-graders suddenly agreed. "It's a sin against the eighth commandment!" It was the same chorus we'd heard every year before and thereafter, for every commandment since we'd learned them from Sister Mary Eunice in second grade. Only Tony Manginardi's longing for exegesis and release had ever made the exercise any different.

"Yes!" she said emphatically. Ruler in hand, she took one step away from Terry and back toward Father, who for a moment seemed to have completely vanished from the room. Every one of the fifty-four hearts in class that day breathed a uniform sigh of relief. But suddenly, she wheeled about, and this time the ruler pointed directly at Terry Murphy's ear. And it was as if the room lurched, and the furtive whispering was replaced in an instant by pitch-black silence.

"Hold out your hand, young man," she said.

Terry couldn't get his hand out of his fist even if he wanted to, so close was Sister now that he feared touching her. Bending down over his shoulder, she snapped the ruler on his neck, curling its brass edge up ever closer to his earlobe, pausing just under his ear. Terry must surely have thought she was St. Peter in the garden of Gethsemane, sword poised, about to slice his ear off. Only a miracle of Father McAuley or Jesus Christ himself could save him now. He stood braced and rigid, ready to take whatever punishment might come. Time seemed to stand still. Then Sister bent down and quietly whispered something in his curled earlobe, which now turned bright red at the ruler's edge. She then stepped back.

"Sit down!" she said.

Perhaps afraid her own temper might actually lead her to do some real damage, she turned abruptly on her heel and walked away. It was milk time.

Exhausted by the spectacle and none too sure Terry's ear had completely escaped violence or the humbling imitation of Christ that the aftermath of such a severe chastening might require, Father McAuley made a hurried exit.

It took months for us to get through the Ten Commandments along with all the sacraments from Confession and Communion down to extreme unction until, if you weren't already dead and buried, you almost wished you were. But every time we came to a new, numbered line of the Baltimore catechism, Tony Manginardi would ask the same string of amazing questions.

"I am the Lord thy God. Thou shalt not have strange gods before me."

"But what if you had strange gods?" he would inquire in a voice that sounded almost convincingly earnest. "But what if you didn't know they were strange and your parents told you that you should worship them and they sent you to fortune-tellers or medicine men or something and they told you like the Indians to worship the corn god and you didn't know it was a false god? Would that be a venial or a mortal sin?"

This was religion. I would tune Tony out in the middle of his questions the way I would drift away from Canio and Uncle Enzo fighting over Garibaldi and Emmanuel II. In my dreamy way, I had concluded that some disputes were too inscrutable for words and that, once loosed, the words had to go on and on until everyone had said all of them in all the ways and combinations in which they could be said. Tony's questions were just like that, except he didn't shout at the top of his voice like grown-ups did, and he had a silly singsong way of asking things because he was afraid if he stopped in midstream, they'd answer just a part of one of his long, endlessly brilliant questions.

———————•◦•———————

The true import of all this—and the event that no doubt kept Doogan in class instead of playing hooky more than occasionally and made proper little children of the rest of us—had occurred one or two years before. By fourth grade we'd gotten used to the idea that we could commit mortal sins and go straight to hell, so we'd come to take confession pretty seriously. It was the only way you could play it safe and get all those damning spots off your soul, especially if some of them might be black and mortal. The priests would give us penance, but it was usually pretty easy—three Our

Fathers, three Hail Marys, and three Glory Bes. You went to confession with the rest of your class every week, and as soon as you got back to the pew, your friends would inevitably ask what you got. "The same," was the usual answer. If you said, "Six," there'd be silence.

If you said, "Two," most gave the jealous response, "Jeez!". But *six* was a lot, so someone would surely ask, "What bad'd you do?" And if you got *eight* or more sets of the three prayers to recite, someone said, "Jeez, *twelve!*" Nobody asked what bad you did then either. Once when my dad was in a good mood, we asked him what he had gotten for his penance.

"The usual," he said. It couldn't have been much because he sort of grinned at Mom. But he swore a lot, so we figured the usual was probably a lot. Whatever your penance was, though, it was usually pretty easy, not like something Tony Manginardi could think up, such as crawling to church on your bare knees or anything like a martyr. Even guys like Murphy and Doogan, bad as they were, didn't brag about what they got, though they seldom missed a chance to brag about everything else.

Every day after morning prayers and the Pledge of Allegiance, there were *announcements*. One morning the announcement was that the words "under God" would be added to the pledge. We would say, "One nation ... under God," from now on. They told us President Eisenhower said that was the way it was to be done because we weren't "a godless country." All the nuns and Bishop Fulton J. Sheen on TV seemed happy about this change as though they'd suddenly looked up and noticed God's face in the flag or had seen a cross there or something. Now we'd beat those godless Commies for sure! That was just after they caught the Rosenbergs spying, and lots of people were grinning about that too. But if you thought about those two people, somebody's mom and dad, getting electrocuted, it made you feel all queasy and squishy inside like you had eaten something that made you feel like you might barf.

Anyway, after the pledge we had announcements, usually over the speaker. They told us about simple stuff. "Please expect a fire drill between 2:00 and 2:15 today." Or "Recess will be canceled for all fourth- and fifth-graders for measles shots at 10:00 a.m." Or "All seventh-graders will go to confession at the confessional in the left aisle next to the Pieta. Now."

Sometimes, though the messages were heard by everybody, it was clear they were really meant for Sister Mary Cyril or Sister Mary Annette. When that happened, Sister would answer very loud, looking up at the ceiling, but it was like she was talking to no one in particular. It was as though she was suddenly following a pillar of fire through the desert or had become Moses speaking to the burning bush. Or perhaps it was as if she was hearing voices lost to her but suddenly heard dimly through the loudspeaker. After the formal announcements, Sister would sometimes make other announcements of her own. Or she would just start reading class.

"Group 1."

Group 1 was the smartest and always sat next to the cloakroom. They got to do everything first. After them came Group 2 and then 3 and then 4, who were the dumbest. If you were in the back of the group, you were probably *the* dumbest in it, we somehow believed. Except, of course, if you had a bad reputation from the year before or had bad eyeglasses or something. Then you got put up front.

I mostly found myself in the middle of the middle. Later when we got to high school, we were put in groups too, and we spent the whole first year trying to figure out which groups were the smartest because otherwise you didn't know where you stood. But by the time we were fourteen, sports and cars had become more important, so most of us quit trying to figure it out.

The thing that happened one or two years before confirmation and gave such importance to all this began in Sister Mary Immaculata's announcements one day. What made it strange was she wasn't announcing some new rule or other, but she was talking about someone in particular, somebody in our class. You hardly ever heard that in announcements. Sister was saying that someone was coming back and that we should be nice to this person and not ask too many questions. I hadn't been paying attention when she started, so I didn't know who she was talking about. Suddenly, whole parts of the room got silent, kids whispering to one another, trying to catch up. Then everything went quiet. It was as though thick blue paint had gushed out from somewhere, oozing over everyone till it was up to our necks so we couldn't shuffle stuff in our desks or lean over and drop books anymore. The sudden tide of blue paint kept everybody's mouth shut tight, ears wide open and listening.

Pretty soon I got it. It was Ellen Tufts. She hadn't been in school for two weeks, and now her mother was dead. We were all supposed to be nice to her because she was being brave and coming back to school, even though the funeral was that Wednesday. I looked around, but no one seemed to know exactly why it was brave ... or wasn't. It was something we'd just never thought of before. Sister Immaculata said we weren't supposed to say anything to her, except how sorry we were. We were only supposed to talk about it if it came up.

I don't remember Ellen coming back to class, though she must have. I do remember what happened the day of the funeral. Every Sunday the fourth-graders all sat in pews 31 to 39 on the left side of the aisle in church. Except if you were in the goody-goody part of fourth, then you sat in the same rows on the right side. So as soon as we got to school the day of the funeral, we didn't even take our coats off or anything. We just lined up as we always did and marched right over to church.

After we were there for a while, the priest and some altar boys went down the aisle to the front door and led the coffin in. Along with it came Ellen's father and a lot of other people. Relatives, we figured. Ellen came in too, walking all by herself a few feet behind her mother's casket. She was sort of small and crouched in her pale blue Easter coat, clutching her gloves and a shiny new purse, which didn't seem to do her much good. Even though I'd never paid any attention to her, I remembered then that she was shy like I was. Even shyer. She hardly ever even looked at you.

Ellen had always been quiet in class. Even when the rest of us were making a racket, she only whispered, and when she answered questions, you could barely hear her. But now here she was walking right down the 243 feet of St. Thomas Aquinas Church to the altar, right through the middle of us. It was like being the only one in a block-long parade and everybody wondering what you were doing there anyway. I thought it was bad enough her mother had died, but I couldn't figure out why they were doing this to her. What'd she do to deserve this? She couldn't help it! At least someone could have walked beside her so she wouldn't stick out. Anyway, they made her walk all the way to the front and sit there, and when the requiem Mass was over, they made her walk all the way back, every pair of our fifty-three eyes and the other fifty-three goody-goody pairs of eyes staring at her as she passed.

No sin Tony Manginardi ever figured out or crazy penance he could imagine ever matched what happened to Ellen Tufts that day. And rough and tumble as we were, everybody knew it.

After Ellen Tufts's mother died, I began going to Mass every day like my mother. Yet I kept wondering why it was that everybody seemed to see Jesus when they went to Communion. Even though I bowed my head and tried, I couldn't. Canio, of course, had a few strong ideas about this, all thought inappropriate to the subject. And Gerald, whose rages at my projects were driving me to fathers outside the house, was no help either.

CHAPTER 21

REESEVILLE, WISCONSIN

The quality I probably loved most about Canio was the kind of otherworldliness he somehow combined with an exquisite and precise manifestation of style. It was a quality I remember distinctively displayed amongst the animals and acres of the farm in Reeseville.

As far as I know, my grandparents visited the farm only once, though those acres of Wisconsin dairy farm had been purchased with a down payment contributed in large part by Canio and Marie. That summer Canio arrived in a brown suit and tie, wearing the fedora that was his style at the time and carrying a Cuban cigar. After a three-and-a-half-hour drive from Chicago on a sweltering summer day in 1953, this was exactly the way he looked when he stepped out of our '52 Chrysler (which had been a gift from Grandpa Heaney) and onto the gravel driveway beside our Wisconsin farmhouse. It was perfectly silent when the motor shut down, except for a bird or two chirping. In the sun and open air and quiet, he told us he was immediately transported to the hills of Italy.

I've referred to my life on the farm already, but now I need to tell the story of Sugarbush. It was a 135-acre tract on a hilltop in central Wisconsin that had once constituted the daily toil of a homesteading farmer, his wife, and fourteen or so offspring. The farmer's name was "something" Klug. I never heard his first name. Landgrabber Klug was how he was known then and perhaps in local legend now. Probably given as a land grant after the Civil War, Klug's homestead had been built by hand and horse on the second highest hilltop in Dodge County, the highest being reserved for Trinity Evangelical Lutheran Church. The two-story brick farmhouse, set on a full basement, was built of split fieldstone laid seven feet below ground and three feet above. From there, for two stories farther up, it was yellow Watertown brick, a prized commodity in its day and unique to the area. Being brick and seemingly indestructible with walls two feet thick, it immediately attracted the attention of my father, whose worst domestic fear seemed to be that of fire. In the remote countryside, it was a sensible consideration.

Klug's house had begun as an opening in the earth, made by drawing off a piece of the hillside with a scratch bucket. That opening actually took days and weeks of toil by a man pressing down on the back of what looks like a wide shovel as it was pulled across the earth by a team of horses. Back and forth across the same ground, uprooting the endless earthborn boulders, the same earth, the same granite, hours, days, and weeks at a time. The barns had been built the same way and probably before the house as the Klug family found what shelter it could in a one-room log cabin that survived until a few years before we arrived in 1950.

Becoming Sugarbush didn't begin there, however, but in a forest of maple trees, which still stands in the pasture three quarters of a mile below the farmstead where the Beaver Dam River widens into Mud Lake, then winds its way southward among the Native American burial grounds and the marshes with their wild ducks, which now more than anything else hold dominion over the watershed. In the forest the maple trees are still thick around the remnants of a boiling house, where in early spring, huge vats of maple sap were cooked down to syrup and then hauled on a stone boat by the hundreds of gallons at a time, transported across the still frozen Mud Lake to Watertown. That was a day's journey of fifteen miles. On the way back, the sledge and horses would draw a load of the pale yellow Watertown brick for Klug's farmhouse, though this time they would climb an additional 210 feet and a half of a mile farther to the hilltop. Generally, the soil beneath the dray horses was sound and the work worthy in sun and snow. But one spring a team and wagon lost footing beside the woods and disappeared in quicksand a few hours later. It must have been a horrible sight as all hands stood by, helpless to save the horses as they sank, thrashing and squealing into the sand. As successive generations of farmers and hunters have come and gone on this hilltop, they've stood and pointed to that spot, the place where the horses perished. And one day I also stood and pointed, resigning tenure to this land, to what by then must surely have been regarded as hallowed ground.

The 135 acres and thirteen-room farmhouse and now collapsing barns had been the lifeblood of numerous German folk before us, and now the ideal and realized dream of my parents.

My room was the one past the woodstove in the corner of the second story, which had been converted into a separate apartment. It was 1950, and Dad was standing in the middle of the big room, which had once been an upstairs dormitory for Klug's boys but now had become our kitchen with a sink and cold-water tap. Like a figure twirling in Renaissance perspective, Dad extended his arms toward the corners. "The front of the house faces southeast," he said, "but you can always tell where you are by pointing to the corners—north, south, east, and west." Regina and I were seven and eight, and we had no idea why we needed to know east from west. It was clear to us that the house and orchards were here, the well and barns across the road. County Trunk G was being paved for the first time, so we had to jump over rows of gravel to get across it. We knew where we were. Here! Like most city children, we marked space by the streets we ran, and we cared about east or west only because Austin was the West Side. Dad spinning in the midst of the kitchen was our introduction to the country.

But we were, we soon realized, in need of some sense of location. Southwest of my room and five miles across the valley, you could sometimes hear the mournful whistle of a train, the Burlington Northern for Chicago, Milwaukee, and St. Paul, as it passed, and on very clear days, you could hear the ground rumble as freights, a mile or two long, pounded over it. When that sound disappeared in the heat of the summer (though you were never quite sure exactly when it disappeared), there was nothing at all to hear, and your ears would stretch for some familiar sound if only to confirm that you were all still alive and not caught in some still and wordless dream.

My room was blue, the trim and windows a deep red. I liked it at first, and I might have continued to do so but for the fact that it had been the product of a subterfuge. One of my parents had wanted the colors—I don't know which one—and so they'd suggested Battleship Blue to me for what they seemed to regard as appropriate for a gray-thinking boy who built model battleships. He would like the idea. The red was unexplained, though there must have been a lot of it since it soon also covered the orange crates and sheets of plywood from which we made desks and kitchen cabinets. Battleship blue did have a romantic sound to it, I had to admit, until I read *gray* on the can. I didn't like being considered a child in a new and unfamiliar place where I was trying to establish my identity or a child who could be tricked with colors. Besides, battleships weren't the only thing I was interested in, just one thing. There were other things too—radios and telegraphs and other neat stuff.

But first, I had to learn tractors.

Across the road, blocking a view of most of the valley, was a building as tall as the house, but deeply cragged and unpainted. The pig barn. It was gray and formidable in every light and weather when we arrived. But formidable as it was, it couldn't be taken seriously because the pigs, when they weren't rutting in the mud, snorting, grunting, or otherwise finding some porcine satisfaction, were flopping about in ways you could only laugh at. Even at night, when they were inside, you could still hear them grunting and rollicking through their dreams across from my blue room. The thing about a pig is that when it squeals, it's mostly unhappy, and when it's happy, it stops. It was one of my first lessons in animal husbandry. Where pigs are concerned, that's all you know in life and all you need to know. But then again, I was never much of a hog farmer.

Next to the pig barn was the well, and beside that, there was a steep path down to the cow barn, steep even for a tractor. And in the early days, though truckloads of gravel had been dumped to stabilize it, milk trucks frequently got mired down there in the spring. Besides the buildings I've described, there were several others—a granary, a machine shed, and a leaning corncrib. When we arrived, they were all surrounded by brush and rusting farm implements, long since worn out, outdated, and now and then tattered with scraps of tar paper blown from the peeling roofs. Wolfram, a distant heir of Landgrabber Klug, had left the place in shambles, which was lucky for us, as we would have paid far more dearly had he done any better. We all supposed that our tenant farmers, the Kulows, would "get the place shipshape fairly quickly." Arnum Kulow, however, far less sentimental about the laboring man and the just fruits of his labors, thought otherwise.

Though life on a dairy farm, as we called it then (but really what might be called mixed farming now), was systematic and rigorous to the point of monotony, farm life for children was never really boring. There were too many machines to ride, adventures with animals, bogs and creek beds, places to hide, Indian mounds to spook you, and wooded ravines to hide in, or there was just fishing to make life interesting. I loved the place, though not as much as my sister did, mostly because she was better with animals and because she was also wily and won her way with the farmers. But I did love the adventure and the freedom of it. It was as though when you took a breath, the air in your face came streaming across the valley, and when you searched the shadows, Indians and ghosts were everywhere. I was eight, and this was Treasure Island, my manhood and my adventure. But my relentless questions must have been tiresome.

A man carrying 9.8 gallons of milk in a ten-gallon bucket doesn't want to be asked why there aren't pipes from the milking machines to the milk house as I asked more than once of Arnum Kulow or one of the other farmers. But my curiosity was sincere as well as insatiable. "And why not from cow's teats to babe's mouth?" a weary Arnum once replied in a handsome answer, lugging his load to the milk house. Since I had yet to plumb the depths of irony, I was apt to actually imagine such things.

"Well, it wouldn't be pipes all the way," I qualified. "Some of it would have to be hoses." The challenge, as I saw it, was how to couple them. Regina's approach, on the other hand, was more practical. She'd ask if she could throw down the hay, and of course, she got a yes. Then she added, "And after that, can I bring the tractor down?" Or she'd say, "Can I feed the calves milk?" Or "Can I go to the cheese factory with Lila?" All of these offers endeared her to the farm workers, while I was off somewhere deep in scientific thought. Would milk, pumped a long distance, freeze in pipes? Or because it's moving, would it be okay? Where would you place pipes in the city? Along the street or in the alleyway? Whether I was pondering these problems in my battleship gray room or sitting on the floor of the dairy barn, I was clearly inhabiting a wildly different world than that of the Kulows.

For the next twelve years, my parents had a succession of partnerships, all of them devised in ways familiar to Midwestern rural communities then. There were two chiefly inequitable ways in which these partnerships were set up—fifty-fifty and so-called cash farming. We always had the first kind while we lived at Sugarbush. In cash farming back in the 1950s, a farmer might rent land for ten to twelve dollars an acre, and the owner would pocket the money, good years and bad, allow the land its abuse and the buildings to receive minimal maintenance, most of it volunteered by the tenant farmer. Alternatively, you went fifty-fifty. Under this arrangement, the owner contributed the land, half the livestock, and paid half the cash outlays. The tenant contributed the machinery, his family's labor, and the other half of everything else. Since the productivity of most farmland can be vastly improved by the labor of a couple of seasons, the really valuable portion of these partnerships was the skill and gritty determination brought by humans to the machines, the work of husbandry, and fifteen-hour days of brutal toil.

When my parents began farming, they thought that most young men eager to start out and with good reputations would do. And there were lots of them. Farm families were large. It eases the labor, and three generations can find themselves working a plot of land before the deed suddenly passes—often to the oldest son. Since dividing it up frequently resulted in acreage too small for anyone's profitable use, these Midwestern families naturally produced lots of tenant farmers who had to look elsewhere for a livelihood doing what they knew how to do. But it was, it was said, the quality of the man that counted.

Reeseville was a small enough place, able to guard and protect its own, so even Arnum Kulow, an outsider from as far away as Watertown (fifteen miles) who had slept his way into adulthood, might not have discovered it, let alone a farm owner from Milwaukee (forty-five miles east) or from Chicago (120 miles west).

Dad went with Arnum to a few auctions, got the hang of buying cows (or at least Arnum's hang of it) and went into the grade-B dairy business. For pigs he bought half of Arnum's. For chickens he gave up the first year's eggs to buy his share of a coop full of them. It was a banner year for Arnum, and it firmly planted us in the farming business right up to the tops of our shiny, urban galoshes. Arnum had a pair of dray horses. We counted them as machinery. And since gas for the tractor was a cost split fifty-fifty, Dad figured the cost of feed for the horses should be split the same way. Arnum brought some hay with him and promised some oats the first winter though the farm he came from was a long way away, and Dad eventually found himself contributing cash for horse feed too. Dad felt he was being reasonably generous, though he was always counting his layout of funds carefully. But these transactions would yield the first of many bitter feelings to follow as the differences between Dad and Arnum in training, resources, and what's often called class were enormous. As the partnership progressed, Arnum and Lila's comments alternated between the mild "Ah, what's it to you? There's plenty more where that came from!" and comments with more of an edge on them like "Why should we pay for feed when you came here with none to begin with?" Dad, new to this, often tried to adjust inequality in terms of equity. "I thought it was supposed to be fifty-fifty," he would say. "Doesn't that mean you pay for half the feed too?"

"But we came in the fall, and there was none," said the Kulows. "We've already got all we can from Clyman, and that was all ours too."

"But we didn't buy the cows until the spring," Dad would counter.

"Then what's to feed the hogs, the horse, and the chickens?" (There was only one horse by then.)

"But the horse is machinery," Dad reasoned. "So that expense should be all yours." But he didn't say this out loud because he was new here and was starting from scratch. So on it went—on and on in squabbles that began in the perception that he was "moneybags," as Arnum's son told me, and "had promised them all they wanted just to get them here" and was now being stingy.

Soon enough, there would be more disputes—plow shears to have sharpened at the blacksmith, long rows of shears waiting for the rich fields of damp loam and stone to be seeded, fertilizer to buy, and a tractor belching smoke and in need of a carburetor. Fixing the tractor, unfortunately, was one of the winter tasks that Arnum "just hadn't gotten around to."

I've drawn you into this bickering only to show how strange this new world was to us and how difficult to keep in balance. Kathryn used to say that "the first man was a farmer and the last one will be a farmer too," an expression intended as an explanation to us, but also, I think, as a reassurance to herself. Besides, that expression left a commercial artist (who was not seen as a real man in Dodge County), not to mention a farmer's wife, both out of the picture. In fairness to them all, not even Father Simioni, the itinerant Catholic priest who served St. Columbkill's, could say whether God and Adam had been on a fifty-fifty or a cash basis … or whether somewhere there was a third way.

In fact, our arrival in Dodge County had breached a mythic divide. Crossing the border from Chicago to southeastern Wisconsin was no mere geographical act. And our blindness to that divide was accentuated by our naiveté, supposing that a common language, a tolerance of diverse ethnicity, progressive politics, and a love of the land held America together. Perhaps these sentiments did accomplish that at some lofty level, where politics and statehood could escape the incongruity felt between barnyard shit and the Nunn Bush shoes walking through it. I'm being crude, I know, but I'm afraid it's an apt image for the encounter of people who were a world of demands apart—one trying to reduce their toil and sustenance to the price of a two-dollar hundred-weight of milk, the other the time it takes to draw a shoe. On their behalf, Arnum Kulow and Gerald Grieco alike, it must be said, did what justice they could do.

To compound matters, Kathryn began a garden, and she also started to repaint what were seemingly hundreds but actually just the fifty-two shutters that had once provided some thin shield against the bitter-cold Sugarbush winters. For Lila Kulow, this was silly, a waste of time, and an affront. Under the "halves" arrangement (the local term for fifty-fifty), the garden had been grudgingly divided. And muttering words like "What does she know about how to raise a garden?" under her breath, Lila went about planting her half. When the cherry trees produced fruit in early June, the two families agreed to pick on alternate days, but following the logic and custom observed far and wide in the county, Lila didn't pick when it rained. So come sunup the next day, she would be in the orchard happily picking away when we marched in with our buckets, thinking it was our day. And much the same would have occurred with the wild strawberries if the patch hadn't been divided into two clearly defined areas. Finally, to top all this, Kathryn, who had always taken some pride in her dress, wore clothes for this work that, while they were seen as nearly tatters to her, looked like church clothes alongside the denim and muslin weave of farm women. I won't belabor these simple differences any further. Most of them amounted to "small potatoes," as Kathryn used to say. But from where I sit today, those words would actually have seemed more appropriate coming from the likes of Lila and the Boetchers, Schallers, Riggies, and Calhouns, who (like us, I'll admit) measured every thread and hundredweight of difference.

———————•●•———————

Kathryn was nervous and trying not to show it. I knew because even though she was carrying the chicken tightly cradled in her arms, she wouldn't look at Regina and me. She walked across the uneven side yard, steadying herself with each step, her eye fixed on the wood block, actually an oak log, upended near the wood pile. The chicken looked around in the indifferent way that chickens usually do. As she walked, Kathryn stroked its crown to keep it quiet, though without any particular affection. She was approaching a part of farm life she would rather have avoided, but perhaps remembering her father and brother, who had kept a few fowl in the backyard, she was approaching it as matter-of-factly as she could. This was what needed to be done. "The first man was a farmer, and the last one will be." She was determined to take her place in that long and respectable line of human activity.

Just at that moment, Angus Klug, another of the Wisconsin Klugs, came around the corner of the house, a camera under his arm. ("How did he get here?" Kathryn exclaimed later. "I never even heard his car pull up the driveway!") There couldn't have been anything more incongruous. This long, spindly fellow with a face so stretched and creased it looked more like a willow tree, had suddenly appeared, dressed in freshly washed, light blue coveralls, a stranded straw hat, and of all things, carrying a cardboard camera. We were amazed. Even the chicken looked up.

Where had he come from? Apparently, while we were intent on Kathryn and the chicken she'd captured, he'd pulled up on the other side of the house. Well, I've said it was Angus Klug. To tell the truth, at that moment we didn't know who it was. Kathryn only recognized him as the farmer whose house and barn could be seen to the north, on the hillside across Lau Creek. It wasn't much of a farm as it ran down to the marsh, just a little pasture really and a lot of bottom land. But Klug knew us, his neighbors, because we had land on the creek too. "The fifteen acres," we called it, which as it turned out produced only one crop in my father's lifetime, land not worth the taxes.

Klug, sensitive to the chicken's situation and to ours, it seemed, knew to step back immediately and doffed what was left of his hat with the usual greetings. To tell the truth, this was far more than most farm women expected and seemed almost like church to us, the sort of thing men did after Mass on the steps of St. Thomas Aquinas and a reasonable way to open a conversation. In fact, those greetings once served the same function as snappy remarks in a bar do now, but they were a lot easier to pull off. On the steps of St. Thomas, there were almost always plenty of relatives around to plug those awkward holes in the conversation, and a woman who was greeted in this way knew the meaning and had resourceful friends to help review the choices in front of her. Just now, though, Klug was being so friendly that it was hard to tell whether he was here to get the chicken, just to display his winning smile, or to air some problem with the marshland. Since we had been visited recently by Rhode (he pronounced it "ROW-dee"), who owned the next farm south, we were becoming used to these borderline fence disputes with neighbors. In fact, this one would end comically, but we didn't know it at the time. So what was Klug up to anyway?

"The nerve of him!" Kathryn said later in a comment that seemed to remedy the embarrassment she'd felt as he'd walked up to the summer kitchen. "Who does he think he is, coming around here offering to take pictures?" Dressed to kill chickens wasn't exactly the way she hoped to be immortalized for posterity.

Angus Klug was a garrulous, smooth-moving sort of guy, and had we known then about Landgrabber Klug, we might have taken his sudden appearance in our farmyard on this windswept hillside for the ghost of his distant cousin. To this day, I still await Landgrabber's ghost. Whether he walks Sugar Bush's fields or not, who can say? But I would prefer to think he does, that he might claim what grace he may of his time and labors. And after sixty years and more of the stewardship of his painstaking creation, I'd be happy to assign some honor to him, even if only in the form of an apparition.

But the Klug we found standing before us that day was flesh and blood, and what's more, he was on a mission. Along with the camera had come a little booklet that told the amateur photographer just how to sell these captured images. Step by step, that booklet laid it out. And so to avoid future mistakes, he had decided to begin by honing his technique on the only strangers he knew in Dodge County. And what luck! They lived just over the next hill. To Angus, it must have felt like grace and predestination all rolled up in one—a fitting reward for the abstemiousness with which this pious Lutheran, somewhat Reformed soul who had but a tiny farm to work and had maintained his slim, modest earthly presence.

So here he was, come upon the perfect moment, Kathryn with a chicken in one hand, a short ax and chopping block in front of her. What better time to memorialize the occasion just as his little instruction book had said.

"Pictures don't cost much," he announced. "And for just a bit more, you get the camera with a roll of film in there all ready to go!"

He didn't know it, of course, but ours was a house full of cameras. Even if Kathryn had wanted the photograph he was about to take of her, she was sure it wouldn't have been with a half-dead chicken. And half dead it was at this point because holding it to the chopping block, she'd taken a swing and missed, cutting its head only part way off. Aware, no doubt, that it had blundered into the midst of its first big photo opportunity, the chicken took off around the yard, up the steps of the summer kitchen, and then back toward the plum trees, sure-footed as hell and spurting blood all the way.

No matter how it had come about, Klug was a conscientious farmer and thus rightly offended by the botched attempt at beheading the witless critter. There was something fundamental in him that wasn't about to let a chicken get away scot-free (if seriously maimed), no matter what the short ax had wrought or who happened to be swinging it. Dropping both his camera and his carefully prepared sales pitch, he began scampering around the side yard after the chicken until he'd scooped it up, still bloodied but squawking. With a single quick twist, he wrung its neck like any proper farmer would and slammed it on the stump. And so there it lay, the limp sack of feathers it had suddenly become.

His chivalrous gesture had left Kathryn suddenly humiliated, and no matter how persuasive his sales pitch, this farmyard fiasco was the last thing she wanted a picture of. There she would be standing in front of her children, Angus Klug, and what would no doubt be half the town, she thought, all of them thinking she couldn't even cook up a simple dinner. Her career as a farmer had suddenly taken a humiliating turn for the worse.

In the following days, Angus Klug visited a lot of other farmhouses, apparently encouraged by his debut performance with the city folk, and

Kathryn heard tell of his camera far and wide in the next few weeks. "It wasn't the best way to get a picture of me," she would say, aware he had probably added the whole silly scene to whatever the instruction book had taught him. Much to her surprise, however, most of the farm women were quietly sympathetic, not mentioning the details of the incident at all. Like her, they didn't much take to this old guy meddling in what they thought of as their private domestic business, not to mention disturbing the ghosts of a hundred other chickens that had one way or another come to grace their dinner tables. Old Klug was free to snap his pictures, but they would take Kathryn's side as they would that of any woman on farmstead or city block, only trying to put a full meal on her table. *Him and his camera! Who did he think he was, taking pictures anyway?*

They'd have none of it.

━━●•●━━

But I began this chapter with Canio and Marie arriving on their one and only visit to Gerald's farm. Despite the drive from Chicago in sweltering ninety-degree heat, Canio's appearance was impeccable as usual.

Somehow our grandparents' arrival that day caught my mother by surprise. She had been making her way downstairs with a porcelain pail full of kitchen refuse when they pulled up. Gerald, who'd driven the distance, and his mother disappeared upstairs with the luggage, leaving Kathryn, who was totally unfit for guests, to tend to my grandfather. There she was—a pail of gnats and garbage in one hand, dressed in a pinkish cotton print, her hair wrapped in a turban like Lucille Ball. The turban at least was in style then, but it also served as some protection for her poor hair against the oat dust the wind carried along with bits of earth uprooted from the open fields.

Dressed like a farm wife, pig slops in hand, Kathryn stared at Canio for a moment at an utter loss about what to say. About the only time you ever saw a three-piece suit on a farm in Dodge County was on Christmas Day or at a funeral, and even then it was more likely to be worn by the family lawyer or someone from Juneau, the county seat. Certainly, no one here wore vests or smoked cigars, Cuban or otherwise. If any of these showed up at all, they were only in magazines.

Feeling underdressed for no sensible reason she could imagine, Kathryn did her best to show our grandfather around, garbage pail in hand, and make him feel comfortable. And as we walked across the road to the barns, Regina and I competed to show off our newfound agricultural expertise. He didn't seem to know much about farming, farm buildings, equipment, or livestock, but he did evince some interest in the fruit trees (cherry, plum, and apple), in the animals, and in the ever-widening gardens.

Always perfectly at ease no matter how incongruous the situation, Canio stepped lightly about the farmyard, cigar held chest-high, a picture of composure, ending the first round of his tour at the pigsty, where Kathryn's kitchen slops created considerable attention. His jacket on his arm now, cigar in hand, he joined in calling the porkies, and Kathryn, who could survive almost any discomfort, couldn't help but laugh at the picture of the two of them, his suit, her Lucille Ball turban, and all the pigs in rapt attention.

Perhaps desperate for a sociable solution or sensing his reliable equanimity, she was about to lead the way back across the road from the pig barn. But Canio was otherwise engaged. Taking it all in with polite curiosity, he ignored the eggshells and watermelon rind flung into the brown slush of the pigsty, and he began to tell one of his perennial stories, this one about the little piggies. It was typical of him that no matter how foul things might be, he remained the artist, able to turn the miasmal into the mythological and find comfort there. Whatever it was that had brought him to Dodge County, he could find a pleasant framework through which to see. As I think of it now, it was as though his very organs of vision became detached, and he with them, separated from all that was painful, liminal, and obvious to the senses.

CHAPTER 22

WHITE FLIGHT

I awoke one night on Washington Boulevard to a tremendous pounding and rattling that nearly threw me out of bed. There was a low thud and groan of metal that shook the house as though a half a dozen buses had simultaneously rumbled down Washington Boulevard only to halt at our front door. But what was that thud? Somehow I fell back to sleep, and I think Canio did likewise. The next morning we found out that a drunk had hit the front porch after losing control of his car on the boulevard. The brick house at 50-0-7 had large, two-foot-wide brick balustrades topped with cast cement slabs that weighed about five hundred pounds each. They were so steady and constant that even on hot summer afternoons we used to lie on them just to cool off. To us they were permanent, cool, and immovable. The next morning, however, the balustrades were heaps of rubble scattered in front of the house, and the car, whatever was left of it, had been towed away. What's more, the driver, who had run from the scene, was nowhere to be found. I could just barely scramble across the rubble on the steps and get off to school.

I looked back from the sidewalk as I took the last step through the rubble and saw Canio, his head leaning just now out the front door. He took in the damage long enough to register complete disgust, and then he went back inside to finish dressing. A few minutes later, suit, vest, and tie in usual order, he walked out the back door and along Lavergne to his usual bus stop, leaving it all behind to my father's care. Whatever had happened, he seemed uninterested in the details. For my part, I couldn't understand how someone who owned a house could care so little about it or take so little interest in what was surely his most valuable asset.

Dad eventually sued the drunk driver who had jolted us out of bed at 3:00 a.m., to no avail. We were in the Korean War then, and the fellow disappeared into the army, which in those days was all that was needed to escape a civil suit. So far as I know, Grandpa never looked at the porch again, and he spoke about it only once when Grandma asked if she should go ahead and pay the masons who'd repaired it. He assented, never even asking how much. This detachment, so completely absent in his son Gerald, was a prominent feature of the aesthetic he lived by. There was something ethereal and, I think, deeply spiritual about Canio's happiness.

———————◆◆◆————————

Why was Jack Donaldson standing there in his gray tweed vest and fedora?

It was Saturday, sometime between five or six o'clock. The long amber shadows glimmered on the cookie crumble walls, and green gilt whorls gleamed from the hall rug as we ran up. It was the time of day when the sisters would drop by for coffee, but that would never happen on Saturday. He'd come without Aunt Flo or Grandma's other sisters. Today there were no smells in the hall like the aunts who always smelled sweet from something and talked in French words like *eau de cologne* and *jasmine*, and who when you kissed them tasted like coal dust and baking powder—so thick you'd lick your hands and rub your face to brush it off. On weekdays Flo or Lou, and Carmen and Louise would bring apple and peach slices. I liked apple. And macaroons, which we didn't ask for because they were too hard to say and trying made people laugh at you. And sometimes there were chocolate cupcakes with swirls we liked. But by then we were old enough to buy Hostess cupcakes on our own. Or Regina and I would take our quarter allowance and buy hot dogs at Al's. For a while after he'd bought the store, Al still sold all the different kinds of candy, but now he only sold hot dogs and fries made out of oily potatoes instead. *Motor oil*, we thought.

But this was Saturday. Husbands were home. There were pies baking and Sunday meals to prepare. No time for gossip over coffee and apple slices today.

Saturdays were the days that Lenny, Bill, and the other big guys in the neighborhood showed up in the alley. They shined their sedans, built wooden shelves for the parlor, or just played softball in the alley, which was where we played kick the can all the other days of the week. With their long arms, twice as long as ours, and with bats even longer, they'd slug a softball flat-sided, knocking its coat off. It sailed, wagging, high over the three-story buildings and into the glaring sunlight that reached into every corner in the alley, blinded every player. The ball seemed to float for several minutes before plunging earthward and out of sight, while the batter, like a mythical Gehrig swelled with pride at a perfect, blinding swing, would lope lackadaisically from cardboard first to tin-can second around the alley bases and back to home.

Sometimes the beaming batter wouldn't even run, just step aside and announce, "Home run!" to no one in particular. And Tommy Collins would scream, "No fair! Outta bounds, you ____!" "You go get it!" "No, you! You fat _____!" Tommy would come back, growing more furious. But the batter just ignored our moans and Tommy's exasperated protests. They were the big guys, and so they were the only ones who got to hit when we were little and only let us play just to shag the ball.

"It ain't fair. You're foul!". In fact, this particular foul ball was now buried deep in the coffee grounds of one of the far-back garbage cans. "I ain't gettin' it," Tommy protested. But that complaint never availed. The big guys would make one of us stand in one of the other cans so that we could bend deep and get the ball out of the barrel next to it. Or they'd pick you up by the belt and push you in headfirst to get it. Tommy might put up a fuss at first, but then he'd scramble after the ball pretty quickly before they hung him by the feet and plunged him headfirst to the bottom of the barrel.

And I was glad. Tommy Collins had it coming. *Revenge is sweet,* I'd think. *Hit him another one.*

I could hear the guys gathering in the alley now. But why was Jack just standing there in the doorway in his tweed suit with its tall tweed cuffs while flecks of golden sunlight danced on his hair and shoulders? And where were the sisters? They always came with him on weekends. During the week, sure, they came on their own for coffee with Marie in the late afternoon. We could hear them chatting outside as we dashed in from school or played hide-and-seek in the alley. "Olee, olee, ocean. Free, free, free!" somebody would yell, and suddenly, somebody else would come flying around the brick corner—Johnny Mulkerin maybe or Frankie—and plow right into their flowery skirts as billowy as pillows. Johnny's brother Tommy had the longest legs and got back quickest. He'd never be *it* again.

But they hadn't come along with Jack this Saturday. And Jack wasn't sitting down. He just remained standing at the dining room door, ignoring invitations to come in and stay for a while. His soft fedora kept spinning in his hand instead of finding its usual place of rest on the credenza.

———————•———————

Jack Donaldson was a liquor salesman who had changed his name from Donafrio during the 1920s when the Italians were getting all the bad press. He kept it that way through prohibition when the war came and after Grandpa got his naturalization papers. I used to try to count the creases in Jack's face because there were so many of them, and I often wondered how he shaved in all those cracks. But no matter how many there were, he was always clean-shaven and friendly, even when he was serious.

"Out of Garfield Park and up to Crawford," he was saying, trying to keep his voice as matter-of-fact and sensible as possible.

Regina and I stared as he talked to Grandpa and Grandma. Grandma wrung her hands in a wash towel and waved him off.

"You of all people! You should know better than that." She snapped a corner of the towel at him and wrung her hands all the way into the kitchen. Jack kept talking, his eyes rolling from face to face and back to where hers had been as though she were still standing there.

"It's more than that, Marie." His voice was a little louder now so she'd be sure to hear. "Flo can't come home late from the hairdresser now that Bill is married. It isn't safe anymore after dark."

Canio's eyes followed Marie to the freezer chest and glanced at her peppers simmering on the stove.

"And it's too much for us now. Flo wants a smaller apartment, less to keep up now that Richard's away," Jack said. "We haven't really needed all those rooms since Bill got married."

"And who do you think will look after Richard's wife and little one if you move away?" Grandma shouted from the kitchen. She was slicing hard at a loaf of bread and pointing at the wall with her knife as if he were there, pointing to get his attention. In an even softer voice, Jack bent around the doorpost. His hat, which was rubbery till now, went limp in his hand.

"Richard won't be working nights much longer, Marie, and they can drive the baby over."

"And drive this way for dinner and that way for after dinner. Drive this and drive that. Drive, drive, drive. What do we need all this for?"

Jack was prepared. He'd heard it all before. First from his sister-in-law, Lou, who said Marie would never allow it. Then from Flo, who had told Marie time and again that she wanted to move. And now Jack was here to try to sum up all the arguments and make things final. In fact, it was all over but the shouting, which meant that there was a lot more shouting ahead of them.

Years later I understood something Aunt Rita had said. Canio would never move. It was a truth that was reinforced by the way he tied his shoes in his armchair every morning, put on his fedora in winter, and had coffee at the kitchen table. Reinforced by his walks to the corner for the morning and evening papers, by the easy bus ride from the corner into the Loop as the climbing sun shortened the long morning shadows under the trees of Washington Boulevard, by the bus ride into the Loop that brought the rest of his life and career to him each day.

But it was all summed up for me in Grandpa's armchair. In the dining room at the edge of his studio, it never moved. We called it the grizzly bear because the knap of the velvet was so prickly it had to be folded down when you slid into the chair to keep it off your bare arms and legs. The lacquer lampshade beside it moved up or down on a bronzed weight, suiting the time of day.

Grandma Marie and Aunt Rita and even Kathryn had made occasional attempts to get rid of the old armchair. It was dusty, they argued. And it was worn out. It wasn't healthy for the children.

Each evening after dinner, which usually consisted of spaghetti with meatballs, fried chicken, salad, and Chianti, we would be brimming with energy and loud voices, popping and giggling around the table. But before we were allowed to run around the house at nightfall or slip into the bluestone shadows of the yard in summer, we were shunted off to the easy chair "to rest awhile … for the digestion." Regina and I would sit there squirming, trying not to let our damp legs touch, or poking one another while we played at reading the papers. Regina's favorite part was adjusting the light by reaching over me and bouncing the bronze weight off the back of the chair. The light would come swooping down, and she'd pull it up and down again until someone barked at us from the table. As often as not, they'd call us back for dessert, which was usually fresh fruit, which Regina loved, and ice cream, which I'd try to eat by itself. The best was Dressel's cakes that Dad brought all the way from the bakery on 12th Street.

But whatever was said about the chair's retirement brought no response from Grandpa, or on a bad day, he'd just give an *"Ah! Madonne!"*—an Italian epitaph muttered under his breath that was meant to assure the health-conscious women they hadn't a prayer of changing him. He and Marie would sometimes get into loud and ferocious arguments that we would time, running up and down the stairs to the second floor to check the clock in the kitchen. But some things were beyond argument. And the chair and the newspapers and having coffee with fruit at the porcelain table in the kitchen were among them.

Canio was like a clock here with his armchair and his lamp, as predictable as the sun and the moon. And the round of his day was as unchallenged and predictable as the round of the holidays themselves. Christmas would come with its twinkling lights and the frost on the windows in the front room at the other end of the hall. But this domain of his remained untouched. Baseball came and went. *Amos and Andy*, Roosevelt, TV, and air-conditioning. Some of these came to stay, and some vanished in time. But nothing upset his constancy. Other lives moved like satellites around him, and although he'd engage them vigorously, his own routine was never shaken, though there were times when, seriously engaged with some matter, he would seem to step outside of himself and the constellation of his daily rituals to resolve a problem.

———————•●•———————

Though she seldom broke the flow of his day, Aunt Flo was one of those who could reshape it. With her large flowering voice and easy infectious laughter, of all the Navigatos, she was most like Canio's sister, Gussie, and like her, she had always been an easy path to joy for him. She would come in the back way, and almost without stopping, merely dropping some faint greeting as a kind of tribute, she would slip into his easy chair. She was the sister after all, and she went there almost brazenly without so much as dropping her shopping bag before she dropped fully into his place. If he was working in the studio, so much the better.

"Shhh. Don't disturb!" she'd say to us and await his attention.

If he'd gone to the back door to let her in, he would not be disturbed either because he'd seen her coming up the walkway and through the yard and was already curious about what she'd bought with Jack's money. I didn't understand what produced the small, uncomfortable laugh that would follow when he said this. Maybe it was a way of getting the better of Jack, or maybe a kind of one-upmanship, anticipating what his own wife would have spent before she got home as well. So when he heard her approach, he would take a brief pen stroke or two at one of the drawings that filled his days and his evenings, and then flipping it aside, he'd rise and bring her in at the back door.

Except in winter, Flo was usually hot from carrying the bags and walking, and she would flourish handkerchiefs and damp cologne as she collapsed in the easy chair, leaving Grandpa to see to it that she was comfortable. His eyes always studied people, lingered longer than most people's eyes would on someone's clothes, a vein throbbing, the shading of eyebrows, the color of skin in this light, the shape of lips in that, pondering the possible reason for some difference in tonality. He was a master of these details, and being an artist, he was permitted to study them in ways that would surely have embarrassed others had they been aware. In varying degrees of light and of mental state, these shadings were notes to him as he contemplated their variations.

Flo didn't seem to mind the attention as he formed what solicitous chitchat he could so as to study her fully. Catching her breath in the armchair, she would smooth her skirt down over her vast lap, looking from him to the television in the corner, inspecting again her yellow taffeta dress and glancing down the long hallway from whence she knew Marie would eventually appear. Crossing his gaze two or three times as if in some mysterious way preparing for him, she would never quite fix her full gaze on Canio. She acted as though she were his model, only slowly acknowledging his presence.

Her answers to his inquiries would be circumspect, even abrupt, until he finally turned away or she found one of us to distract her. She had come to speak with her sister, and even if she held forth occasionally from her brother-in-law's armchair, she felt no obligation to include him. In this way she negotiated two worlds, relying on her influence in both. Whether comfortably or not, I never knew.

Of course, that was what made our uncle Jack's arrival this day so unusual, such a departure from Canio's routine as it was … and thus a break from the usual rhythms and expected events of the household. Even Jack's suit and vest on a Saturday afternoon, despite the fact that he'd come from work, seemed completely out of place. And in yet another departure from tradition, he stood in the dining room, never quite refusing a seat but never taking one either.

Regina and I listened, completely uncomprehending, too young to absorb the details or put together their meaning. Jack tried to explain to

Grandpa and then to Kathryn, who walked in in the middle of things and pretended not to notice that anything out of the ordinary was afoot. She'd come ostensibly to get Regina and me washed up for dinner. But the rest of them went on and on, Grandpa taking Jack's side quietly, which infuriated Marie, and then taking Marie's side and finally getting disgusted with the whole thing, leaving Jack to stand there with his hat and tweed suit and Marie in the kitchen as he went back to his drawings. I don't honestly know how or when Jack left. But he did. And Flo and Marie didn't speak for months after.

Regina and I were too young to care about whatever was going on in Garfield Park or whether people got mugged or beat up on Crawford Avenue. Mother took us to Dr. Bailey's to have our teeth fixed, and he said things were bad. And yet, he wasn't planning to move. As far as we knew, the only bad thing there was getting drilled by Dr. Bailey.

When I was eleven, I was finally allowed to take the bus down Washington Boulevard a mile to Crawford Avenue and two miles farther east of that to Allied Radio, so I could buy condensers and B batteries and tubes for my radios. No one seemed to mind, and I never got in fights there like the ones I got into in the neighborhood.

But the Donaldsons moved, and so did Richard and his wife. And eventually, we did too.

Years later when Jack's grandchildren were getting married, Lenny and Bill and all of Jack's sons changed their name back to Donafrio, and their kids did too.

Whatever it was that Jack did wrong that Saturday, the crisis of the moment must have ended pretty quickly.

But when the shadows were long in the hallway and the light flickered like linen on the cookie crumble walls, Flo and Lou and Aunt Louise were no longer laughing in the kitchen or waiting for the evening breeze to prompt them to households and ovens of their own. They had moved away, and the only sound now was of Grandma's pots bubbling in the kitchen. The house, which seemed to have taken on a brown hue in the gathering dusk, felt unusually empty, alone with the hum of buses and countless unseen faces that trudged home along the boulevard.

Occasionally, in the days that followed, Canio would meet one of them as he walked back from the newsstand with his evening papers. Only rarely were they there when he arrived. Only now, Flo would bundle herself up and out of the armchair when he came in so that he could read by the glow of the lacquered lamp. Night would fall, and Canio would ponder the day alone in the pale light of *The Sun Times* and *The Chicago Daily News*.

———————•———————

If Jack had hoped to repair fresh wounds that day, he might have taken more account of these long-standing, comforting routines. Instead he became a harbinger of their demise. The fact was that there would have been no good time for the news he brought. Like Kathryn, Canio would never have moved from the neighborhood because of gang fights in Garfield Park or blacks walking by Featherstone's on Saturday evening. He simply wasn't afraid of people. And the house and his place there meant much more to him than property values. But to the rest of the family, these were idealistic, impractical considerations.

For some of the people in Austin, the break was not seen as inevitable. Parts of the community stayed intact. But for my family, the neighborhood our parents and grandparents had known and aspired to would all but disappear. By the late 1950s, the community we had known was changing rapidly, and much of the white community had determined to move as racial tensions, inflamed by blockbusting realtors and redlining bankers, led people to flee Austin as from a lost world.

———————•———————

Lawrence Walsh was the only friend I knew who stayed after the blockbusting and white flight of the late 1950s came to our neighborhood. Like Canio, he wasn't afraid of different people.

Lawrence Walsh was fearless. Once when a bunch of us were leaving Peanut Park, he was jumped by some guy who was tougher than him. We let the two of them duke it out for a while. Lawrence was from west of the park, and we were from the other side, so we didn't really know the other guy or what it was all about. Lawrence did okay for a while, but we didn't know how long he'd last. We all respected him more for the funny stuff he said rather than for his fighting. He got some good licks in though, and we figured he had the guy beaten. But then he tripped, and the guy was on top of him, beating his head into the grass.

"Come on, Lawrence. Say uncle," we shouted. We figured he'd had enough.

But he wouldn't give in. The guy just kept sitting on his belly and punching him in the face, Lawrence kicking and twisting to get outta there, but he never let out a word, not even a moan. Finally, the other guy just got tired and walked off. Lawrence lay there awhile. He looked so bad that Mulkerin or somebody said we should call an ambulance. But he shook us off, and after a while, he pulled himself up.

"Why didn't you say uncle?" we kept asking as he stumbled away.

"Not for that guy," he said. "I'll never say uncle for him, no matter how much he beats me."

Thirty years later at a high school reunion, I reminded him about that day and what he had said. "You were amazing," I told him. "Nobody had guts like that!"

"Yeah, and stupid," he said. "Real stupid."

I wanted to argue with him for Uncle Jack, for the bombs of Robert LoGerardo, for the fallen heroes of Peanut Park, for all the lost and faceless names in bronze that waited in silence on the monument. For what? Affirmation? Or resolution?

But my voice collapsed. Who was I to argue? Lawrence had stayed, unafraid of gangs, of thefts, of anyone, while the rest of white Austin fled to the suburbs. It was his to say what was worth fighting for and what was not.

chapter 23

LINDEN AVENUE, OAK PARK

In 1958, we moved to Oak Park, west of Austin. And at sixteen my time was far different than the time of Canio.

There were few Italian families in Oak Park. Doc Pecora lived on the corner two houses away, and his office was just a block or so farther north of Oak Park on North Avenue. In his full round, white smock, he looked across the desk at me just now with his large, inquiring Neapolitan eyes, eyes just like Grandma Marie's and Aunt Flo's. I know these eyes, these people. They see a lot and take no nonsense for an answer. Our Dad, who always knew what he was looking for, had quickly made friends with the few Italians he could find in Oak Park, while he made business deals with the Irish and the Germans, who had long been there and whom he knew had a long way to go to trust us. That was all right. He'd charm them just as he had others in German Wisconsin. Besides, with friends like Doc Pecora, who was he to complain?

"How're the girls treating you?" Doc asked, surprising me as he glanced up from his script. "Pretty good, I'll bet. No trouble there."

In the pause he realized I was framing an answer. *What does he know about that?* I wondered. Suddenly, I was back in Austin just as it had been, where everybody knew everybody else's business. Or maybe Dad had told him.

Though it felt a bit intrusive at first, a strange coziness came over me, a sense of being watched and cared for that I'd forgotten in my headlong flight from the old neighborhood. Doc Pecora probably knew about the terrible fights I was having with my father in those days.

Dad and I sparred with one another through our two arrogances—my father's an arrogance of the better educated son of immigrant parents, mine the resolute inability to focus on money and success and debilitating guilt that the grandchildren of immigrants often demonstrate. Through my apprenticeship at the shop and labor on the farm, I had gained the empowerment of mastering electricity and other practical skills. But I had also developed early on a disposition to retreat into my mind and imagination as a place of safety from the pressure of my father's rage and the oppressiveness of social structures in the family and the neighborhood. In there, in the mind and imagination, I sought knowledge of the scope of the human, and thus, I was soon set on a life in the priesthood and disdained the narrowly defined "American market success" story.

Dad's dreams of an engineer in the family or a doctor were being dashed once more. There were terrible meals at our house then. I would sit in stunned, defensive silence, and he would try to make sense of what I was doing, we were doing, and he was doing. The furious silence, one that went on for months, was punctuated periodically by meaningless explosions at the dining room table. For him, all his work, this beautiful house, this village of opportunity brought with it no promise, no assurance that a dream would be sustained.

On Sunday, Dad would drive to 50-0-7 and pick up Canio and Marie. Now for me they had names, though they had been Grandma and Grandpa before. Marie would have been up early, dressed for church in a new beige suit from Field's. Canio would shower while she was praying and put on his best three-piece suit. That spring, carrying his light gray matching overcoat and new fedora, he would appear in the large glass front door as Dad pulled up. I don't think he wore a Borsalino that year, though it might have been one. Men's hats, when men wore dress hats then, had broad, curled brims, often with a bead of matching gray satin on the edge.

But the fedora was on its way out. The haberdasher at Madison and Cicero was going out of business, and no respectable businessman we knew would buy a hat at Sears. Nor were they likely to go all the way downtown to have one fitted. The former was too cheap, the latter too extravagant.

Canio and Marie arrived around noon that Sunday. I had already been on the phone once or twice with the guys that morning, figuring out where we'd hook up, who could get the car, and whether it was just us or who had a chick involved. Guys talked that way all the time then, but not in front of women—except, I suppose, in the forgetfulness of a brag. Meanwhile, the polite girls we knew used far more offensive words for other women, carefully graded to indicate the degree to which someone was despised.

Whatever our plans were that Sunday, the basketball season was winding down, and that meant springtime and Tower Beach were already on our minds. Long, warm evenings in the parking lot at Thatcher Woods wouldn't be far behind. At this point we'd almost lost Dan Kepp to Marilyn Messina. Joe Caruso had met Jeannie Dwyer and planned to ask her to the junior prom. Mary Jo Long, whom Noreen Nagle introduced to me when she figured we weren't going to work out, was a sort of front seat item with me. And Dan Schilf and Jack Brett had a few girls whose voices they longed to hear. I was still in love with my first love, now so far removed I didn't even know how to find her, and in the psychic unease of those years, had decided to forget her completely. There was too much to do to wait around worrying about that. The deeper reasons for that incredible first experience and for its awful denial would take years to uncover. Years for me anyway. Other people were sharper about these things and saw them more quickly. And then perhaps there was no possible substitute for the transparency and the flavor of her skin since she was so close to my first touch with the world.

As I bounded down the stairs, Canio and Marie appeared, dressed for Easter. Though they'd come to see their grandchildren, this one was in a rush to make a ball game. Regina and my younger brother, Tommy, who was about seven then, could take care of them. If it was Easter—and it may have been—Canio may well have departed from custom and gone to church that Sunday, not out of any interest but as he did once or twice a year to please Marie. Meanwhile, Kathryn, Gerald, and my sister were somewhere between their separate morning Masses.

It was a bright and beautiful day, and having no need of more sermons and without so much as taking their coats off, Canio and Marie decided to take a walk through the neighborhood. As I look back on it, they seemed eager to enjoy the success their son and daughter-in-law had achieved and now were sharing with them.

Taking a stroll was an ancient and amiable pleasure for them both, recalling times in their youth when people dressed of a summer evening and went about, enjoying the festiveness of a chance encounter, the opportunity to exchange a knowing smile, perhaps even flirt a bit with those you'd grown up with and who now enjoyed this passing relief from the stillness of the evening table as much as you did. In these momentary meetings, there was suddenly so much to see, to talk about politely now, and to reminisce about. For Canio, these walks surely recalled his own memories of *la passeggiata* as it had been practiced in his childhood and is still practiced in Brindisi di Montagna, his birthplace, to this day. There, various cohorts of children, young adults, and village leaders stroll with their wives and their husbands, their pals and their betrothed along the streets leading in and out of the town square. On those evenings in Brindisi, the church is usually dark, and the crowds gather to have a little coffee or to listen for a moment to something of national import, to a strident Mussolini in one era, to a soccer game in another. In the life of this tiny village, much of this was a distant, easily commented on thing. Although for Canio, who left the village long before radio burst from the mind of Marconi, *la passeggiata* would have had references that are now lost to us, though perhaps very close to those of Carlo Levi in *Christ Stopped at Eboli*.

Their walk this day was not in the evening but on a Sunday morning and not in Brindisi di Montagna but in German, English, and especially Protestant Oak Park. Though Oak Park fancied itself a village, it was not a village like those in Basilicata or any part of Italy for that matter. Walks of quiet reminiscence were not what these households had in mind.

Canio and Marie, strolling through the neighborhood, were borne on a cloud of memory, delighting in the perfume of flowering crab trees and of passersby, borne along on the grandeur of wide lawns edged in yellow crocuses, amid substantial gabled houses shrouded in lilacs. Happily absent were the stone fronts and walkways abutting tenement doors, the winding cobblestone streets of their ancestors. All that was dreamily gone from them now as they were thrust along with their grandchildren into a world wholly flowering and well beyond the dreams they'd ever allowed themselves.

Gerardo's grandson, Gerald, had a very different view of all this. Few men in Oak Park conducted business from home, yet he was loath to take up the expense, inconvenience, and the necessity of going out at lunchtime for a warm meal that a rented office off the village square entailed. His office was still at home, now in the back study. What's more, he was new here, and his relationships with "these burghers" and even men like Doc Pecora were still tenuous. Observing Canio and Marie stroll through the neighborhood, Gerald was embarrassed and unsure of the impression his family was making on his neighbors, and he became less and less fond of his parents' Old World walks, fearing he would be identified with a way of life long since abandoned, a way of life that would leave him in a bad light among his new neighbors.

———•————

This change of form, honored in a newfound place, was sensed as well by Louie Esposito and Rocky Marotta, my old employers from the washing machine and repair shop. When they came to help out with the new washer or to have a look at the television, they knew enough to park in the alley behind the house, or perhaps they were told to. "You don't have to worry about parking. Just pull up behind the garage," you could hear Gerald saying on the phone in his office. Now counted among the men who still worked in Austin and understood to be invisible, they were to be even less visible in executive, managerial Oak Park.

For me, admiration and allegiance had long since shifted to these men who had guided me from desire to adulthood, and I saw myself still aspiring to their capabilities. Consequently, when one of my sister's new friends developed a crush on me, her father was perplexed. "What to do with this mechanic across the alley." He hadn't bought a home in upscale Oak Park to marry his daughter off to Midas Muffler.

And there was a larger irony. When Rocky pulled up in the alley, it was with a considerable fortune in the bank. He'd built a string of Laundromats in Chicago, and he was probably worth two or three times the wealth of these suburban households by then. He was the one who should have been protecting his reputation. But Rocky was an instinctively quiet, even humble man who avoided attention and seemed accustomed to slipping in and out unnoticed. He sent his children to college, though he himself had only finished trade school, and he left the world to itself as quietly and unostentatiously as he lived in it. And he built his children a fortune.

As for Henry Heitbommer, I never saw him again. With two words he had started it all, the possibility of understanding the world in just two words of circuitry—*full duplex*. For some reason, probably his own sense of how hard it was to be a kid then, he had taught me to talk to grown-ups as though I knew what I was doing and to memorize words I couldn't understand until I could make my way through them. Words memorized, though dimly understood or perhaps misunderstood, become a mantra of hope as well as a vessel of imagination and understanding. Slipped into books and conversations with other men or sought in the complexities of others' conversations, words gathered currency and took on a life of their own. In those years I learned as much in this way as I learned in school. And I owned the outcome of that learning in ways classroom lessons would take years to achieve. Henry had a long career at Argonne Labs, though he died rather young.

Old Schneiderman's Bakery, Dressel's, the meat market, and Featherstone's soon disappeared from our daily thoughts, fading monuments that gradually receded into the haze of our past. Yet the strangely anonymous memorial in Peanut Park along with the church steeples and school yards would remain clear memories, though the frescoes of St. Thomas have by now been painted over and the bronze plaques of the monument to the two world wars worn away. In the last analysis, they were just hardware, transferable to other playmates, veterans, and congregations, people who now rightly claim those places as their own. These markers, though they came to us as a birthright, were sold, commodified, and abandoned because racism was more important than the bonds that held us together. The former weight and the precise measure of those bonds is now occasionally felt in a gathering, now occurring less and less frequently, a meeting of the aging diaspora of the old neighborhood, a diaspora aptly named since it got what it preferred, specifically the answer to its isolated, dreadful, and murmuring prayers.

———————◆◆◆———————

In the end, it must have broken my grandfather's heart to see us move away, to see us move on, to visit us in an alien place so close to 50-0-7 Washington Boulevard. But the fact was that I was long gone, first to the farm and then to Louie and the shop and then to my first love and the girls who necked at the movies with anyone and didn't care. Now I was long on the rich satisfactions of abandon. And every word I uttered had become a treason to Canio's world and its former hold on me. Like boats that boys carve out of soap, we sailed away, the wind puffing our sails of ivory flakes, lost in the thrill of abandon we adored. Full of ourselves, full of our values, full of our populous generation, we weren't meant for the world of Austin.

I had hoped to grow up the dashing uncle. After all, I was tall like Jack. And Uncle Tom was my favorite, and he was dashing too, his long fingers tapping cigarettes on a silver case and his legs crossed and trousers pleated. I thought I had a fair chance of being an elegant uncle to my nieces and nephews. But as the 1960s progressed, I would first abandon my dream of becoming a priest and later my Catholic marriage, which ended in a civil divorce, and so I grew further and further distant from all this life and dogma and history and turmoil until I wasn't dashing anymore, more like dashing off in the end.

In the early 1970s, the struggles over sexuality and relationships and parenthood and professional aspiration finally drove me to seek help. I would not be writing this now or have a fraction of the happiness I've experienced were it not for an eminent Chicago biodynamic psychiatrist. Patient with all this, though not too patient, he got me off the couch and back to my senses in less than a year. Of course, therapy continues. Good therapy probably never really concludes but rather is just transmuted into self-sustaining, persistent, and informed reflection. Analysis carried nothing like the terror and discomfort I'd anticipated, though that had kept me away from it far too long. Ultimately, this work took the form of a kind of ongoing personal wellness inventory, which still remains effective for me despite the tendency of the nightmares and demon habits to reappear.

I suppose that if there is a lesson to be learned from these childhood memories, it is that we seldom understand our children, no matter what our household imperatives, and we seldom (or not nearly enough) reflect on their experiences with them. Nor do we encourage the kind of self-reflection that therapy enables. In my childhood—and I suspect this is still the case for many people—most of us were assumed to be growing up *naturally*, our parents naively believing that childhood would find a natural way of its own. What sharing of our interior life there was with parents, ended up being too confusing, imprecise, and constrained by learned or inherited inhibitions, to capture and convey the true dimensions of our inner life. Looking at David, my eldest son, and Tony, who is nine years younger, I see now what I needed to know fifty years ago. The life of the spirit is not meant to grow in a crowd but intimately among a few shared souls.

CHAPTER 24

THE CASTLE AND THE HAT

Sometimes when Canio pulled a softball from his desk drawer, its gray skin falling off, or a league ball for a game of catch, that old postcard would reappear in a bundle of string and water tape. It was *the castle* in the place where he'd been born with a strange, mysterious name we tried to read on the postmark, Brindisi di Montagna. I couldn't understand how his house in Italy could be so special as to get a postcard all to itself and a colored one too! His finger would glide along the edge to reaffirm hidden but important details. It was the castle near where he, his mother, and Aunt Gussie had lived in Italy, and then correcting us in order to make it more familiar to us, he'd say it was in Brindisi, his home before America.

What I knew about castles at seven or eight, I'd learned from my cousin Topper Heaney, who built all kinds of them. Consequently, I had quite particular views on fixed fortifications, and I was planning something along those lines myself. To me, good castles had high walls, moats and parapets, castellations on the towers, and slits for archers. Topper's always had two other important features, dungeons and drawbridges, both of which had trap doors so you could show prisoners where the dragons lived and drop unruly captives in the moat. Canio's castle followed a different model, however. Except for the rampart, none of Topper's military engineering applied. Only the tall window openings and moss-covered arches remained, three or four stories of them. Try as I might, examining that post card, I could find no other battlements.

Whatever the castle had been, it was high on a hill with orchards and vineyards, and Canio's house was just below, not quite in the picture at all. A certain silence came over him when he showed us that scene, drawn from a time so immediate and concrete to him yet so inexplicably absent in all that it represented. In a way, it must have embodied some essential mystery of his life as an artist, the reality of images, and the invisibility, the ephemera, the whirlwind that made art necessary. Brindisi was a place long since past, and after World War II, no one knew, perhaps it barely existed. In any case, it was completely inaccessible. So far as we knew, the breakup of Canio's studio in 1939, the war, the fear of fascism and the threat of an Italian internment, similar to what had happened to Japanese Americans, had ended whatever contact he had with Italy. His fingers might as well have touched a picture of heaven, for there was as much mystery of separation between those famous fingers drawn of Michelangelo in the Sistine Chapel as there was in Canio's hand slipping along that colored postcard.

By the time I was in my late twenties, with no further information to confirm it, I'd come to find this story of Italy largely unconvincing. I believed instead that the castle was probably a communal farm of the sort where several families lived on the upper floors, their livestock in the pens and courtyard below. Aunt Gussie had just died, and Grandma Marie was the last living link with Italy. Except for her cooking, she was the one least enamored of things Italian.

I first considered finding Brindisi in the 1970s, at a time when the world around us made returns of all kinds seem out of sync and nostalgic. By then, the Vietnam War was hundreds of marches, demonstrations, bail bonds, body bags, and beaten heads old. What political voices we had, including Martin Luther King, Robert Kennedy, and Gene McCarthy, had been assassinated or silenced. And by 1972, jobs were becoming scarce for long-haired hippy types. People who had done little more than show up for an antiwar demonstration had had their phone lines tapped. Friends began hiding guns.

Meanwhile, Nixon's Plumbers, their dirty tricks and the cover-up called Watergate, were just being uncovered. The only voices ameliorating cynicism for some of us were people like Walter Cronkite, who'd concluded the war was tearing America apart and who had become openly critical of the CIA, the Pentagon, and the questionable legality of the war itself. Meanwhile, communes and co-ops were springing up everywhere as people hunkered down for another longer war against *the system.*

It was a difficult time not to be cynical. Parents of the middle class, anchoring one end of the so-called generation gap, wondered what had gotten into their children. They were rethinking their wills, holding onto their pocketbooks, and not fronting down payments for houses despite the boom in housing that was landing young families in suburbs and inner cities. Those down payments would only grudgingly come forth a few years later when the housing boom of the mid-1970s (and not a little greed) entered the picture.

As someone said in the 1976 film *Network,* we were "mad as hell," and we weren't gonna "take it anymore!" Hearing that orchestrated cacaphony of scripted exasperation burst forth from the actors stationed at an array of apartment building windows made us laugh. Hollywood had no idea. Now with one official lie after another being exposed on what seemed almost a daily basis, I had begun to doubt many things I had once innocently taken as true.

Consequently, when my new partner, Sidonie, and I visited Europe together in 1976, the postcard, now itself a mythical fantasy in my cynical scenario, had gone missing. If the farm collective had indeed existed as I had once supposed, it would hardly have merited a postcard. What's more, where would an immigrant laborer have found the money to buy the six-flat building we called 13-48? That story now went unexplained as well. We traveled south—ten cities in seventeen days. With a change of clothes and a dog-eared copy of *Europe on $7 a Day,* we clutched our Europasses. The train eventually slipped out of the Swiss Alps into Italy and suddenly seemed to come off the tracks with a bump. Crossing the border from welded Swiss rails and switching onto whatever Italy had, it felt as though the car had been derailed and run aground. A few moments later, when we pulled into an Italian border station, people began throwing their belongings in at the windows and then swarming in to fill and overfill the car. As we proceeded along the route, the crowding only grew worse. People bounced and joggled, becoming indistinguishable from boxes, bags, and luggage all the way to Venice and then on to Rome.

When I told Gerald about this on our return, he was nonplussed. "What did you expect?" he said. "All the good ones left?" I knew better then, but I had no better answer.

It wasn't until 1995 that we ventured farther south from Rome. By then, a hundred years had passed since Canio had left his home for Chicago. So far as any of us knew, not a trace was left there of Gerardo, Canio, or any of the family. Southern Italy was more accessible to us in 1995 through Carlo Levi's *Christ Stopped at Eboli* than through any family member who was still alive or in our living memory. What's more, the only indication that there might be some distinction between the Griecos' actual Italian home and the port of Brindisi was buried in a note we found among immigration papers that Aunt Gussie had filled out in error and left among her love letters for some reason. So we were headed for Brindisi, at the Eastern end of the Appian way, the historic seaport connecting Greece to Rome.

From London, Sidonie and I would also travel in early summer to Ireland, specifically to Cahir, the ancestral home of my mother's side of the family, where another castle, beautifully restored, can indeed be found and where the remaining Heaneys operate a prosperous dairy farm. But in early April, we made our way to Brindisi, hoping to find some trace of the Griecos.

Sifting through regional maps in London in search of Brindisi di Montagna and supposing it to be a mountain suburb of the seaport or a mountain village along the nearby shore, Sidonie, who has an uncanny feel for maps and unerring sense of direction, began to notice the locations of various ruins, castles in particular, that were well marked even in the poorest parts of the Italian countryside. Her eyes, wandering across a succession of maps, soon discovered the village a hundred miles inland, clustered about the ruins of a castle, perhaps the one first seen on Canio's postcard. The Brindisi of my grandfather was in the heart of Basilicata a few kilometers from Potenza, once a garrison in the Punic Wars and now the regional capital. But for Gussie's note and Sidonie's mapping eye, we might never have found it.

That April we drove east from Naples toward Potenza. It was raining madly from a glowering sky, and as we reached higher elevations, the rain turned into sleet and then a blizzard capping the mountaintops with snow. As the clouds descended lower and lower, they turned the green and calcine hillsides black and amber, finally obliterating every detail in white. Not what we'd expected. It felt more like a snowstorm in the desert. We had planned to stop in Potenza for the night, but when we got there, knowing the village was just a few kilometers farther east, we decided to press on for a first look. As we drew closer, trying to refocus through the snow and raindrops on the window, my eyes melted in surprise and happiness. On a snow-covered hillside, I saw what no one in the family had seen for more than a century, the ruins of a castle just as it had appeared on the postcard cradled in Canio's hands. Not only was it as I remembered, but happily, it could be seen quite clearly from the highway a few miles below. We took a right and began climbing.

At the end of the zigzagging switchbacks that led to the village's entrance, we came to a sign in three languages that welcomed us. It was an old sign that was a bit rusted in places but had been partially repainted. The streets were narrow, too narrow to allow us to drive up to the castle, so we parked in the grammar school parking lot where we could hear the voices of students chanting their lessons. Like everyone else, we walked through the village, our spring clothes wrapped tightly around us against the unexpected wind.

Dad had died the previous May, and I'd taken to occasionally wearing his fedora. Here in the cold, I pulled it down hard on my head. It was my second favorite hat, not a Borsalino, and it didn't fit quite right. But it felt good, and it had survived the gusts and rain of a wet spring in London.

Hiking through the cobbled streets, we hadn't seen a soul out in the weather. We eventually reached the largest archway of the ruins, its limestone keys alternating with shims of terra cotta as are so often found in Norman castles. Once up inside the main arch, it seemed we were at least safe from the weather.

Even through the blizzard, there was a pleasant view of the newer houses behind the castle, and in front of it a wide panorama of the gray and coiling Basento valley. Faintly in the distance, you could make out other mountain villages nestled in the surrounding hills, and below us ran the highway and railroad that linked Naples and Brindisi. Standing there, it seemed to me that we few Griecos and these roads were the last visible link across Basilicata and Campagna—from the Griecos to the Navigatos—and a past that was all but lost to us. Just then a gust of wind whipped through the arch and swept Gerald's hat off my head and into my hand. Though I'd caught it that way in London a half dozen times before, the blast whipped at it again, this time ripping it away from me and down the stony ramparts of the hillside, me scrambling after it but without any luck. It disappeared somewhere in the rocks below, perhaps below that, somewhere in the village or perhaps in the orchard where Canio's fig trees still grow. Try as I might, I could never find that hat.

With that gust of wind, something of Gerald returned to his ancestral home.

<hr />

It would take another six or seven years before this part of Italy would be discovered on the travel pages of the *New York Times* and in the tour books. But in the spring of 1995, the treasures of Paestum, the exquisite Tomb of the Diver, the Lucani ritual sites, and the villages that gave birth to Horace and Pythagoras beckoned and awed us, even though they seemed off the map so far as the guidebooks were concerned. It was a fortunate irony because what was available were the magnificent narratives of Carlo Levi, who long ago recognized the stark beauty of the south in his paintings and who captured the resilience of its people in the deft characterizations and anguish of *Christ Stopped at Eboli*.

And it would take me another six or seven years to come to an understanding of Canio's secret and the impact he had on me. It seems to me that my grandfather's curiosity and unrelenting grasp of life and insistence on the quality of happiness was pre-Christian, perhaps not Greek but Lucani, informed by the desolate hope that only the experience of life on this earth can give you—that the earth with its malaria, its inexplicable diseases, its sorrows and disappointments, nevertheless continues to nurture you just enough.

Soon after I returned from my second journey to Brindisi di Montagna a few years later, I had a confrontation with my father in a dream. And realizing I was shouting at a dead man, I panicked and then froze. In that hypercognitive state, I let him have the last word, which was witty and cynical on his part. And whatever it was, it woke me up.

chapter 25

IN DEATH

Canio died in 1960. When he lay dying, they sent me to the rectory for a priest to bring him the last rites. I kept hoping Father Rabitt would answer the door because he was supposed to be the smartest priest in the parish and a canonical lawyer for the diocese. I wanted to ask him if he thought Grandpa would go to heaven, even if he just said the rosary now because he was scared and because Father Domicelli had converted him in the hospital. But when I got to the rectory, Father McAuley was there instead. He was a slight man in his thirties with a brash voice. Even after he shaved, he looked like he needed one.

"I'll be there in a moment," he said without looking at me, standing in the twilight of the rectory door. There was a thick iron grate over the tiny window with diamond shapes in it like the ones in the confessional.

"Wait here," he said. It was a cold damp day in April, and on the stoop I tapped my feet to keep warm.

He came back wearing a purple scapular around his shoulders with white tassels and embroidery, carrying the sacrament under his black coat. He led the way now, and I was surprised to see that his cassock looked stringy as it dragged down the steps. It seemed to me he could have done better for Grandpa, but then who were we to get anything special?

"Father?" I said.

I didn't think God would mind if we talked about whether or not he was going to save Grandpa's soul.

"Shhhhhh!" he said. "I'm carrying the sacrament."

So I kept quiet while we waited for the light at Leamington. I was stuck, and it was hard to keep quiet. This was one question Tony Manginardi had never managed to ask, and though I didn't realize it at the time, walking in the shadow of Father McAuley that gray day was the beginning of a priesthood of my own.

A few days or so before Canio died, Kathryn brought him some lunch. Clutching the rosary that Father Cunio had given him, he was lucid, though in considerable pain. For a few weeks after his prostate had been removed, he'd returned to life in the neighborhood, taking his usual walks and even getting back to work. We were all in a bliss of miraculous recovery. But then he suddenly weakened and the cancer, which we knew was malignant, returned. On the day Kathryn last spoke with him, the doctors had come and gone. There was nothing more they could do. Grandma Marie was relieved a little. Though desperate to see him live, wrapping her hands in a rosary as she walked from room to room about the house, she took some consolation in the fact that her novenas had been answered. Canio had received the sacraments and confessed his sins.

That day as she brought him a little soup, Kathryn asked if he would like to say some prayers.

"I'd do anything to live," he said.

Though not a person given to judgment of others, Kathryn was disturbed by this, by the hint of superstition in his words. Or was it cynicism? Poor Canio, who laid no claim to understanding the beauty and mystery of the world, who, if he understood it at all, did so in terms more akin to Ruskin or Teilhard de Chardin, was still being tested by the Baltimore catechism.

That catechism was a set of questions and answers that began with "Why did God make me?" and enumerated a few hundred other articles of faith, most of which Tony Manginardi and the rest of our classmates had memorized before completing second grade and taking first Communion. The answer was, "God made me to know Him, to love Him, to serve Him in this world, and to be with Him in the next." This image of a God the King requiring slavish affection, destined to an eternity of babysitting, was as foreign to Canio as it was to Teilhard, who knew very well the

Babylonian origins of this monarchical vision. It had first appeared in the ancient Sumerian city of Ur, and it had then been taken up by the descendants of Abraham and passed on to us, generation by generation, down to the twentieth century. Along with Canio's dislike for the politics of the Roman papacy had come his recognition of the inability of papal authorities to allow God to grow or at least grow in our consciousness. Or as some wag once put it, "For God so loved the world that He sent his only begotten Son on a midcourse correction."

That evening Canio slipped into unconsciousness.

Canio's last words, as reported by Kathryn, were repeated among us in the days following his death. But Kathryn never said what she thought of his remark. Years later when I asked her directly, she said she didn't know. "I can see now what a wonderful man he was ... and how much he meant to you and Regina," she said. "I only wish I had gotten to know him better."

Aunt Flo, though a Navigato, always said, "Canio knew how to live." True enough, but those words irked her sister Marie so much that she would sometimes storm out of the room.

"Ah! Well, you don't have to live with him!" Marie would say.

Well, she wouldn't always storm out. Sometimes she would only retreat to the kitchen as if she'd just realized she had left something on the stove. But nothing but her heart was burning. "You were always a know-it-all," she would mutter under her breath. And everyone around her knew that Florence was right. Canio knew how to live, no matter the commotion, no matter the explosions around him. As I learned much later, he had expected this adaptation of me, and it was this knowledge I had resisted in all the years when I hoped he would stand in my defense against my father. In fact, he had been modeling a stronger, more enduring, more satisfying defense for me—a world of art, of hope, and of imagination, a defense that steels us all against what cruelty might come. Fifty years on, Flo Donaldson's words seem prophetic. Amid intense emotions as in vast emptiness, Canio knew how to live, and so he taught us at newstands, amidst racism, at pitch penny, and in love.

Gerald died in May of 1994. Not long before he passed, he had scrambled out of bed one day, seeming to have regained his old athletic self against all odds, apparently fully recovered only to discover the rapid return of the pain and near paralysis of Parkinson's disease. Ever angry as we had always known him to be, he was angry again this time "and sick of laying around." His condition deteriorated quickly, and he died a few days later. "Do not go gentle into that good night." I thought of Dylan Thomas in those days. "Rage, rage, against the dying of the light." For our dad, there had been no need of Dylan Thomas.

My days had long been haunted by the recurring pattern of my father's encounter with the world, by his brawling rage. Too often, in the course of my own life, I myself have become aggravated, crabby, morose, contemptuous, easy to anger, and short-tempered. Rather than gradually achieving release from my father's authority as I matured, I often exhibited the features of Gerald's controlling affect as well. I adopted his mean conviction about the truth of meritocracy, which is to say, no belief in meritocracy at all but a belief in an oppressive feudal outcome. "Who you know is where you go." Out of this too predictable psychology came my decision to *never be like him*. And over time that became a decision never to love him. Both decisions, of course, had always been impossible and therefore never achievable.

In the months preceding Gerald's death, Sidonie had begun to take down bits and pieces of this story. Knowing the power of story to relieve, to unburden what is good from the baggage of what is debilitating, to "give that two-humped camel, fear, a Christian's day of rest," as my buddy Denny Dooley put it, she typed up that which she knew had shaped me and had informed two generations of relationships in ways that neither religion nor psychotherapy had relieved.

With Dad's death nearing, Sidonie had embarked on a strategy that might make his coming passing bearable, perhaps even transformative for me. In fact, she had hoped for some reconciliation between Dad and me, a possibility we talked about by phone several times. I was in Chicago (where Dad was dying), and she detained by professional obligations overseas. Her suggestions gave me the opportunity to explore some of the gentleness of my father and to reflect on the still unnamed origins of his temperament. How she was able to do this was not clear to me then, though it surely had something to do with her own father's sudden death and with the grief and grieving that had come to her, though I wouldn't understand this until years later.

The day of Dad's funeral, there was a reading from the book of Ecclesiasticus, also known as the book of Sirach, which only Catholics seem to include in the Old Testament. Having pointed out the irony of including a contested element of scripture in the requiem Mass for Gerald, whose family swam in seas of theological dispute, I put my best foot forward for his eulogy. There must have been some in the sanctuary that day, not the least of them some friends of my youth who knew what had happened between us and dreaded what might come next. And yet I stumbled toward my own inadequate act of reconciliation, born of the graciousness of words crafted out of mourning.

———◆———

Kathryn, who had spent days and years acceding to Gerald's every whim, ending the day when she could barely stand, seemed a person beside herself. She had attended to his funeral with all the minute considerations you'd bring to a wedding or a fiftieth anniversary. When it came to the eulogy, I was the oldest, so as usual, I went first. She said later she hadn't been able to hear me, though everyone around her had. So I gave her my notes.

Well, if her mind had been elsewhere during my remarks, it was understandable. For the first time in years, she was free. She had better things to think about. Kathryn, who always loved to travel, was beginning to realize she might finally have the freedom to simply toss some things in a suitcase ... and *go*. And for a period after Gerald died, she did just that.

In the family Bible, where she had dutifully recorded the names and dates of deceased family members, from Charles Konning forward, Kathryn would now have the last word. After entering the notation of her husband's death, she squeezed in her own name at the bottom of the page, leaving the date for us to complete. It was just as her mother had done in a little notebook of her own.

That date came four years later in 1998. Kathryn's life, like Eva Mae's before her, had collapsed slowly into reverie and death. The Heaneys were characteristically optimistic and private. "Put your best foot forward" also meant that they would retreat from their spouses to their bedrooms and to private tears in times of grief and despair. For my father, Gerald, and for the Italians, grief and disappointment took a different form, one filled with cynicism, argument, and claims of betrayal flung in many directions until the rafters shook with fists thrust at a bewildered God. The only guidance that seemed to embrace both cultures was the expression "Time heals all wounds." The only safe conclusion was "But when? And at what cost to the present?" Even long experience made it difficult to predict the cure with real confidence.

Kathryn died more from weariness and her refusal to eat than from any medical cause. Sleeping in our midst, her children and grandchildren in attendance, she suddenly sat up to watch the cartoons purring softly on the television set. For a few hours, it was as if she'd regained her curiosity and wonder, commenting on one of the cartoon characters, "What a wise guy! Who does he think he is!" or on the antics of another, "The nerve!" I don't really recall exactly what she said, but it was as though she'd suddenly become herself again. I remember that as we assembled dinner from the covered dishes and thoughtfully packaged leftovers friends had sent over, how we were suddenly buoyed by the thought she might yet recover, that her optimism and spirit were on the mend. But as with Canio, that hope proved illusory.

Toward the end of her life, Kathryn stood before the mirror, putting on the last touches of makeup as she prepared to go to Mass. "I'm a vain old woman," she said. Like Canio, in her last years, she stared at people unabashedly. Still deliciously vain, she was now entitled to be so—vain not in an oppressive way but in a well-constructed, proper way, appropriate to her world, her community, her religious views, and herself.

The fact was that she had made her world as best she could, and she now left many pieces of it behind in the photographic record made by her husband, in the words and memories retained and shared now by her children, and finally, in the lives that had sprung from her and Gerald's marriage. It was a world she had the right to look back at and to be vain about, and though it might not have conformed to her strictest moments of belief, it was a world she had entered into lavishly and fully to the limits that courage would permit. "Put your best foot forward," they had said, and she had. The filial debts she left would be paid by her children not out of guilt or fear but in their own creative ways—in their continued deep affection for one another, in Sugarbush, and in the reflective world she created around them.

Whether in her joys or her faults, Kathryn's life is like the long arc of a bouquet still flying through the air to me, arcing from her grandparents' generation to that of her grandchildren—flowers of confidence and faith, flowers of optimism and of sorrow. "Hail, Holy Queen," she used to say. Happy as we were that the rosary was over, we felt the truth of her quiet exclamation, that our life, our sweetness, and our hope was enough. "Hail, Holy Queen." In the long arc of that bouquet, the sorrow and pain of her prayer could finally be relinquished.

Grief makes us reflect as no other emotion can. It makes us cleave to what is most valuable in life. If we let it, it allows us to examine the trivialities and frameworks along which we've strung our lesser natures. It takes the measure of us, of our ability to grow, to nurture others, and to see those we have loved as a new revelation. Even in their dying, Canio and Kathryn crystallized something fundamental about the human spirit for me, indefatigably themselves, true to their most visible and present characteristics, asserting what body and soul alone could never fully capture.

CHAPTER 26

THE DREAM OF HAPPINESS

For years I had a recurring dream that seemed to take me through several rooms. One of them was the room that Canio gave me. It took years to realize this, partly because as often as the dream occurred, I seldom remembered how I got to that room. Now I think I know how. It's a room with a beautiful view to the northeast, the view from my room at Sugarbush, trees and hillside and the Reeseville water tower on the far horizon four and a half miles away. But in the dream the view from this room looks out over a city, over streetlights and boulevards, city lights streaming like water down to the lake. When I go there in dreams, I've lain down to think things through, to get away from something. Whether it is day or night in my dream or in my waking reverie, that room is filled with creamy green sunlight, the kind that little children play in.

One Sunday morning at the farm, it was probably the last day of Canio's visit, I was furiously reading from a new batch of books I'd gotten from the library the day before. I was eight, and for some reason I was convinced that, like Alessandro Volta, I could make a battery. Not just a battery from the formulas I was reading, but some long-lasting, never-needs-recharging kind of battery. It was the kind of dream wild-eyed boys often have.

Canio came in. He must have been dressed for church, even though he never went. He had on his three-piece suit. Perhaps he was dressed for the drive to Chicago.

"You don't really have to make things," he said as though he were standing in the middle of my thoughts. There was a pause, and as I had done on so many other occasions, I refused to look up.

"Happiness is all that's required."

He was always interrupting me—as I sawed beams for the iceboat I built in the basement, for instance, or pounded shelves together on the back steps.

"I'd be happy to just get this battery finished," I said, pretending to concentrate so as to be able to shut him out.

After a while he left.

In the midst of the truths Socrates sought in his dialogues with students or the curious, there arose a great wisdom born of personal confidence, insights, and mutual respect, carefully examined. His dialogues relied most on the trust, the trust between mentor and student, borne from teacher to teacher, and the trust of students in one another that they would participate seriously and listen with respect to one another's ideas and questions. In my case, save for the efforts of a few reflective men, my trust in the sincerity of my fellow human beings in their pursuit of important truths came only late in adolescence when most of my habits of thought, formed by early experiences, were deeply embedded, long since implacably ingrained.

In the rare moments of such unguarded sincerity I had experienced in conversations with Rocky and Louie in the shop and in some long, solitary moments spent at the farm, the sense of deep consciousness, of intimate and important reflection pressed in and transformed me. But most indelible was this moment I came to understand only in later years. It had occurred when I was eleven. Canio, speaking over my shoulder, penetrating the distance at which I held him then, said with his eyes as surely as he said with his lips what I most needed to know. "Happiness is all that's required."

So that room has stayed in me, a kind of mean and creative place from which I'd chased him. Dusty, not much of a place to go back to, which in fact is just what that upstairs room at Sugarbush had become by the 1990s.

It's a curious idea, that only happiness is required. Not long and hard work as Canio's father had known and Gerald had obsessively repeated.

Nor did Canio say that the master creativity he saw in Sessions or Rodin or the fierce determination to render the figure perfectly found in his own pen and ink illustrations was required.

"Happiness," he said, "is all that's required." With five words, he was sealing for me an armory that could keep me safe from an imperious world that endlessly invited, demanded, and pressed for achievement and the impressive performance even as he opened a heart that always honored human longing. Beyond my capacity for understanding at the time, these were words through which the heart was plainly meant to see the only thing that really mattered.

⸺•⸺

Fifty years of struggles, dreams, and obsessions would pass before I began to understand him and his secret. With the name and talent of his own grandfather, drawing from the age of thirteen and always loving to draw, Canio probably never gave up the happiness, the marvel he experienced as images slid from beneath his hand.

And if I will never be totally sure what he meant that August Sunday at Sugarbush in 1953 or what had prompted that haunting statement, it's because in the happy confusion of this oft-recurring dream, guilt subsides, and light and color return even to doomed occasions. The creative room I go to now is not blue, angry, and windswept the way my bedroom at Sugarbush was with its failed battery and lost grandfather. It is bright yellow, as bright as the sun and sea, accessible to myself and to others … and as playful as Canio ever wished it to be on that distant Sunday morning.

CHAPTER
27

LAST WRITES

There is too much to love. Too much love to remain unhappy. Too much love to ever give up. All around Canio, people took their dissatisfactions and their pain to church out of guilt or unhappiness, or to war out of their need to transcend their fear and foreboding, or to politics to forestall their sense of smallness and frustration. Or they followed other means of redemption out of the shame of their sins and the need of forgiveness. But happiness, he said, is all that's required.

Is it possible that many of us, feeling meaningless in the scheme of things, useless and unfulfilled as one sometimes does, have bought into the wrong myth? Is it possible that we're flailing ourselves through the universe when we were meant to be laughing our way instead, that the cosmic plan is better illustrated by the Dali Lama. "All humans want to be ha-ha-happy," he often says before he chuckles, happy despite conflict and wars, despite genocide and the disappearance of his culture. In this simple universal law, he grasps firmly at what is magnificently human. So why is he laughing? Perhaps because he has arrived at a broader view, discovering first and foremost that life is to be celebrated, that our purpose here is not and never has been our private, self-aggrandizing purposes, no matter how noble the cause, the language, or the culture that surrounds us. It is to reflect God's love of the ultimate omelet, even if our particular portion happens to be no more than just another item on a Denny's menu. He is laughing because God's love is vastly proletarian, seemingly indiscriminate, a love of every atom and quark in creation, of every Canio in a beret.

In another tradition, St. Paul wrote to a stranded Christian community in Philippi of love, knowledge, and peace.

> Rejoice in the Lord always; again I say to you Rejoice. Let your gentleness be known to everyone. The Lord is near. Do not worry about anything, but in everything by prayer and supplication with thanksgiving, let your requests be known to God. And the peace of God which surpasses all understanding will guard your hearts and your minds in Christ Jesus. Finally, beloved, whatever is true, whatever is honorable, whatever is just, whatever is pure, whatever is pleasing, whatever is commendable, if there is any excellence and if there is anything worthy of praise think about these things … and the God of peace will be with you. (Philippians 4:4–9 NRSV)

St. Paul also projects a vision of happiness and a proletarian love of atoms and quarks and Canios.

Jesus, no more than a human, albeit a singular human linked to the divine, reminded and enabled people to focus on God's goodness, linked them to the divine despite the overwhelming fatalism they felt (and that we feel most of the time) when faced with our own shortcomings, the successes of others, and the mounting violence of the world. Despite the worst that is done by some, he pointed to and placed faith in others. He encouraged them to overcome their doubt, and through that love of others, of the infinite in others, to open themselves to the faith that they could glimpse some image of the infinite and so set themselves free of fatalism at the core. Does this love of others involve disappointments? Yes. Betrayal? Sure. Will we tire of it? Quite possibly. Is it frustrating? Undoubtedly. Necessary? Absolutely.

Whether through the Dali Lama or Jesus, we might better understand what is behind the maldistribution of resources and a whole list of other injustices committed in the darkness of existential angst if we grasp this message of love and hope and resignation. Needless to say, whatever consolation we might find, wherever we might find it, we still have to contend with evil, rampant violence, and the overwhelming degradation some humans visit upon others. Our senses and our moral beings continue to be bombarded with that recognition, especially in news reports of body counts, the politics of mass incarceration, and images of endless movements of refugees. Our responsibilities, laughing or weeping, remain there. But the point is to view the universe first as celebration and as God's loving, and then to view these other huge dislocations and injustices as human aberrations arising from a culture of injustice and greed, formed by buying into any number of misguided ethics—of work and reward, of vengeance and triumph, of righteousness and chosen-ness, of class and classlessness.

Where we love God and love all of God's manifestations, we love more capaciously in idleness, reveling in the fact that we exist. And we appeal to God more out of pain or possibility than we ever do out of greed, the need for self-aggrandizing work, the quest for revenge, or the smugness of righteousness. The point is to embrace a belief that the principle of goodness has made us possible and that in its immense evolution of millions of changes within us and hundreds of evolving changes we ourselves pursue and experience, this goodness makes us better.

Oh, for the messiness of love and laughter and imagination, which is the afterlife of Canio's secret that lives in the soul of this grandchild.

AFTERWORD

This book arose from the conviction that there are no commonplace lives, merely commonplace descriptions of them. And since identity, whether biographically or autobiographically conceived, is prima facie swept up in words, it can be no other way. My topic has been the mystery of words in a world of ordinary explanation. As children, we began with words that we memorized and resolutely believed, words that gave us our identity but which nevertheless also sustained mysteries. There is something similar that happens when a slice of lime turns an ordinary beer into a delicacy tingling on the lips or the way a jalapéno, consumed in the desert sun, turns the air about your head to a soothing breeze. In commonplace events there is a similar mystery set on the edge between convention and consciousness, between sensation and mythology.

In retrospect, we are constantly fixed at each point in a time and place which we then reimagine as a constancy or perhaps an inconstancy of others, whom we also imagine in their entries and exits from our lives and also in our own adherence to—or perhaps violation of—an ethical vision of responsibility. Conceiving of ourselves either as islands of self (or selves) huddled in inward-turned isolation in a hostile world or as the robust, fearless heroes of literature and newsprint believing their press releases, most of us come sooner or later to feel meaningless in the scheme of things, useless and unfulfilled in the larger context. Alone and insufficient. Whether our self-concept is one of the mighty or the inconsequential, this adherence to the idea of an island self amounts to buying into the wrong myth.

Our very bodies carry not only the physical imprint of others, but the meanings of stories lived vicariously through our parents, siblings, and grandparents. They inhabit our bones, these people, our synapses, our

221

shared chemistry, and most profoundly and accessibly, our imaginations. All of us are far more than individuals, the conventional figures of literature. We are far more than what fabled heroes and rogues permit us to be. Rather we are more like living illusions interwoven among one another and our own biological constraints, more like multivalent, co-bonded atoms whose physical identity is lost in some biochemical or chemical mission, ever mysteriously entangled with one another and with something larger that involves other souls. And these entangled identities have a life—and even a half-life—that continues through time and generations.

I have come to the ironic recognition that it is in this zone of exchange with others, whether in alliance or misalliance, that we seem to see ourselves most clearly. And in those contexts, those arrangements, we attempt to take responsibility for the scope of our action. In that self-imagining, we conjure others to us just as we conjure ourselves. To do otherwise is to break faith with words, our own and those of others, whether family members, lovers, friends, acquaintances, or antagonists. To refuse this responsibility is to break faith with those we love, those through whom we confront our being. The critical dimension of self-knowing is the complexity of our entwined lives and through that complexity, the hidden dimensions of human maturation. You may look for me here, but you can surely also see me in another elsewhere.

We can draw a character in context, knowing that all our drawing will liquefy and disappear, a kind of performance art blown away or drifting nostalgically downstream like a paper boat. What remains is not identity but an abiding responsibility for a complex past, and along with it a curious love for all those whose stories are in our bones and synapses. And so I have given you Canio Grieco, my very commonplace grandfather. These are the stories I've come to tell of him and those around him. They have been the ground of my efforts at loving. They have given me ways to understand myself, those I love, and strangers in a crowd. They have kept before me some glimpse of happiness.

A final note: Many of the people in *Canio's Secret* are given their real names. But in other instances, I've chosen to assign people different names and sometimes to conflate several personalities into one person.

EDITOR'S NOTE

In 1994, Greg started writing this memoir of his grandfather, Canio Grieco. At the time I was writing a story about my grandmother, Arline Kinsel Paulen. For the two of us, our relationship has been forged in large part out of our informing narratives, the stories we told of our parents and grandparents, our backgrounds, our childhoods, our loves, our failures, and our dreams, the stories we imagined of ourselves and for ourselves. These narratives, offered, revised, sometimes rejected and reimagined, have bound us together now for more than four decades. Our stories gave us ways to enter each other's histories and cleave to the other's body. They gave us ways to understand one another and to calibrate the degrees of our differences. They gave us imagined pasts through which we could maintain independence as our lives became more and more imbricated in one another's. They gave us a way to understand, where possible, the verbal basis of a life lived together and the experience enfolded in our shared decisions.

We began to ask very complex questions about relationships. How do people with two widely different interpretive modes operate in a world where judgments about people (i.e., child-rearing, familial politics, friendships, and professional networks) become the most important areas of joint decision making? How do you proceed where the reliability of judgments about people, situations, consequences, and ethics affect everyday decisions and where the confidence engendered by these mutual understandings ultimately form the basis of economic exchange, professional sacrifices on one side or the other, assessment of life's choices, and workmanlike pride in one's personal accomplishments?

Operationally, of course, in celebratory toasts, political meetings, or conversations after movies, we could disgree, and we often did. But the habit of mutuality turned out not to be a context of the immediately identifiable and the immediately shared but a willingness to be persistently reflective about the shared values themselves. So while our sons, our family, and our friends might at times have found us disagreeing (even disagreeable), for us there had always been some sense of hopeful anticipation about the outcome of these encounters, some nonresolution to the story that is more satisfying in its complexities than easy and repetitious assent … and often more creative in its tensions.

"There are perhaps two ways to get along," Greg's lawyer Jimmy Gitlitz, told us when we were pursuing our only serious attempt at separation. "One is by talking a great deal about everything and the other by choosing carefully where not to talk at all." Ours had been the former mode. And while our efforts seemed at times to be a matter of juggling puffballs and kingpins at once, it had been, taken as a life, a way of floating on air. We couldn't juggle snowflakes, but the moments we tried had come to be the ones that truly counted.

Sometime in 2002, Greg came close to finishing his memoir of his grandfather Canio. Then life intruded, and it remained in unaccessed files until I opened them up a few years ago. First came forgetfulness of where he had parked his car and hours spent roaming the streets to find it. Then came distressing signs of memory loss, and the periodic full-body sobbing at the recognition that he was *losing* his mind. Then came the raging paranoia and dark psychosis followed by the diagnosis of frontotemporal dementia. In 2006, doctors told us that he had three to five years. But until what? Until he died? Until he would lose all memory and live in total disinhibition? The deterioration that has unfolded has taken much longer and eluded certain diagnosis. Maybe it's another kind of dementia, maybe Alzheimer's. But in the last year, the dementing process has gained on him. The stories he tells so powerfully in this memoir have floated away on evaporating snowflakes.

So the time had clearly come to edit his book into a final shape and publish his story of Canio, Austin, and his childhood. The writing is all Greg's. The organization into chapters and final editing is mine.

I hope I have adequately captured the long arc of the narrative he hoped to tell.

It has been a bittersweet project. As an academic, I have spent four decades writing books. I know how to put a sentence together. But rereading Greg's prose, I marvel at the shape and rhythm of the sentences, the intensity of distilled affect, the evocation of neighborhood, the precision of portraiture, the multiple voices—of the child and of the adult looking back and at the gracious love so hauntingly and generously extended into a past that was in service of the future. In returning to his book, I have returned to the stories that indelibly shaped our relationship.

When I worked on the manuscript last summer, Greg had achieved some modicum of the happiness Canio had long ago recommended to him. Perhaps it was the medication. It may have been. Then he seemed to live in a continuous present of his life. Everything to which he directed his attention gave him pleasure. Every meal tasted good. Every concert or movie or play was fully engrossing. Every moment spent with family and friends was an occasion to give others the pleasures of what remained of his wit and affection. By this summer there are only a few of us he still recognizes. There is no longer the quick wit, no longer the searing blue eyes. Soon there will no longer be the memory of Canio. Sometimes if I riff on something he has said, the dulling plane of his face will break in a smile at his pleasure in the play of language.

In rereading his memoir, in inhabiting these pages over these months of preparation, I feel only too keenly the vastness of loss that Tony, David, and I—and all those who love Greg—have experienced. I do not have his gift for prose to describe that sense of loss. What I can do now, at this very moment, is take Canio's wise advice and find happiness where it comes. Preparing this book for Greg is the happiness that has been required of me now.

I owe a debt of gratitude to the estate of the photographer Joan Albert for permission to use the probing photograph of Greg that appears on the back cover. Greg and Joan met at St. Mary's College when both were involved in theater productions there. They remained lifelong friends.

I would also like to acknowledge Greg's best friend, Dennis Dooley, whose friendship reaches back to their days at Fenwick High School on the West Side of Chicago. Den, whom I knew when he taught in the English department at Case Western Reserve University in the late 1960s, introduced me to Greg way back in the summer of 1971. A longtime freelance writer and magazine editor, Den gave his expertise and time to editing the final version of Greg's book. It was truly a gift of love and friendship, for which I am overwhelmingly thankful.

—Sidonie Smith, March 2018

CPSIA information can be obtained
at www.ICGtesting.com
Printed in the USA
BVHW03s0311170418
513561BV00018B/298/P